CAPTAIN SIR RICHARD F. BURTON'S

Captain Sir Richard F. Burton's

King Vikram and the Vampire

Classic Hindu Tales of Adventure, Magic, and Romance

EDITED BY HIS WIFE,
ISABEL BURTON

"Les fables, loin de grandir les hommes, la Nature et Dieu, rapetissent tout."
LAMARTINE *(Milton)*.

"One who had eyes saw it; the blind will not understand it.
A poet, who is a boy, he has perceived it; he who understands it will be
his sire's sire."—Rig-Veda (I. 164, 16).

*WITH THIRTY-THREE ILLUSTRATIONS
BY
ERNEST GRISET,
AND A PHOTOGRAVURE FRONTISPIECE
BY
ALBERT LETCHFORD*

PARK STREET PRESS
ROCHESTER, VERMONT

Park Street Press
One Park Street
Rochester, Vermont 05767

First edition published in 1870; this edition is a facsimile of the 1893
limited edition published by Tylston and Edwards of London.

LIBRARY OF CONGRESS CATALOGING-IN-PUBLICATION DATA
Vetalapañcaviṃśati. English
Captain Sir Richard F. Burton's King Vikram and the vampire :
classic Hindu tales of adventure, magic, and romance.
p.   cm.
Facsim. of: limited ed. London : Tylston and Edwards, 1893.
ISBN 978-0-89281-475-6
1. Tales—India. 2. Vampires—India—Folklore. 3. Hindus—Folklore.
I. Burton, Richard Francis, Sir, 1821–1890.   II. Title.
GR305.V453   1992
398.21—dc20   92-28955
                               CIP

Printed and bound in the United States

10 9 8 7 6 5 4 3

Park Street Press is a division of Inner Traditions International, Ltd.

CONTENTS.

LIST OF ILLUSTRATIONS.

PREFACE.

THE Baital-Pachisi, or Twenty-five Tales of a Baital is the history of a huge Bat, Vampire, or Evil Spirit which inhabited and animated dead bodies. It is an old, and thoroughly Hindú, Legend composed in Sanskrit, and is the germ which culminated in the Arabian Nights, and which inspired the "Golden Ass" of Apuleius, Boccacio's "Decamerone," the "Pentamerone," and all that class of facetious fictitious literature.

The story turns chiefly on a great king named Vikram, the King Arthur of the East, who in pursuance of his promise to a Jogi or Magician, brings to him the Baital (Vampire), who is hanging on a tree. The difficulties King Vikram and his son have in bringing the Vampire into the presence of the Jogi are truly laughable; and on this thread is strung a series of Hindú fairy stories, which contain much interesting information on Indian customs and manners. It also alludes to that state, which induces Hindú devotees to allow themselves to be buried alive, and to appear dead for weeks or months, and then to return to life again; a curious state of mesmeric catalepsy, into which they work themselves by concentrating the mind and abstaining from food —a specimen of which I have given a practical illustration in the Life of Sir Richard Burton.

The following translation is rendered peculiarly valuable and interesting by Sir Richard Burton's intimate knowledge of the language.   To all who understand the ways of the East, it is as witty, and as full of what is popularly called "chaff" as it is possible to be.   There is not a dull page in it, and it will especially please those who delight in the weird and supernatural, the grotesque, and the wild life.

My husband only gives eleven of the best tales, as it was thought the translation would prove more interesting in its abbreviated form.

ISABEL BURTON.

August 18th, 1893.

PREFACE

TO THE

FIRST (1870) EDITION.

———

" THE genius of Eastern nations," says an established and respectable authority, " was, from the earliest times, much turned towards invention and the love of fiction. The Indians, the Persians, and the Arabians, were all famous for their fables. Amongst the ancient Greeks we hear of the Ionian and Milesian tales, but they have now perished, and, from every account we hear of them, appear to have been loose and indelicate." Similarly, the classical dictionaries define " Milesiæ fabulæ" to be " licentious themes," " stories of an amatory or mirthful nature," or " ludicrous and indecent plays." M. Deriége seems indeed to confound them with the " Mœurs du Temps" illustrated with artistic *gouaches,* when he says, " une de ces fables milésiennes, rehaussées de peintures, que la corruption romaine recherchait alors avec une folle ardeur."

My friend, Mr. Richard Charnock, F.A.S.L., more correctly defines Milesian fables to have been originally " certain tales or novels, composed by Aristides of Miletus "; gay in matter and graceful in manner. " They were translated into Latin by the historian Sisenna, the friend of Atticus, and they had a great success at Rome. Plutarch, in his life of Crassus, tells us that after the

defeat of Carhes (Carrhæ?) some Milesiacs were found in
the baggage of the Roman prisoners.   The Greek text
and the Latin translation have long been lost.   The only
surviving fable is the tale of Cupid and Psyche,[1] which
Apuleius calls 'Milesius sermo,' and it makes us deeply
regret the disappearance of the others."   Besides this
there are the remains of Apollodorus and Conon, and a
few traces to be found in Pausanias, Athenæus, and the
scholiasts.

I do not, therefore, agree with Blair, with the dictionaries, or with M. Deriége.   Miletus, the great mari-
time city of Asiatic Ionia, was of old the meeting-place
of the East and the West.   Here the Phœnician trader
from the Baltic would meet the Hindu wandering to
Intra, from Extra, Gangem; and the Hyperborean would
step on shore side by side with the Nubian and the
Æthiop.   Here was produced and published for the use
of the then civilized world, the genuine Oriental apologue,
myth and tale combined, which, by amusing narrative
and romantic adventure, insinuates a lesson in morals or
in humanity, of which we often in our days must fail to
perceive the drift.   The book of Apuleius, before quoted,
is subject to as many discoveries of recondite meaning as is
Rabelais.   As regards the licentiousness of the Milesian
fables, this sign of semi-civilization is still inherent in
most Eastern books of the description which we call
"light literature," and the ancestral tale-teller never
collects a larger purse of coppers than when he relates
the worst of his "aurei."   But this looseness, resulting
from the separation of the sexes, is accidental, not necessary.   The following collection will show that it can be
dispensed with, and that there is such a thing as com-
parative purity in Hindu literature.   The author, indeed,

---

[1] *Metamorphoseon, seu de Asino Aureo, libri XI.* The well known
and beautiful episode is in the fourth, the fifth, and the sixth books.

almost always takes the trouble to marry his hero and
his heroine, and if he cannot find a priest, he generally
adopts an exceedingly left-hand and Caledonian but legal
rite called "gandharbavivaha.[1]"

The work of Apuleius, as ample internal evidence
shows, is borrowed from the East. The groundwork of
the tale is the metamorphosis of Lucius of Corinth into
an ass, and the strange accidents which precede his recovering the human form.

Another old Hindu story-book relates, in the popular
fairy-book style, the wondrous adventures of the hero and
demigod, the great Gandharba-Sena. That son of Indra,
who was also the father of Vikramajit, the subject of this
and another collection, offended the ruler of the firmament
by his fondness for a certain nymph, and was doomed to
wander over earth under the form of a donkey. Through
the interposition of the gods, however, he was permitted
to become a man during the hours of darkness, thus
comparing with the English legend—

> Amundeville is lord by day,
> But the monk is lord by night.

Whilst labouring under this curse, Gandharba-Sena
persuaded the King of Dhara to give him a daughter in
marriage, but it unfortunately so happened that at the
wedding hour he was unable to show himself in any but
asinine shape. After bathing, however, he proceeded to
the assembly, and, hearing songs and music, he resolved
to give them a specimen of his voice.

The guests were filled with sorrow that so beautiful
a virgin should be married to a donkey. They were
afraid to express their feelings to the king, but they could
not refrain from smiling, covering their mouths with their
garments. At length some one interrupted the general
silence and said:

---

1 This ceremony will be explained in a future page.

"O king, is this the son of Indra? You have found a fine bridegroom; you are indeed happy; don't delay the marriage; delay is improper in doing good; we never saw so glorious a wedding! It is true that we once heard of a camel being married to a jenny-ass; when the ass, looking up to the camel, said, 'Bless me, what a bridegroom!' and the camel, hearing the voice of the ass, exclaimed, 'Bless me, what a musical voice!' In that wedding, however, the bride and the bridegroom were equal; but in this marriage, that such a bride should have such a bridegroom is truly wonderful."

Other Brahmans then present said:

"O king, at the marriage hour, in sign of joy the sacred shell is blown, but thou hast no need of that" (alluding to the donkey's braying).

The women all cried out:

"O my mother![1] what is this? at the time of marriage to have an ass! What a miserable thing! What! will he give that angelic girl in wedlock to a donkey?"

At length Gandharba-Sena, addressing the king in Sanskrit, urged him to perform his promise. He reminded his future father-in-law that there is no act more meritorious than speaking truth; that the mortal frame is a mere dress, and that wise men never estimate the value of a person by his clothes. He added that he was in that shape from the curse of his sire, and that during the night he had the body of a man. Of his being the son of Indra there could be no doubt.

Hearing the donkey thus speak Sanskrit, for it was never known that an ass could discourse in that classical tongue, the minds of the people were changed, and they confessed that, although he had an asinine form he was unquestionably the son of Indra. The king, therefore,

---

1 A common exclamation of sorrow, surprise, fear, and other emotions. It is especially used by women.

gave him his daughter in marriage.[1] The metamorphosis brings with it many misfortunes and strange occurrences, and it lasts till Fate in the author's hand restores the hero to his former shape and honours.

Gandharba-Sena is a quasi-historical personage, who lived in the century preceding the Christian era. The story had, therefore, ample time to reach the ears of the learned African Apuleius, who was born A.D. 130.

The *Baital-Pachisi*, or *Twenty-five* (tales of a) *Baital*[2] —a Vampire or evil spirit which animates dead bodies— is an old and thoroughly Hindu repertory. It is the rude beginning of that fictitious history which ripened to the *Arabian Nights' Entertainments*, and which, fostered by the genius of Boccaccio, produced the romance of the chivalrous days, and its last development, the novel— that prose-epic of modern Europe.

Composed in Sanskrit, "the language of the gods," alias the Latin of India, it has been translated into all the Prakrit or vernacular and modern dialects of the great peninsula. The reason why it has not found favour with the Moslems is doubtless the highly polytheistic spirit which pervades it; moreover, the Faithful had already a specimen of that style of composition. This was the Hitopadesa, or *Advice of a Friend*, which, as a line in its introduction informs us, was borrowed from an older book, the *Panchatantra*, or *Five Chapters*. It is a collection of apologues recited by a learned Brahman, Vishnu Sharma by name, for the edification of his pupils, the sons of an Indian Raja. They have been adapted to or translated into a number of languages, notably into Pehlvi and Persian, Syriac and Turkish, Greek and Latin,

---

[1] Quoted from *View of the Hindoos*, by William Ward, of Serampore (vol. i. p. 25).

[2] In Sanskrit, *Vétála-pancha-Vinshati*. "Baital" is the modern form of "Vétála."

b

Hebrew and Arabic.   And as the *Fables of Pilpay*,[1] they are generally known, by name at least, to European littérateurs.   Voltaire remarks,[2] "Quand on fait réflexion que presque toute la terre a été infatuée de pareils contes, et qu'ils ont fait l'éducation du genre humain, on trouve les fables de Pilpay, Lokman, d'Ésope bien raisonnables."

These tales, detached, but strung together by artificial means—pearls with a thread drawn through them —are manifest precursors of the Decamerone, or Ten Days.   A modern Italian critic describes the now classical fiction as a collection of one hundred of those novels which Boccaccio is believed to have read out at the court of Queen Joanna of Naples, and which later in life were by him assorted together by a most simple and ingenious contrivance.   But the great Florentine invented neither his stories nor his "plot," if we may so call it. He wrote in the middle of the fourteenth century (1344-8) when the West had borrowed many things from the East, rhymes[3] and romance, lutes and drums, alchemy and knight-errantry.   Many of the "Novelle" are, as Orientalists well know, to this day sung and recited almost textually by the wandering tale-tellers, bards, and rhapsodists of Persia and Central Asia.

The great kshatriya ·(soldier) king Vikramaditya,[4] or Vikramarka, meaning the "Sun of Heroism," plays in India the part of King Arthur, and of Hárún al-Rashíd further West.   He is a semi-historical personage.   The son of Gandharba-Sena the donkey and the daughter of the King of Dhara, he was promised by his father the

---

1 In Arabic, *Bidpai el Hakim.*

2 *Dictionnaire philosophique,* sub v. "Apocryphes."

3 I do not mean that rhymes were not known before the days of Al-Islam, but that the Arabs popularized assonance and consonance in Southern Europe.

4 "Vikrama" means "valour" or "prowess."

strength of a thousand male elephants. When his sire
died, his grandfather, the deity Indra, resolved that the
babe should not be born, upon which his mother stabbed
herself. But the tragic event duly happening during the
ninth month, Vikram came into the world by himself,
and was carried to Indra, who pitied and adopted him,
and gave him a good education.

The circumstances of his accession to the throne, as
will presently appear, are differently told. Once, however,
made King of Malaya, the modern Malwa, a province of
Western Upper India, he so distinguished himself that
the Hindu fabulists, with their usual brave kind of speaking, have made him "bring the whole earth under the
shadow of one umbrella."

The last ruler of the race of Mayúra, which reigned
318 years, was Rája-pál. He reigned 25 years, but giving himself up to effeminacy, his country was invaded
by Shakáditya, a king from the highlands of Kumaon.
Vikramaditya, in the fourteenth year of his reign, pretended to espouse the cause of Rája-pál, attacked and
destroyed Shakáditya, and ascended the throne of Delhi.
His capital was Avanti, or Ujjayani, the modern Ujjain.
It was 13 kos (26 miles) long by 18 miles wide, an area
of 468 square miles, but a trifle in Indian History. He
obtained the title of Shakári, "foe of the Shakas," the
Sacæ or Scythians, by his victories over that redoubtable
race. In the Kali Yug, or Iron Age, he stands highest
amongst the Hindu kings as the patron of learning.
Nine persons under his patronage, popularly known as
the "Nine Gems of Science," hold in India the honourable position of the Seven Wise Men of Greece.

These learned persons wrote works in the eighteen
original dialects from which, say the Hindus, all the
languages of the earth have been derived.[1] Dhanwantari

---

1 Mr. Ward of Serampore is unable to quote the names of more
than nine out of the eighteen, namely: Sanskrit, Prakrit, Naga,

enlightened the world upon the subjects of medicine and of incantations. Kshapanaka treated the primary elements. Amara-Singha compiled a Sanskrit dictionary and a philosophical treatise. Shankubetálabhatta composed comments, and Ghatakarpara a poetical work of no great merit. The books of Mihira are not mentioned. Varáha produced two works on astrology and one on arithmetic. And Bararúchí introduced certain improvements in grammar, commented upon the incantations, and wrote a poem in praise of King Mádhava.

But the most celebrated of all the patronized ones was Kalidása. His two dramas, Sakuntala,[1] and Vikram and Urvasi,[2] have descended to our day; besides which he produced a poem on the seasons, a work on astronomy, a poetical history of the gods, and many other books.[3]

Vikramaditya established the Sambat era, dating from A.C. 56. After a long, happy, and glorious reign, he lost his life in a war with Shalivahana, King of Pratisthana. That monarch also left behind him an era called the "Shaka," beginning with A.D. 78. It is employed, even now, by the Hindus in recording their births, marriages, and similar occasions.

Paisacha, Gandharba, Rakshasa, Ardhamágadi, Apa, and Guhyaka —most of them being the languages of different orders of fabulous beings. He tells us, however, that an account of these dialects may be found in the work called *Pingala.*

1 Translated by Sir Wm. Jones, 1789; and by Professor Williams, 1856.

2 Translated by Professor H. H. Wilson.

3 The time was propitious to savans. Whilst Vikramaditya lived, Mágha, another king, caused to be written a poem called after his name. For each verse he is said to have paid to learned men a gold piece, which amounted to a total of 5,280*l.*—a large sum in those days, which preceded those of *Paradise Lost.* About the same period Karnáta, a third king, was famed for patronizing the learned men who rose to honour at Vikram's court. Dhavaka, a poet of nearly the same period, received from King Shriharsha the magnificent present of 10,000*l.* for a poem called the *Ratna-Malá.*

King Vikramaditya was succeeded by his infant son
Vikrama-Sena, and father and son reigned over a period
of 93 years. At last the latter was supplanted by a
devotee named Samudra-pála, who entered into his body
by miraculous means. The usurper reigned 24 years and
2 months, and the throne of Delhi continued in the hands
of his sixteen successors, who reigned 641 years and 3
months. Vikrama-pála, the last, was slain in battle by
Tilaka-chandra, King of Vaharannah.[1]

It is not pretended that the words of these Hindu
tales are preserved to the letter. The question about
the metamorphosis of cats into tigers, for instance, proceeded from a Gem of Learning in a university much
nearer home than Gaur. Similarly the learned and still
living Mgr. Gaume (*Traité du Saint-Esprit*, p. 81) joins
Camerarius in the belief that serpents bite women rather
than men. And he quotes (p. 192) Cornelius à Lapide,
who informs us that the leopard is the produce of a lioness
with a hyena or a pard.

The merit of the old stories lies in their suggestive-
ness and in their general applicability. I have ventured to
remedy the conciseness of their language, and to clothe
the skeleton with flesh and blood.

---

1 Lieut. Wilford supports the theory that there were eight Vik-
ramadityas, the last of whom established the era. For further particulars, the curious reader will consult Lassen's *Anthologia*, and
Professor H. H. Wilson's *Essay on Vikram* (New), As. Res. ix. 117.

TO MY UNCLE,

ROBERT BAGSHAW, OF DOVERCOURT,

THESE TALES,

THAT WILL REMIND HIM OF A LAND WHICH

HE KNOWS SO WELL,

ARE AFFECTIONATELY INSCRIBED.

VIKRAM

AND

THE VAMPIRE.

INTRODUCTION.

THE sage Bhavabhuti—Eastern teller of these tales—after making his initiatory and propitiatory congé to Ganesha, Lord of Incepts, informs the reader that this book is a string of fine pearls to be hung round the neck of human intelligence; a fragrant flower to be borne on the turband of mental wisdom; a jewel of pure gold, which becomes the brow of all supreme minds; and a handful of powdered rubies, whose tonic effects will appear palpably upon the mental digestion of every patient. Finally, that by aid of the lessons inculcated in the following pages, man will pass happily through this world into the state of absorption, where fables will be no longer required.

He then teaches us how Vikramaditya the Brave became King of Ujjayani.

Some nineteen centuries ago, the renowned city of Ujjayani witnessed the birth of a prince to whom was given the gigantic name Vikramaditya. Even the Sanskrit-speaking people, who are not usually pressed for time, shortened it to " Vikram," and a little further West it would infallibly have been docked down to " Vik."

Vikram was the second son of an old king Gan-

dharba-Sena, concerning whom little favourable has
reached posterity, except that he became an ass, married
four queens, and had by them six sons, each of whom was
more learned and powerful than the other.   It so happened that in course of time the father died.   Thereupon
his eldest heir, who was known as Shank, succeeded to
the carpet of Rajaship, and was instantly murdered by
Vikram, his " scorpion," the hero of the following pages.[1]

By this act of vigour and manly decision, whch all
younger-brother princes should devoutly imitate, Vikram
having obtained the title of Bir, or the Brave, made
himself Raja.   He began to rule well, and the gods so
favoured him that day by day his dominions increased.
At length he became lord of all India, and having firmly
established his government, he instituted an era—an
uncommon feat for a mere monarch, especially when
hereditary.

The steps,[2] says the historian, which he took to arrive
at that pinnacle of grandeur, were these :

The old King calling his two grandsons Bhartari-hari
and Vikramaditya, gave them good counsel respecting
their future learning.   They were told to master every-

---

1 History tells us another tale.   The god Indra and the King of
Dhara gave the kingdom to Bhartari-hari, another son of Gandharba-Sena, by a handmaiden.   For some time, the brothers lived
together; but presently they quarrelled.   Vikram being dismissed
from court, wandered from place to place in abject poverty, and at
one time hired himself as a servant to a merchant living in Guzerat.
At length, Bhartari-hari, disgusted with the world on account of the
infidelity of his wife, to whom he was ardently attached, became a
religious devotee, and left the kingdom to its fate.   In the course of
his travels, Vikram came to Ujjayani, and finding it without a head,
assumed the sovereignty.   He reigned with great splendour, conquer-
ing by his arms Utkala, Vanga, Kuch-bahar, Guzerat, Somnat, Delhi,
and other places; until, in his turn, he was conquered, and slain by
Shalivahan.

2 The words are found, says Mr. Ward, in the *Hindu History*
compiled by Mrityungaya.

thing, a certain way not to succeed in anything. They were diligently to learn grammar, the Scriptures, and all the religious sciences. They were to become familiar with military tactics, international law, and music, the riding of horses and elephants—especially the latter—the driving of chariots, and the use of the broadsword, the bow, and the mogdars or Indian clubs. They were ordered to be skilful in all kinds of games, in leaping and running, in besieging forts, in forming and breaking bodies of troops; they were to endeavour to excel in every princely quality, to be cunning in ascertaining the power of an enemy, how to make war, to perform journeys, to sit in the presence of the nobles, to separate the different sides of a question, to form alliances, to distinguish between the innocent and the guilty, to assign proper punishments to the wicked, to exercise authority with perfect justice, and to be liberal. The boys were then sent to school, and were placed under the care of excellent teachers, where they became truly famous. Whilst under pupilage, the eldest was allowed all the power necessary to obtain a knowledge of royal affairs, and he was not invested with the regal office till in these preparatory steps he had given full satisfaction to his subjects, who expressed high approval of his conduct.

The two brothers often conversed on the duties of kings, when the great Vikramaditya gave the great Bhartari-hari the following valuable advice [1]:

" As Indra, during the four rainy months, fills the earth with water, so a king should replenish his treasury with money. As Surya the sun, in warming the earth

---

[1] These duties of kings are thus laid down in the *Rajtarangini.* It is evident, as Professor H. H. Wilson says, that the royal status was by no means a sinecure. But the rules are evidently the closet work of some pedantic, dogmatic Brahman, teaching kingcraft to kings. He directs his instructions, not to subordinate judges, but to the Raja as the chief magistrate, and through him to all appointed for the administration of his justice.

eight months, does not scorch it, so a king, in drawing
revenues from his people, ought not to oppress them. As
Vayu, the wind, surrounds and fills everything, so the
king by his officers and spies should become acquainted
with the affairs and circumstances of his whole people. As
Yama judges men without partiality or prejudice, and
punishes the guilty, so should a king chastise, without
favour, all offenders. As Varuna, the regent of water, binds
with his pasha or divine noose his enemies, so let a king
bind every malefactor safely in prison. As Chandra,[1] the
moon, by his cheering light gives pleasure to all, thus
should a king, by gifts and generosity, make his people
happy. And as Prithwi, the earth, sustains all alike, so
should a king feel an equal affection and forbearance
towards every one."

Become a monarch, Vikram meditated deeply upon
what is said of monarchs :—" A king is fire and air ; he is
both sun and moon ; he is the god of criminal justice ; he
is the genius of wealth ; he is the regent of water ; he
is the lord of the firmament ; he is a powerful divinity
who appears in human shape." He reflected with some
satisfaction that the scriptures had made him absolute,
had left the lives and properties of all his subjects to his
arbitrary will, had pronounced him to be an incarnate
deity, and had threatened to punish with death even ideas
derogatory to his honour.

He punctually observed all the ordinances laid down
by the author of the Niti, or institutes of government.
His night and day were divided into sixteen pahars or
portions, each one hour and a half, and they were disposed
of as follows :—

Before dawn Vikram was awakened by a servant
appointed to this special duty. He swallowed—a thing
allowed only to a khshatriya or warrior—a Mithridatic

---

1 Lunus, not Luna.

every morning on the saliva,[1] and he made the cooks taste every dish before he ate of it. As soon as he had risen, the pages in waiting repeated his splendid qualities, and as he left his sleeping-room in full dress, several Brahmans rehearsed the praises of the gods. Presently he bathed, worshipped his guardian deity, again heard hymns, drank a little water, and saw alms distributed to the poor. He ended this watch by auditing his accounts.

Next entering his court, he placed himself amidst the assembly. He was always armed when he received strangers, and he caused even women to be searched for concealed weapons. He was surrounded by so many spies and so artful, that of a thousand, no two ever told the same tale. At the levée, on his right sat his relations, the Brahmans, and men of distinguished birth. The other castes were on the left, and close to him stood the ministers and those whom he delighted to consult. Afar in front gathered the bards chanting the praises of the gods and of the king; also the charioteers, elephanteers, horsemen, and soldiers of valour. Amongst the learned men in those assemblies there were ever some who were well instructed in all the scriptures, and others who had studied in one particular school of philosophy, and were acquainted only with the works on divine wisdom, or with those on justice, civil and criminal, on the arts, mineralogy or the practice of physic; also persons cunning in all kinds of customs; riding-masters, dancing-masters, teachers of good behaviour, examiners, tasters, mimics, mountebanks, and others, who all attended the court and awaited the king's commands. He here pronounced judgment in suits of appeal. His poets wrote about him:

The lord of lone splendour an instant suspends
His course at mid-noon, ere he westward descends;

---

1 That is to say, "upon an empty stomach."

And brief are the moments our young monarch knows,
Devoted to pleasure or paid to repose!

Before the second sandhya,[1] or noon, about the
beginning of the third watch, he recited the names of the
gods, bathed, and broke his fast in his private room;
then rising from food, he was amused by singers and
dancing girls. The labours of the day now became
lighter. After eating he retired, repeating the name of
his guardian deity, visited the temples, saluted the gods,
conversed with the priests, and proceeded to receive and
to distribute presents. Fifthly, he discussed political
questions with his ministers and councillors.

On the announcement of the herald that it was the
sixth watch—about 2 or 3 P.M.—Vikram allowed himself
to follow his own inclinations, to regulate his family, and
to transact business of a private and personal nature.

After gaining strength by rest, he proceeded to review
his troops, examining the men, saluting the officers, and
holding military councils. At sunset he bathed a third
time and performed the five sacraments of listening to a
prelection of the Veda; making oblations to the manes;
sacrificing to Fire in honour of the deities; giving rice
to dumb creatures; and receiving guests with due ceremonies. He spent the evening amidst a select company
of wise, learned, and pious men, conversing on different
subjects, and reviewing the business of the day.

The night was distributed with equal care. During
the first portion Vikram received the reports which his
spies and envoys, dressed in every disguise, brought to
him about his enemies. Against the latter he ceased not
to use the five arts, namely—dividing the kingdom,
bribes, mischief-making, negotiations, and brute-force—
especially preferring the first two and the last. His
forethought and prudence taught him to regard all his

---

1 There are three sandhyas amongst the Hindús—morning, mid-
day, and sunset; and all three are times for prayer.

nearest neighbours and their allies as hostile. The powers beyond those natural enemies he considered friendly because they were the foes of his foes. And all the remoter nations he looked upon as neutrals, in a transitional or provisional state as it were, till they became either his neighbours' neighbours, or his own neighbours, that is to say, his friends or his foes.

This important duty finished he supped, and at the end of the third watch he retired to sleep, which was not allowed to last beyond three hours. In the sixth watch he arose and purified himself. The seventh was devoted to holding private consultations with his ministers, and to furnishing the officers of government with requisite instructions. The eighth or last watch was spent with the Purohita or priest, and with Brahmans, hailing the dawn with its appropriate rites; he then bathed, made the customary offerings, and prayed in some unfrequented place near pure water.

And throughout these occupations he bore in mind the duty of kings, namely—to pursue every object till it be accomplished; to succour all dependants, and hospitably to receive guests, however numerous. He was generous to his subjects respecting taxes, and kind of speech; yet he was inexorable as death in the punishment of offences. He rarely hunted, and he visited his pleasure gardens only on stated days. He acted in his own dominions with justice; he chastised foreign foes with rigour; he behaved generously to Brahmans, and he avoided favouritism amongst his friends. In war he never slew a suppliant, a spectator, a person asleep or undressed, or anyone that showed fear. Whatever country he conquered, offerings were presented to its gods, and effects and money were given to the reverends. But what benefited him most was his attention to the creature comforts of the nine Gems of Science: those eminent men ate and drank themselves into fits of enthusiasm, and ended by immortalising their patron's name.

Become Vikram the Great he established his court
at a delightful and beautiful location rich in the best of
water. The country was difficult of access, and artificially
made incapable of supporting a host of invaders, but four
great roads met near the city. The capital was surrounded with durable ramparts, having gates of defence,
and near it was a mountain fortress, under the especial
charge of a great captain.

The metropolis was well garrisoned and provisioned,
and it surrounded the royal palace, a noble building
without as well as within. Grandeur seemed embodied
there, and Prosperity had made it her own. The nearer
ground, viewed from the terraces and pleasure pavilions,
was a lovely mingling of rock and mountain, plain and
valley, field and fallow, crystal lake and glittering stream.
The banks of the winding Lavana were fringed with
meads whose herbage, pearly with morning dew,
afforded choicest grazing for the sacred cow, and were
dotted with perfumed clumps of Bo-trees, tamarinds,
and holy figs: in one place Vikram planted 100,000 in a
single orchard and gave them to his spiritual advisers.
The river valley separated the stream from a belt of
forest growth which extended to a hill range, dark with
impervious jungle, and cleared here and there for the
cultivator's village. Behind it, rose another sub-range,
wooded with a lower bush and already blue with air,
whilst in the background towered range upon range, here
rising abruptly into points and peaks, there ramp-shaped
or wall-formed, with sheer descents, and all of light
azure hue adorned with glories of silver and gold.

After reigning for some years, Vikram the Brave
found himself at the age of thirty, a staid and sober
middle-aged man. He had several sons—daughters are
naught in India—by his several wives, and he had some
paternal affection for nearly all—except of course, for his

eldest son, a youth who seemed to conduct himself as though he had a claim to the succession. In fact, the king seemed to have taken up his abode for life at Ujjayani, when suddenly he bethought himself, "I must visit those countries of whose names I am ever hearing." The fact is, he had determined to spy out in disguise the lands of all his foes, and to find the best means of bringing against them his formidable army.

  * * * * * * *

We now learn how Bhartari Raja becomes Regent of Ujjayani.

Having thus resolved, Vikram the Brave gave the government into the charge of a younger brother, Bhartari Raja, and in the garb of a religious mendicant, accompanied by Dharma Dhwaj, his second son, a youth bordering on the age of puberty, he began to travel from city to city, and from forest to forest.

The Regent was of a settled melancholic turn of mind, having lost in early youth a very peculiar wife. One day, whilst out hunting, he happened to pass a funeral pyre, upon which a Brahman's widow had just become Sati (a holy woman) with the greatest fortitude. On his return home he related the adventure to Sita Rani, his spouse, and she at once made reply that virtuous women die with their husbands, killed by the fire of grief, not by the flames of the pile. To prove her truth the prince, after an affectionate farewell, rode forth to the chase, and presently sent back the suite with his robes torn and stained, to report his accidental death. Sita perished upon the spot, and the widower remained inconsolable—for a time.

He led the dullest of lives, and took to himself sundry spouses, all equally distinguished for birth, beauty, and modesty. Like his brother, he performed all the proper devoirs of a Raja, rising before the day to finish his ablutions, to worship the gods, and to do due obeisance to

the Brahmans.   He then ascended the throne, to judge
his people according to the Shastra, carefully keeping in
subjection lust, anger, avarice, folly, drunkenness, and
pride ; preserving himself from being seduced by the
love of gaming and of the chase ; restraining his desire
for dancing, singing, and playing on musical instruments,
and refraining from sleep during daytime, from wine, from
molesting men of worth, from dice, from putting human
beings to death by artful means, from useless travelling,
and from holding any one guilty without the commission
of a crime.   His levées were in a hall decently splendid,
and he was distinguished only by an umbrella of peacock's
feathers ; he received all complainants, petitioners, and
presenters of offences with kind looks and soft words.   He
united to himself the seven or eight wise councillors, and
the sober and virtuous secretary that formed the high
cabinet of his royal brother, and they met in some secret
lonely spot, as a mountain, a terrace, a bower or a forest,
whence women, parrots, and other talkative birds were
carefully excluded.

And at the end of this useful and somewhat laborious
day, he retired to his private apartments, and, after
listening to spiritual songs and to soft music, he fell
asleep.   Sometimes he would summon his brother's
" Nine Gems of Science," and give ear to their learned
discourses.   But it was observed that the viceroy re-
served this exercise for nights when he was troubled with
insomnia—the words of wisdom being to him an infallible
remedy for that disorder.

Thus passed onwards his youth, doing nothing that
it could desire, forbidden all pleasures because they were
unprincely, and working in the palace harder than in the
pauper's hut.   Having, however, fortunately for himself,
few predilections and no imagination, he began to pride
himself upon being a philosopher.   Much business from
an early age had dulled his wits, which were never of the

most brilliant ; and in the steadily increasing torpidity of
his spirit, he traced the germs of that quietude which
forms the highest happiness of man in this storm of
matter called the world. He therefore allowed himself
but one friend of his soul. He retained, I have said, his
brother's seven or eight ministers ; he was constant in
attendance upon the Brahman priests who officiated at
the palace, and who kept the impious from touching
sacred property ; and he was courteous to the commander-
in-chief who directed his warriors, to the officers of
justice who inflicted punishment upon offenders, and to
the lords of towns, varying in number from one to a
thousand. But he placed an intimate of his own in
the high position of confidential councillor, the ambassador to regulate war and peace.

Mahi-pala was a person of noble birth, endowed
with shining abilities, popular, dexterous in business,
acquainted with foreign parts, famed for eloquence and
intrepidity, and as Menu the Lawgiver advises, remarkably handsome.

Bhartari Raja, as I have said, became a quietist and
a philosopher. But Kama,[1] the bright god who exerts
his sway over the three worlds, heaven and earth and
grewsome Hades,[2] had marked out the prince once more
as the victim of his blossom-tipped shafts and his flowery
bow. How, indeed, could he hope to escape the doom
which has fallen equally upon Brahma the Creator,
Vishnu the Preserver, and dreadful Shiva the Three-eyed
Destroyer[3] ?

By reason of her exceeding beauty, her face was a
full moon shining in the clearest sky; her hair was the
purple cloud of autumn when, gravid with rain, it hangs
low over earth ; and her complexion mocked the pale

1 The Hindu Cupid.
2 Patali, the regions beneath the earth.
3 The Hindu Triad.

waxen hue of the large-flowered jasmine. Her eyes were
those of the timid antelope ; her lips were as red as those
of the pomegranate's bud, and when they opened, from
them distilled a fountain of ambrosia. Her neck was like
a pigeon's ; her hand the pink lining of the conch-shell ;
her waist a leopard's ; her feet the softest lotuses. In a
word, a model of grace and loveliness was Dangalah
Rani, Raja Bhartari's last and youngest wife.

The warrior laid down his arms before her ; the poli-
tician spoke out every secret in her presence. The
religious prince would have slaughtered a cow—that sole
unforgivable sin—to save one of her eyelashes : the absolute
king would not drink a cup of water without her permission ; the staid philosopher, the sober quietist, to win from
her the shadow of a smile, would have danced before her
like a singing-girl. So desperately enamoured became
Bhartari Raja.

It is written, however, that love, alas ! breeds not
love; and so it happened to the Regent. The warmth of
his affection, instead of animating his wife, annoyed her ;
his protestations wearied her ; his vows gave her the
headache ; and his caresses were a colic that made
her blood run cold. Of course, the prince perceived
nothing, being lost in wonder and admiration of the
beauty's coyness and coquetry. And as women must
give away their hearts, whether asked or not, so the lovely
Dangalah Rani lost no time in lavishing all the passion of
her idle soul upon Mahi-pala, the handsome ambassador
of peace and war. By this means the three were happy
and were contented ; their felicity, however, being built
on a rotten foundation, could not long endure. It soon
ended in the following extraordinary way.

In the city of Ujjayani,[1] within sight of the palace,

---

1 Or Avanti, also called Padmavati. It is the first meridian of
the Hindus, who found their longitude by observation of lunar
eclipses, calculated for it and Lanka, or Ceylon. The clepsydra was
used for taking time.

dwelt a Brahman and his wife, who, being old and poor, and having nothing else to do, had applied themselves to the practice of austere devotion.[1] They fasted and refrained from drink, they stood on their heads and held their arms for weeks in the air; they prayed till their knees were like pads; they disciplined themselves with scourges of wire; and they walked about unclad in the cold season, and in summer they sat within a circle of flaming wood, till they became the envy and admiration of all the plebeian gods that inhabit the lower heavens. In fine, as a reward for their exceeding piety, the venerable pair received at the hands of a celestial messenger an apple of the tree Kalpavriksha—a. fruit which has the virtue of conferring eternal life upon him that tastes it.

Scarcely had the god disappeared, when the Brahman, opening his toothless mouth, prepared to eat the fruit of immortality. Then his wife addressed him in these words, shedding copious tears the while:

"To die, O man, is a passing pain; to be poor is an interminable anguish. Surely our present lot is the penalty of some great crime committed by us in a past state of being.[2] Callest thou this state life? Better we die at once, and so escape the woes of the world!"

Hearing these words, the Brahman sat undecided, with open jaws and eyes fixed upon the apple. Presently he found tongue: "I have accepted the fruit, and have brought it here; but having heard thy speech, my intellect hath wasted away; now I will do whatever thou pointest out."

The wife resumed her discourse, which had been in-

---

1 In the original only the husband "practised austere devotion." For the benefit of those amongst whom the "pious wife" is an institution, I have extended the privilege.

2 A Moslem would say, "This is our fate." A Hindu refers at once to metempsychosis, as naturally as a modern Swedenborgian to spiritism.

terrupted by a more than usually copious flow of tears.
" Moreover, O husband, we are old, and what are the
enjoyments of the stricken in years?   Truly quoth the
poet—

> Die loved in youth, not hated in age.

If that fruit could have restored thy dimmed eyes, and
deaf ears, and blunted taste, and warmth of love, I had
not spoken to thee thus."

After which the Brahman threw away the apple, to
the great joy of his wife, who felt a natural indignation at
the prospect of seeing her goodman become immortal,
whilst she still remained subject to the laws of death ; but
she concealed this motive in the depths of her thought,
enlarging, as women are apt to do, upon everything but
the truth.   And she spoke with such success, that the
priest was about to toss in his rage the heavenly fruit
into the fire, reproaching the gods as if by sending it they
had done him an injury.   Then the wife snatched it out
of his hand, and telling him it was too precious to be
wasted, bade him arise and gird his loins and wend him
to the Regent's palace, and offer him the fruit—as King
Vikram was absent—with a right reverend brahmanical
benediction.   She concluded with impressing upon her
unworldly husband the necessity of requiring a large sum
of money as a return for his inestimable gift.   " By this
means," she said, " thou mayst promote thy present and
future welfare.[1]"

Then the Brahman went forth, and standing in the
presence of the Raja, told him all things touching the
fruit, concluding with " O, mighty prince ! vouchsafe to
accept this tribute, and bestow wealth upon me.   I shall
be happy in your living long !"

Bhartari Raja led the supplicant into an inner strong-

---

[1] In Europe, money buys this world, and delivers you from the
pains of purgatory ; amongst the Hindus, it furthermore opens the
gate of heaven.

room, where stood heaps of the finest gold-dust, and bade him carry away all that he could ; this the priest did, not forgetting to fill even his eloquent and toothless mouth with the precious metal. Having dismissed the devotee groaning under the burden, the Regent entered the apartments of his wives, and having summoned the beautiful Queen Dangalah Rani, gave her the fruit, and said, "Eat this, light of my eyes! This fruit—joy of my heart!— will make thee everlastingly young and beautiful."

The pretty queen, placing both hands upon her husband's bosom, kissed his eyes and lips, and sweetly smiling on his face—for great is the guile of women— whispered, " Eat it thyself, dear one, or at least share it with me ; for what is life and what is youth without the presence of those we love ? " But the Raja, whose heart was melted by these unusual words, put her away tenderly, and, having explained that the fruit would serve for only one person, departed.

Whereupon the pretty queen, sweetly smiling as before, slipped the precious present into her pocket. When the Regent was transacting business in the hall of audience she sent for the ambassador who regulated war and peace, and presented him with the apple in a manner at least as tender as that with which it had been offered to her.

Then the ambassador, after slipping the fruit into his pocket also, retired from the presence of the pretty queen, and meeting Lakha, one of the maids of honour, explained to her its wonderful power, and gave it to her as a token of his love. But the maid of honour, being an ambitious girl, determined that the fruit was a fit present to set before the Regent in the absence of the King. Bhartari Raja accepted it, bestowed on her great wealth, and dismissed her with many thanks.

He then took up the apple and looked at it with eyes brimful of tears, for he knew the whole extent of his mis-

fortune.   His heart ached, he felt a loathing for the
world, and he said with sighs and groans[1]:

"Of what value are these delusions of wealth and
affection, whose sweetness endures for a moment and becomes eternal bitterness?   Love is like the drunkard's
cup: delicious is the first drink, palling are the draughts
that succeed it, and most distasteful are the dregs.
What is life but a restless vision of imaginary pleasures
and of real pains, from which the only waking is the terrible day of death?   The affection of this world is of no
use, since, in consequence of it, we fall at last into hell.
For which reason it is best to practise the austerities of
religion, that the Deity may bestow upon us hereafter
that happiness which he refuses to us here!"

Thus did Bhartari Raja determine to abandon
the world.   But before setting out for the forest, he
could not refrain from seeing the queen once more, so hot
was the flame which Kama had kindled in his heart.   He
therefore went to the apartments of his women, and having caused Dangalah Rani to be summoned, he asked her
what had become of the fruit which he had given to her.
She answered that, according to his command, she had
eaten it.   Upon which the Regent showed her the apple,
and she beholding it stood aghast, unable to make any
reply.   The Raja gave careful orders for her beheading;
he then went out, and having had the fruit washed, ate
it.   He quitted the throne to be a jogi, or religious mendicant, and without communicating with any one departed
into the jungle.   There he became such a devotee that
death had no power over him, and he is wandering still.
But some say that he was duly absorbed into the essence
of the Deity.

*   *   *   *   *   *

1 This part of the introduction will remind the reader of the two
royal brothers and their false wives in the introduction to the *Arabian
Nights*.   The fate of Bhartari Raja, however, is historical.

We are next told how the valiant Vikram returned to his own country.

Thus Vikram's throne remained empty. When the news reached King Indra, Regent of the Lower Firmament and Protector of Earthly Monarchs, he sent Prithwi Pala, a fierce giant,[1] to defend the city of Ujjayani till such time as its lawful master might reappear, and the guardian used to keep watch and ward night and day over his trust.

In less than a year the valorous Raja Vikram became thoroughly tired of wandering about the woods half dressed : now suffering from famine, then exposed to the attacks of wild beasts, and at all times very ill at ease. He reflected also that he was not doing his duty to his wives and children ; that the heir-apparent would probably make the worst use of the parental absence ; and finally, that his subjects, deprived of his fatherly care, had been left in the hands of a man who, for ought he could say, was not worthy of the high trust. He had also spied out all the weak points of friend and foe. Whilst these and other equally weighty considerations were hanging about the Raja's mind, he heard a rumour of the state of things spread abroad ; that Bhartari, the regent, having abdicated his throne, had gone away into the forest. Then quoth Vikram to his son, " We have ended our wayfarings, now let us turn our steps homewards ! "

---

1 In the original, "Div"—a supernatural being, god, or demon. This part of the plot is variously told. According to some, Raja Vikram was surprised, when entering the city, to see a grand procession at the house of a potter, and a boy being carried off on an elephant, to the violent grief of his parents. The King inquired the reason of their sorrow, and was told that the wicked Div that guarded the city was in the habit of eating a citizen per diem. Whereupon the valorous Raja caused the boy to dismount ; took his place ; entered the palace ; and, when presented as food for the demon, displayed his pugilistic powers in a way to excite the monster's admiration.

2

The gong was striking the mysterious hour of midnight as the king and the young prince approached the principal gate. And they were pushing through it when a monstrous figure rose up before them and called out with a fearful voice, " Who are ye, and where are ye going ? Stand and deliver your names ! "

" I am Raja Vikram," rejoined the king, half choked with rage, " and I am come to mine own city. Who art thou that darest to stop or stay me ? "

" That question is easily answered," cried Prithwi Pala the giant, in his roaring voice ; " the gods have sent me to protect Ujjayani. If thou be really Raja Vikram, prove thyself a man : first fight with me, and then return to thine own."

The warrior king cried " Sadhu ! " wanting nothing better. He girt his girdle tight round his loins, summoned his opponent into the empty space beyond the gate, told him to stand on guard, and presently began to devise some means of closing with or running in upon him. The giant's fists were large as water melons, and his knotted arms whistled through the air like falling trees, threatening fatal blows. Besides which the Raja's head scarcely reached the giant's stomach, and the latter, each time he struck out, whooped so abominably loud, that no human nerves could remain unshaken.

At last Vikram's good luck prevailed. The giant's left foot slipped, and the hero, seizing his antagonist's other leg, began to trip him up. At the same moment the young prince, hastening to his parent's assistance, jumped viciously upon the enemy's naked toes. By their united exertions they brought him to the ground, when the son sat down upon his stomach, making himself as weighty as he well could, whilst the father, climbing up to the monster's throat, placed himself astride upon it, and pressing both thumbs upon his eyes, threatened to blind him if he would not yield.

2—2

Then the giant, modifying the bellow of his voice, cried out—

" O Raja, thou hast overthrown me, and I grant thee thy life."

" Surely thou art mad, monster," replied the king, in jeering tone, half laughing, half angry. " To whom grantest thou life ? If I desire it I can kill thee; how, then, dost thou talk about granting me my life?"

" Vikram of Ujjayani," said the giant, " be not too proud ! I will save thee from a nearly impending death. Only hearken to the tale which I have to tell thee, and use thy judgment, and act upon it. So shalt thou rule the world free from care, and live without danger, and die happily."

" Proceed," quoth the Raja, after a moment's thought, dismounting from the giant's throat, and beginning to listen with all his ears.

The giant raised himself from the ground, and when in a sitting posture, began in solemn tones to speak as follows:

" In short, the history of the matter is, that three men were born in this same city of Ujjayani, in the same lunar mansion, in the same division of the great circle described upon the ecliptic, and in the same period of time. You, the first, were born in the house of a king. The second was an oilman's son, who was slain by the third, a jogi, or anchorite, who kills all he can, wafting the sweet scent of human sacrifice to the nostrils of Durga, goddess of destruction. Moreover, the holy man, after compassing the death of the oilman's son, has suspended him head downwards from a mimosa tree in a cemetery. He is now anxiously plotting thy destruction. He hath murdered his own child——"

" And how came an anchorite to have a child?" asked Raja Vikram, incredulously.

" That is what I am about to tell thee," replied the giant. " In the good days of thy generous father, Gand-

harba-Sena, as the court was taking its pleasure in the
forest, they saw a devotee, or rather a devotee's head, protruding from a hole in the ground.   The white ants had
surrounded his body with a case of earth, and had made
their home upon his skin.   All kinds of insects and small
animals crawled up and down the face, yet not a muscle
moved.   Wasps had hung their nests to its temples, and
scorpions wandered in and out of the matted and clotted
hair; yet the hermit felt them not.   He spoke to no one;
he received no gifts; and had it not been for the opening
of his nostrils, as he continually inhaled the pungent
smoke of a thorn fire, man would have deemed him dead.
Such were his religious austerities.

"Thy father marvelled much at the sight, and rode
home in profound thought.   That evening, as he sat in
the hall of audience, he could speak of nothing but the
devotee ; and his curiosity soon rose to such a pitch, that
he proclaimed about the city a reward of one hundred gold
pieces to any one that could bring to court this anchorite
of his own free will.

"Shortly afterwards, Vasantasena, a singing and
dancing girl more celebrated for wit and beauty than for
sagesse or discretion, appeared before thy sire, and offered
for the petty inducement of a gold bangle to bring the
anchorite into the palace, carrying a baby on his
shoulder.

"The king hearing her speak was astonished, gave
her a betel leaf in token that he held her to her promise,
and permitted her to depart, which she did with a laugh
of triumph.

"Vasantasena went directly to the jungle, where she
found the pious man faint with thirst, shrivelled with
hunger, and half dead with heat and cold.   She cautiously
put out the fire.   Then, having prepared a confection,
she approached from behind and rubbed upon his lips a
little of the sweetmeat, which he licked up with great

relish. Thereupon she made more and gave it to him. After two days of this generous diet he gained some strength, and on the third, as he felt a finger upon his mouth, he opened his eyes and said, ' Why hast thou come here ? '

" The girl, who had her story in readiness, replied : ' I am the daughter of a deity, and have practised religious observances in the heavenly regions. I have now come into this forest ! ' And the devotee, who began to think how much more pleasant is such society than solitude, asked her where her hut was, and requested to be led there.

" Then Vasantasena, having unearthed the holy man and compelled him to purify himself, led him to the abode which she had caused to be built for herself in the wood. She explained its luxuries by the nature of her vow, which bound her to indulge in costly apparel, in food with six flavours, and in every kind of indulgence.[1] In course of time the hermit learned to follow her example; he gave up inhaling smoke, and he began to eat and drink as a daily occupation.

" At length Kama began to trouble him. Briefly the saint and saintess were made man and wife, by the simple form of matrimony called the Gandharba-vivaha,[2]

---

1 In India, there is still a monastic order the pleasant duty of whose members is to enjoy themselves as much as possible. It has been much the same in Europe. "Représentez-vous le couvent de l'Escurial ou du Mont Cassin, où les cénobites ont toutes sortes de commodités, nécessaires, utiles, délectables, superflues, surabondantes, puisqu'ils ont les cent cinquante mille, les quatre cent mille, les cinq cent mille écus de rente ; et jugez si monsieur l'abbé a de quoi laisser dormir la méridienne à ceux qui voudront."—*Saint Augustin, de l'Ouvrage des Moines,* by Le Camus, Bishop of Belley, quoted by Voltaire, *Dict. phil.*, sub v. "Apocalypse."

2 This form of matrimony was recognized by the ancient Hindus, and is frequent in books. It is a kind of Scotch wedding—ultra-Caledonian—taking place by mutual consent, without any form or

and about ten months afterwards a son was born to them.
Thus the anchorite came to have a child.

"Remained Vasantasena's last feat.   Some months
passed : then she said to the devotee her husband, ' Oh
saint ! let us now, having finished our devotions, perform
a pilgrimage to some sacred place, that all the sins of our
bodies may be washed away, after which we will die and
depart into everlasting happiness.'   Cajoled by these
speeches, the hermit mounted his child upon his shoulder
and followed her where she went — directly into Raja
Gandharba-Sena's palace.

"When the king and the ministers and the officers
and the courtiers saw Vasantasena, and her spouse carrying the baby, they recognised her from afar.   The Raja
exclaimed, ' Lo! this is the very singing girl who went
forth to bring back the devotee.'   And all replied : ' O
great monarch ! thou speakest truly ; this is the very
same woman.   And be pleased to observe that whatever
things she, having asked leave to undertake, went forth
to do, all these she hath done ! '   Then gathering around
her they asked her all manner of questions, as if the
whole matter had been the lightest and the most laughable thing in the world.

"But the anchorite, having heard the speeches of
the king and his courtiers, thought to himself, ' They
have done this for the purpose of taking away the fruits of
my penance.'   Cursing them all with terrible curses, and
taking up his child, he left the hall.   Thence he went to
the forest, slaughtered the innocent, and began to practise
austerities with a view to revenge that hour, and, having
slain his child, he will attempt thy life.   His prayers
have been heard.   In the first place they deprived thee
of thy father.   Secondly, they cast enmity between thee
and thy brother, thus dooming him to an untimely end.

---

ceremony. The Gandharbas are heavenly minstrels of Indra's court,
who are supposed to be witnesses.

Thirdly, they are now working thy ruin. The anchorite's design is to offer up a king and a king's son to his patroness Durga, and by virtue of such devotional act he will obtain the sovereignty of the whole world !

"But I have promised, O Vikram, to save thee, if such be the will of Fortune, from impending destruction. Therefore hearken well unto my words. Distrust them that dwell amongst the dead, and remember that it is lawful and right to strike off his head that would slay thee. So shalt thou rule the universal earth, and leave behind thee an immortal name !"

Suddenly Prithwi Pala, the giant, ceased speaking, and disappeared. Vikram and his son then passed through the city gates, feeling their limbs to be certain that no bones were broken, and thinking over the scene that had occurred.

    *   *   *   *   *   *

We now are informed how the valiant King Vikram met with the Vampire.

It was the spring season when the Raja returned, and the Holi festival[1] caused dancing and singing in every house. Ujjayani was extraordinarily happy and joyful at the return of her ruler, who joined in her gladness with all his kingly heart. The faces and dresses of the public were red and yellow with gulal and abir,—perfumed powders,[2]—which were sprinkled upon one another in token of merriment. Musicians deafened the citizens' ears, dancing girls performed till ready to faint with fatigue, the manufacturers of comfits made their fortunes, and the Nine Gems of Science celebrated the auspicious day with the most long-winded odes. The royal hero, decked in regal attire, and attended by many thousands of state

---

1 The Hindu Saturnalia.

2 The powders are of wheaten flour, mixed with wild ginger-root, sappan-wood, and other ingredients. Sometimes the stuff is thrown in syringes.

palanquins glittering with their various ornaments, and escorted by a suite of a hundred kingly personages, with their martial array of the four hosts, of cavalry, elephants, chariots, and infantry, and accompanied by Amazon girls, lovely as the suite of the gods, himself a personification of majesty, bearing the white parasol of dominion, with a golden staff and tassels, began once more to reign.

After the first pleasures of return, the king applied himself unremittingly to good government and to eradicating the abuses which had crept into the administration during the period of his wanderings.

Mindful of the wise saying, " if the Raja did not punish the guilty, the stronger would roast the weaker like a fish on the spit," he began the work of reform with an iron hand. He confiscated the property of a councillor who had the reputation of taking bribes; he branded the forehead of a sudra or servile man whose breath smelt of ardent spirits, and a goldsmith having been detected in fraud he ordered him to be cut in shreds with razors as the law in its mercy directs. In the case of a notorious evil-speaker he opened the back of his head and had his tongue drawn through the wound. A few murderers he burned alive on iron beds, praying the while that Vishnu might have mercy upon their souls. His spies were ordered, as the shastra called " The Prince" advises, to mix with robbers and thieves with a view of leading them into situations where they might most easily be entrapped, and once or twice when the fellows were too wary, he seized them and their relations and impaled them all, thereby conclusively proving, without any mistake, that he was king of earth.

With the sex feminine he was equally severe. A woman convicted of having poisoned an elderly husband in order to marry a younger man was thrown to the dogs, which speedily devoured her. He punished simple infidelity by cutting off the offender's nose—an admirable practice, which is not only a severe penalty to the culprit, but also a standing warning to others, and an efficient preventative to any recurrence of the fault. Faithlessness combined with bad example or brazenfacedness was further treated by being led in solemn procession through the bazár mounted on a diminutive and crop-eared donkey, with the face turned towards the crupper. After a few such examples the women of Ujjayani became almost modest; it is the fault of man when they are not tolerably well behaved in one point at least.

Every day as Vikram sat upon the judgment-seat, trying causes and punishing offences, he narrowly observed the speech, the gestures, and the countenances of the various criminals and litigants and their witnesses. Ever suspecting women, as I have said, and holding them to be the root of all evil, he never failed when some sin or crime more horrible than usual came before him, to ask the accused, "Who is she?" and the suddenness of the question often elicited the truth by accident. For there can be nothing thoroughly and entirely bad unless a woman is at the bottom of it; and, knowing this, Raja Vikram made certain notable hits under the most improbable circumstances, which had almost given him a reputation for omniscience. But this is easily explained : a man intent upon squaring the circle will see squares in circles wherever he looks, and sometimes he will find them.

In disputed cases of money claims, the king adhered strictly to established practice, and consulted persons learned in the law. He seldom decided a cause on his own judgment, and he showed great temper and patience in bearing with rough language from irritated plaintiffs and defendants, from the infirm, and from old men beyond eighty. That humble petitioners might not be baulked

in having accsss to the "fountain of justice," he caused
an iron box to be suspended by a chain from the windows
of his sleeping apartment. Every morning he ordered
the box to be opened before him, and listened to all the
placets at full length. Even in this simple process he
displayed abundant cautiousness. For, having forgotten
what little of the humanities he had mastered in his youth,
he would hand the paper to a secretary whose business it
was to read it out before him; after which operation the
man of letters was sent into an inner room, and the petition was placed in the hands of a second scribe. Once it
so happened by the bungling of the deceitful kayasths
(clerks) that an important difference was found to occur
in the same sheet. So upon strict inquiry one secretary
lost his ears and the other his right hand. After this
petitions were rarely if ever falsified.

The Raja Vikram also lost no time in attacking the
cities and towns and villages of his enemies, but the
people rose to a man against him, and hewing his army
to pieces with their weapons, vanquished him. This took
place so often that he despaired of bringing all the earth
under the shadow of his umbrella.

At length on one occasion when near a village he
listened to a conversation of the inhabitants. A woman
having baked some cakes was giving them to her child,
who leaving the edges would eat only the middle. On
his asking for another cake, she cried, "This boy's way
is like Vikram's in his attempt to conquer the world!"
On his inquiring "Mother, why, what am I doing; and
what has Vikram done?" "Thou, my boy," she replied,
"throwing away the outside of the cake eatest the middle
only. Vikram also in his ambition, without subduing the
frontiers before attacking the towns, invades the heart of
the country and lays it waste. On that account, both
the townspeople and others rising, close upon him from

the frontiers to the centre, and destroy his army. *That* is his folly."

Vikram took notice of the woman's words. He strengthened his army and resumed his attack on the provinces and cities, beginning with the frontiers, reducing the outer towns and stationing troops in the intervals. Thus he proceeded regularly with his invasions. After a respite, adopting the same system and marshalling huge armies, he reduced in regular course each kingdom and province till he became monarch of the whole world.

It so happened that one day as Vikram the Brave sat upon the judgment-seat, a young merchant, by name Mal Deo, who had lately arrived at Ujjayani with loaded camels and elephants, and with the reputation of immense wealth, entered the palace court. Having been received with extreme condescension, he gave into the king's hand a fruit which he had brought in his own, and then spreading a prayer carpet on the floor he sat down. Presently, after a quarter of an hour, he arose and went away. When he had gone the king reflected in his mind: " Under this disguise, perhaps, is the very man of whom the giant spoke." Suspecting this, he did not eat the fruit, but calling the master of the household he gave the present to him, ordering him to keep it in a very careful manner. The young merchant, however, continued every day to court the honour of an interview, each time presenting a similar gift.

By chance one morning Raja Vikram went, attended by his ministers, to see his stables. At this time the young merchant also arrived there, and in the usual manner placed a fruit in the royal hand. As the king was thoughtfully tossing it in the air, it accidentally fell from his fingers to the ground. Then the monkey, who was tethered amongst the horses to draw calamities from their heads,[1] snatched it up and tore it to pieces. Where-

---

1 The Persian proverb is—"Bala e tavilah bar sar i maimun":

upon a ruby of such size and water came forth that the king and his ministers, beholding its brilliancy, gave vent to expressions of wonder.

Quoth Vikram to the young merchant severely—for his suspicions were now thoroughly roused—"Why hast thou given to us all this wealth ?"

"O great king," replied Mal Deo, demurely, "it is written in the scriptures (shastra) 'Of Ceremony' that 'we must not go empty-handed into the presence of the following persons, namely, Rajas, spiritual teachers, judges, young maidens, and old women whose daughters we would marry.' But why, O Vikram, dost thou speak of one ruby only, since in each of the fruits which I have laid at thy feet there is a similar jewel?"

Having heard this speech, the king said to the master of his household, "Bring all the fruits which I have entrusted to thee." The treasurer, on receiving the royal command, immediately brought them, and having split them, there was found in each one a ruby, one and all equally perfect in size and water. Raja Vikram beholding such treasures was excessively pleased. Having sent for a lapidary, he ordered him to examine the rubies, saying, "We cannot take anything with us out of this world. Virtue is a noble quality to possess here below—so tell justly what is the value of each of these gems.[1]"

To so moral a speech the lapidary replied, "Maha-

"The woes of the stable be on the monkey's head!" In some Moslem countries a hog acts prophylactic. Hence probably Mungo Park's troublesome pig at Ludamar.

[1] So the moribund father of the "babes in the wood" lectures his wicked brother, their guardian:

> "To God and you I recommend
> My children deare this day :
> But little while, be sure, we have
> Within this world to stay."

But, to appeal to the moral sense of a goldsmith!

raja¹! thou hast said truly; whoever possesses virtue, possesses everything; virtue indeed accompanies us always, and is of advantage in both worlds. Hear, O great king! each gem is perfect in colour, quality and beauty. If I were to say that the value of each was ten million millions of suvarnas (gold pieces), even then thou couldst not understand its real worth. In fact, each ruby would buy one of the seven regions into which the earth is divided."

The king on hearing this was delighted, although his suspicions were not satisfied ; and, having bestowed a robe of honour upon the lapidary, dismissed him. Thereon, taking the young merchant's hand, he led him into the palace, seated him upon his own carpet in presence of the court, and began to say, " My entire kingdom is not worth one of these rubies: tell me how it is that thou who buyest and sellest hast given me such and so many pearls?"

Mal Deo replied : " O great king, the speaking of matters like the following in public is not right; these things—prayers, spells, drugs, good qualities, household affairs, the eating of forbidden food, and the evil we may have heard of our neighbour—should not be discussed in full assembly. Privately I will disclose to thee my wishes. This is the way of the world; when an affair comes to six ears, it does not remain secret; if a matter is confided to four ears it may escape further hearing; and if to two ears even Brahma the Creator does not know it; how then can any rumour of it come to man?"

Having heard this speech, Raja Vikram took Mal Deo aside, and began to ask him, saying, " O generous man! you have given me so many rubies, and even for a single day you have not eaten food with me; I am exceedingly ashamed, tell me what you desire."

---

1 Maha (great) raja (king): common address even to those who are not royal.

"Raja," said the young merchant, "I am not Mal Deo, but Shanta-Shil,[1] a devotee. I am about to perform spells, incantations and magical rites on the banks of the river Godavari, in a large smashana, a cemetery where bodies are burned. By this means the Eight Powers of Nature will all become mine. This thing I ask of you as alms, that you and the young prince Dharma Dhwaj will pass one night with me, doing my bidding. By you remaining near me my incantations will be successful."

The valiant Vikram nearly started from his seat at the word cemetery, but, like a ruler of men, he restrained his face from expressing his feelings, and he presently replied, "Good, we will come, tell us on what day!"

"You are to come to me," said the devotee, "armed, but without followers, on the Monday evening the 14th of the dark half of the month Bhadra.[2]" The Raja said: "Do you go your ways, we will certainly come." In this manner, having received a promise from the king, and having taken leave, the devotee returned to his house: thence he repaired to the temple, and having made preparations, and taken all the necessary things, he went back into the cemetery and sat down to his ceremonies.

The valiant Vikram, on the other hand, retired into an inner apartment, to consult his own judgment about an adventure with which, for fear of ridicule, he was unwilling to acquaint even the most trustworthy of his ministers.

In due time came the evening moon's day, the 14th of the dark half of the month Bhadra. As the short twilight fell gloomily on earth, the warrior king accompanied by his son, with turband-ends tied under their chins, and with trusty blades tucked under their arms ready for foes, human, bestial, or devilish, slipped out

---

1 The name means, "Quietistic Disposition."

2 August. In the solar-lunar year of the Hindu the months are divided into fortnights—light and dark.

unseen through the palace wicket, and took the road leading to the cemetery on the river bank.

Dark and drear was the night. Urged by the furious blast of the lingering winter-rains, masses of bistre-coloured cloud, like the forms of unwieldy beasts, rolled heavily over the firmament plain. Whenever the crescent of the young moon, rising from an horizon sable as the sad Tamala's hue,[1] glanced upon the wayfarers, it was no brighter than the fine tip of an elephant's tusk protruding from the muddy wave. A heavy storm was impending; big drops fell in showers from the forest trees as they groaned under the blast, and beneath the gloomy avenue the clayey ground gleamed ghastly white. As the Raja and his son advanced, a faint ray of light, like the line of pure gold streaking the dark surface of the touchstone, caught their eyes, and directed their footsteps towards the cemetery.

When Vikram came upon the open space on the river bank where corpses were burned, he hesitated for a moment to tread its impure ground. But seeing his son undismayed, he advanced boldly, trampling upon remnants of bones, and only covering his mouth with his turband-end.

Presently, at the further extremity of the smashana, or burning ground, appeared a group. By the lurid flames that flared and flickered round the half-extinguished funeral pyres, with remnants of their dreadful loads, Raja Vikram and Dharma Dhwaj could note the several features of the ill-omened spot. There was an outer circle of hideous bestial forms; tigers were roaring, and elephants were trumpeting; wolves, whose foul hairy coats blazed with sparks of bluish phosphoric light, were devouring the remnants of human bodies; foxes, jackals, and hyenas were disputing over their prey; whilst bears were chewing the livers of children. The space within

---

1 A flower, whose name frequently occurs in Sanskrit poetry.

was peopled by a multitude of fiends. There were the
subtle bodies of men that had escaped their grosser
frames prowling about the charnel ground, where their
corpses had been reduced to ashes, or hovering in the air,
waiting till the new bodies which they were to animate
were made ready for their reception. The spirits of those
that had been foully slain wandered about with gashed
limbs; and skeletons, whose mouldy bones were held
together by bits of blackened sinew, followed them as the
murderer does his victim. Malignant witches with
shrivelled skins, horrid eyes and distorted forms, crawled
and crouched over the earth; whilst spectres and goblins
now stood motionless, and tall as lofty palm trees; then,
as if in fits, leaped, danced, and tumbled before their
evocator. The air was filled with shrill and strident
cries, with the fitful moaning of the storm-wind, with the
hooting of the owl, with the jackal's long wild cry, and
with the hoarse gurgling of the swollen river, from whose
banks the earth-slip thundered in its fall.

In the midst of all, close to the fire which lit up his
evil countenance, sat Shanta-Shil, the jogi, with the
banner that denoted his calling and his magic staff planted
in the ground behind him. He was clad in the ochre-
coloured loin-wrap of his class; from his head streamed
long tangled locks of hair like horsehair; his black body
was striped with lines of chalk, and a girdle of thigh
bones encircled his waist. His face was smeared with
ashes from a funeral pyre, and his eyes, fixed as those of
a statue, gleamed from this mask with an infernal light of
hate. His cheeks were shaven, and he had not forgotten
to draw the horizontal sectarian mark. But this was of
blood; and Vikram, as he drew near saw that he was
playing upon a human skull with two shank bones,
making music for the horrid revelry.

Now Raja Vikram, as has been shown by his en-
counter with Indra's watchman, was a bold prince, and

he was cautious as he was brave. The sight of a human being in the midst of these terrors raised his mettle; he determined to prove himself a hero, and feeling that the critical moment was now come, he hoped to rid himself and his house for ever of the family curse that hovered over them.

For a moment he thought of the giant's words, "And remember that it is lawful and right to strike off his head

He was playing upon a human skull with two shank bones.

that would slay thee." A stroke with his good sword might at once and effectually put an end to the danger. But then he remembered that he had passed his royal word to do the devotee's bidding that night. Besides, he felt assured that the hour for action had not yet sounded.

These reflections having passed through his mind with the rapid course of a star that has lost its honours,[1]

---

1 The stars being men's souls raised to the sky for a time proportioned to their virtuous deeds on earth.

Vikram courteously saluted Shanta-Shil. The jogi briefly replied, "Come sit down, both of ye." The father and son took their places, by no means surprised or frightened by the devil dances before and around them. Presently the valiant Raja reminded the devotee that he was come to perform his promise, and lastly asked, "What commands are there for us?"

The jogi replied, "O king, since you have come, just perform one piece of business. About two kos[1] hence, in a southerly direction, there is another place where dead bodies are burned; and in that place is a mimosa tree, on which a body is hanging. Bring it to me immediately."

Raja Vikram took his son's hand, unwilling to leave him in such company; and, catching up a fire-brand, went rapidly away in the proper direction. He was now certain that Shanta-Shil was the anchorite who, enraged by his father, had resolved his destruction; and his uppermost thought was a firm resolve "to breakfast upon his enemy, ere his enemy could dine upon him." He muttered this old saying as he went, whilst the tom-toming of the anchorite upon the skull resounded in his ears, and the devil-crowd, which had held its peace during his meeting with Shanta-Shil, broke out again in an infernal din of whoops and screams, yells and laughter.

The darkness of the night was frightful, the gloom deepened till it was hardly possible to walk. The clouds opened their fountains, raining so that you would say they could never rain again. Lightning blazed forth with more than the light of day, and the roar of the thunder caused the earth to shake. Baleful gleams tipped the black cones of the trees and fitfully scampered like fire-flies over the waste. Unclean goblins dogged the travellers and threw themselves upon the ground in their path and obstructed them in a thousand different ways.

---

[1] A measure of length, each two miles.

Huge snakes, whose mouths distilled blood and black venom, kept clinging around their legs in the roughest part of the road, till they were persuaded to loose their hold either by the sword or by reciting a spell. In fact, there were so many horrors and such a tumult and noise that even a brave man would have faltered, yet the king kept on his way.

At length having passed over, somehow or other, a very difficult road, the Raja arrived at the smashana, or burning place pointed out by the jogi. Suddenly he sighted the tree where from root to top every branch and leaf was in a blaze of crimson flame. And when he, still dauntless, advanced towards it, a clamour continued to be raised, and voices kept crying, "Kill them! kill them! seize them! seize them! take care that they do not get away! let them scorch themselves to cinders! let them suffer the pains of Patala.[1]"

Far from being terrified by this state of things the valiant Raja increased in boldness, seeing a prospect of an end to his adventure. Approaching the tree he felt that the fire did nót burn him, and so he sat there for a while to observe the body, which hung, head downwards, from a branch a little above him.

Its eyes, which were wide open, were of a greenish-brown, and never twinkled; its hair also was brown,[2] and brown was its face—three several shades which, notwithstanding, approached one another in an unpleasant way, as in an over-dried cocoa-nut. Its body was thin and ribbed like a skeleton or a bamboo framework, and as it held on to a bough, like a flying fox,[3] by the toe-tips, its

---

1 The warm region below.

2 Hindus admire only glossy black hair; the "bonny brown hair" loved by our ballads is assigned by them to low-caste men, witches, and fiends.

3 A large kind of bat; a popular and silly Anglo-Indian name. It almost justified the irate Scotchman in calling "prodigious

drawn muscles stood out as if they were ropes of coir. Blood it appeared to have none, or there would have been a decided determination of that curious juice to the head; and as the Raja handled its skin, it felt icy cold and clammy as might a snake. The only sign of life was the whisking of a ragged little tail much resembling a goat's.

Judging from these signs the brave king at once determined the creature to be a Baital—a Vampire. For a short time he was puzzled to reconcile the appearance with the words of the giant, who informed him that the anchorite had hung the oilman's son to a tree. But soon he explained to himself the difficulty, remembering the exceeding cunning of jogis and other reverend men, and determining that his enemy, the better to deceive him, had doubtless altered the shape and form of the young oilman's body.

With this idea, Vikram was pleased, saying, "My trouble has been productive of fruit." Remained the task of carrying the Vampire to Shanta-Shil the devotee. Having taken his sword, the Raja fearlessly climbed the tree, and ordering his son to stand away from below, clutched the Vampire's hair with one hand, and with the other struck such a blow of the sword, that the bough was cut and the thing fell heavily upon the ground. Immediately on falling it gnashed its teeth and began to utter a loud wailing cry like the screams of an infant in pain. Vikram having heard the sound of its lamentations, was pleased, and began to say to himself, "This devil must be alive." Then nimbly sliding down the trunk, he made a captive of the body, and asked "Who art thou?"

Scarcely, however, had the words passed the royal lips, when the Vampire slipped through the fingers like a worm, and uttering a loud shout of laughter, rose in the air with its legs uppermost, and as before suspended

---

leears" those who told him in India that foxes flew and trees were tapped for toddy.

itself by its toes to another bough. And there it swung to and fro, moved by the violence of its cachinnation.

"Decidedly this is the young oilman!" exclaimed the Raja, after he had stood for a minute or two with mouth open, gazing upwards and wondering what he should do next. Presently he directed Dharma Dhwaj not to lose an instant in laying hands upon the thing when it next

He once more seized the Baital's hair.

might touch the ground, and then he again swarmed up the tree. Having reached his former position, he once more seized the Baital's hair, and with all the force of his arms—for he was beginning to feel really angry—he tore it from its hold and dashed it to the ground, saying, "O wretch, tell me who thou art?"

Then, as before, the Raja slid deftly down the trunk,

and hurried to the aid of his son, who in obedience to
orders, had fixed his grasp upon the Vampire's neck.
Then, too, as before, the Vampire, laughing aloud, slipped
through their fingers and returned to its dangling-place.

To fail twice was too much for Raja Vikram's temper, which was right kingly and somewhat hot.   This
time he bade his son strike the Baital's head with his
sword.   Then, more like a wounded bear of Himalaya
than a prince who had established an era, he hurried up
the tree, and directed a furious blow with his sabre at the
Vampire's lean and calfless legs.   The violence of the
stroke made its toes loose their hold of the bough, and
when it touched the ground, Dharma Dhwaj's blade fell
heavily upon its matted brown hair.   But the blows
appeared to have lighted on iron-wood—to judge at least
from the behaviour of the Baital, who no sooner heard
the question, "O wretch, who art thou?" than it returned
in loud glee and merriment to its old position.

Five mortal times did Raja Vikram repeat this pro-
fitless labour.   But so far from losing heart, he quite
entered into the spirit of the adventure.   Indeed he would
have continued climbing up that tree and taking that
corpse under his arm—he found his sword useless—and
bringing it down, and asking it who it was, and seeing it
slip through his fingers, six times sixty times, or till the
end of the fourth and present age,[1] had such extreme
resolution been required.

However, it was not necessary.   On the seventh
time of falling, the Baital, instead of eluding its cap-
turer's grasp, allowed itself to be seized, merely remarking
that "even the gods cannot resist a thoroughly obstinate

---

1 The Hindus, like the European classics and other ancient
peoples, reckon four ages :—The Satya Yug, or Golden Age, numbered 1,728,000 years; the second, or Treta Yug, comprised
1,296,000 ; the Dwapar Yug had 864,000 : and the present, the Kali
Yug, has shrunk to 832,000 years.

man.[1]" And seeing that the stranger, for the better protection of his prize, had stripped off his waistcloth and
was making it into a bag, the Vampire thought proper to
seek the most favourable conditions for himself, and asked
his conqueror who he was, and what he was about to do?

"Vile wretch," replied the breathless hero, "know
me to be Vikram the Great, Raja of Ujjayani, and I bear
thee to a man who is amusing himself by drumming to
devils on a skull."

"Remember the old saying, mighty Vikram!" said
the Baital, with a sneer, "that many a tongue has cut
many a throat. I have yielded to thy resolution and I am
about to accompany thee, bound to thy back like a beggar's wallet. But hearken to my words, ere we set out
upon the way. I am of a loquacious disposition, and it
is well nigh an hour's walk between this tree and the
place where thy friend sits, favouring his friends with the
peculiar music which they love. Therefore, I shall try to
distract my thoughts, which otherwise might not be of
the most pleasing nature, by means of sprightly tales and
profitable reflections. Sages and men of sense spend
their days in the delights of light and heavy literature,
whereas dolts and fools waste time in sleep and idleness.
And I purpose to ask thee a number of questions, con-

---

1 Especially alluding to prayer. On this point, Southey justly
remarks (Preface to *Curse of Kehama*): "In the religion of the
Hindoos there is one remarkable peculiarity. Prayers, penances, and
sacrifices are supposed to possess an inherent and actual value, in
one degree depending upon the disposition or motive of the person
who performs them. They are drafts upon heaven for which the
gods cannot refuse payment. The worst men, bent upon the worst
designs, have in this manner obtained power which has made them
formidable to the supreme deities themselves." Moreover, the
Hindu gods hear the prayers of those who desire the evil of others.
Hence when a rich man becomes poor, his friends say, "See how
sharp are men's teeth!" and, "He is ruined because others could
not bear to see his happiness!"

cerning which we will, if it seems fit to thee, make this covenant:

"Whenever thou answerest me, either compelled by Fate or entrapped by my cunning into so doing, or thereby gratifying thy vanity and conceit, I leave thee and return to my favourite place and position in the siras-tree, but when thou shalt remain silent, confused, and at a loss to reply, either through humility or thereby confessing thine ignorance, and impotence, and want of comprehension, then will I allow thee, of mine own free will, to place me before thine employer. Perhaps I should not say so; it may sound like bribing thee, but—take my counsel, and mortify thy pride, and assumption, and arrogance, and haughtiness, as soon as possible. So shalt thou derive from me a benefit which none but myself can bestow."

Raja Vikram hearing these rough words, so strange to his royal ear, winced; then he rejoiced that his heir-apparent was not near; then he looked round at his son Dharma Dhwaj, to see if he was impertinent enough to be amused by the Baital. But the first glance showed him the young prince busily employed in pinching and screwing the monster's legs, so as to make it fit better into the cloth. Vikram then seized the ends of the waist-cloth, twisted them into a convenient form for handling, stooped, raised the bundle with a jerk, tossed it over his shoulder, and bidding his son not to lag behind, set off at a round pace towards the western end of the cemetery.

The shower had ceased, and, as they gained ground, the weather greatly improved.

The Vampire asked a few indifferent questions about the wind and the rain and the mud. When he received no answer, he began to feel uncomfortable, and he broke out with these words: "O King Vikram, listen to the true story which I am about to tell thee."

THE VAMPIRE'S FIRST STORY.

IN WHICH A MAN DECEIVES A WOMAN.

IN Benares once reigned a mighty prince, by name
Pratapamukut, to whose eighth son Vajramukut happened
the strangest adventure.

One morning, the young man, accompanied by the
son of his father's pradhan or prime minister, rode out
hunting, and went far into the jungle. At last the twain
unexpectedly came upon a beautiful " tank [1]" of a prodigious size. It was surrounded by short thick walls of fine
baked brick ; and flights and ramps of cut-stone steps,
half the length of each face, and adorned with turrets,
pendants, and finials, led down to the water. The substantial plaster work and the masonry had fallen into
disrepair, and from the crevices sprang huge trees, under
whose thick shade the breeze blew freshly, and on whose
balmy branches the birds sang sweetly ; the grey squirrels [2]
chirruped joyously as they coursed one another up the
gnarled trunks, and from the pendent llianas the long-
tailed monkeys were swinging sportively. The bountiful
hand of Sravana [3] had spread the earthen rampart with a
carpet of the softest grass and many-hued wild flowers, in

---

1 A pond, natural or artificial; in the latter case often covering
an extent of ten to twelve acres.

2 The Hindústaní " gilahri," or little grey squirrel, whose
twittering cry is often mistaken for a bird's.

3 The autumn or rather the rainy season personified—a hackneyed
Hindu prosopopœia.

which were buzzing swarms of bees and myriads of bright-
winged insects; and flocks of water fowl, wild geese,
Brahmini ducks, bitterns, herons, and cranes, male and
female, were feeding on the narrow strip of brilliant green
that belted the long deep pool, amongst the broad-leaved
lotuses with the lovely blossoms, splashing through the
pellucid waves, and basking happily in the genial sun.

The prince and his friend wondered when they saw
the beautiful tank in the midst of a wild forest, and made
many vain conjectures about it.   They dismounted,
tethered their horses, and threw their weapons upon the
ground ; then, having washed their hands and faces, they
entered a shrine dedicated to Mahadeva, and there began
to worship the presiding deity.

Whilst they were making their offerings, a bevy of
maidens, accompanied by a crowd of female slaves, descended the opposite flight of steps.   They stood there for
a time, talking and laughing and looking about them to
see if any alligators infested the waters.   When convinced that the tank was safe, they disrobed themselves in
order to bathe.   It was truly a splendid spectacle——

"Concerning which the less said the better," interrupted Raja Vikram in an offended tone.[1]

——but did not last long.   The Raja's daughter—
for the principal maiden was a princess—soon left her
companions, who were scooping up water with their palms
and dashing it over one another's heads, and proceeded to
perform the rites of purification, meditation, and worship.
Then she began strolling with a friend under the shade of
a small mango grove.

The prince also left his companion sitting in prayer,
and walked forth into the forest.   Suddenly the eyes of
the Raja's son and the Raja's daughter met.   She started
back with a little scream.   He was fascinated by her

---

[1] Light conversation upon the subject of women is a personal
offence to serious-minded Hindus.

beauty, and began to say to himself, " O thou vile **Kama,**[1] why worriest thou me ? "

Hearing this, the maiden smiled encouragement, but the poor youth, between palpitation of the heart and hesitation about what to say, was so confused that his tongue clave to his teeth. She raised her eyebrows a little. There is nothing which women despise in a man more than modesty,[2] for mo-des-ty——

A violent shaking of the bag which hung behind Vikram's royal back broke off the end of this offensive sentence. And the warrior king did not cease that discipline till the Baital promised him to preserve more decorum in his observations.

Still the prince stood before her with downcast eyes and suffused cheeks : even the spur of contempt failed to arouse his energies. Then the maiden called to her friend, who was picking jasmine flowers so as not to witness the scene, and angrily asked why that strange man was allowed to stand and stare at her ? The friend, in hot wrath, threatened to call the slave, and throw Vajramukut into the pond unless he instantly went away with his impudence. But as the prince was rooted to the spot, and really had not heard a word of what had been said to him, the two women were obliged to make the first move.

As they almost reached the tank, the beautiful maiden turned her head to see what the poor modest youth was doing.

Vajramukut was formed in every way to catch a woman's eye. The Raja's daughter therefore half forgave him his offence of mod——. Again she sweetly smiled, disclosing two rows of little opals. Then descending to the water's edge, she stooped down and plucked a lotus. This she worshipped ; next she placed it in her

---

1 Cupid in his two forms, Eros and Anteros.

2 This is true to life ; in the East, women make the first advances, and men do the *bégueules.*

hair, then she put it in her ear, then she bit it with her
teeth, then she trod upon it with her foot, then she raised
it up again, and lastly she stuck it in her bosom. After
which she mounted her conveyance and went home to her
friends; whilst the prince, having become thoroughly
desponding and drowned in grief at separation from her,
returned to the minister's son.

"Females!" ejaculated the minister's son, speaking
to himself in a careless tone, when, his prayer finished,
he left the temple, and sat down upon the tank steps to
enjoy the breeze. He presently drew a roll of paper from
under his waist-belt, and in a short time was engrossed
with his study. The women seeing this conduct, exerted
themselves in every possible way of wile to attract his
attention and to distract his soul. They succeeded only
so far as to make him roll his head with a smile, and to
remember that such is always the custom of man's bane;
after which he turned over a fresh page of manuscript.
And although he presently began to wonder what had
become of the prince his master, he did not look up even
once from his study.

He was a philosopher, that young man. But after all,
Raja Vikram, what is mortal philosophy? Nothing but
another name for indifference! Who was ever philosophical about a thing truly loved or really hated?—no one!
Philosophy, says Shankharacharya, is either a gift of
nature or the reward of study. But I, the Baital, the
devil, ask you, what is a born philosopher, save a man of
cold desires? And what is a bred philosopher but a man
who has survived his desires? A young philosopher?—
a cold-blooded youth! An elderly philosopher?—a leuco-
phlegmatic old man! Much nonsense, of a verity, ye
hear in praise of nothing from your Rajaship's Nine Gems
of Science, and from sundry other such wise fools.

Then the prince began to relate the state of his case,
saying, "O friend, I have seen a damsel, but whether she

be a musician from Indra's heaven, a maiden of the sea, a daughter of the serpent kings, or the child of an earthly Raja, I cannot say."

" Describe her," said the statesman in embryo.

" Her face," quoth the prince, " was that of the full moon, her hair like a swarm of bees hanging from the blossoms of the acacia, the corners of her eyes touched her ears, her lips were sweet with lunar ambrosia, her waist was that of a lion, and her walk the walk of a king-goose.[1] As a garment, she was white; as a season, the spring; as a flower, the jasmine; as a speaker, the kokila bird; as a perfume, musk; as a beauty, Kamadeva; and as a being, Love. And if she does not come into my possession I will not live; this I have certainly determined upon."

The young minister, who had heard his prince say the same thing more than once before, did not attach great importance to these awful words. He merely remarked that, unless they mounted at once, night would surprise them in the forest. Then the two young men returned to their horses, untethered them, drew on their bridles, saddled them, and catching up their weapons, rode slowly towards the Raja's palace. During the three hours of return hardly a word passed between the pair. Vajramukut not only avoided speaking; he never once replied till addressed thrice in the loudest voice.

The young minister put no more questions, "for," quoth he to himself, " when the prince wants my counsel, he will apply for it." In this point he had borrowed wisdom from his father, who held in peculiar horror the giving of unasked-for advice. So, when he saw that conversation was irksome to his master, he held his peace and meditated upon what he called his " day-thought." It was his practice to choose every morning some tough

---

[1] Raja-hans, a large grey goose, the Hindu equivalent for our swan.

food for reflection, and to chew the cud of it in his mind at times when, without such employment, his wits would have gone wool-gathering. You may imagine, Raja Vikram, that with a few years of this head work, the minister's son became a very crafty young person.

After the second day the Prince Vajramukut, being restless from grief at separation, fretted himself into a fever. Having given up writing, reading, drinking, sleeping, the affairs entrusted to him by his father, and everything else, he sat down, as he said, to die. He used constantly to paint the portrait of the beautiful lotus gatherer, and to lie gazing upon it with tearful eyes; then he would start up and tear it to pieces and beat his forehead, and begin another picture of a yet more beautiful face.

At last, as the pradhan's son had foreseen, he was summoned by the young Raja, whom he found upon his bed, looking yellow and complaining bitterly of headache. Frequent discussions upon the subject of the tender passion had passed between the two youths, and one of them had ever spoken of it so very disrespectfully that the other felt ashamed to introduce it. But when his friend, with a view to provoke communicativeness, advised a course of boiled and bitter herbs and great attention to diet, quoting the hemistich attributed to the learned physician Charndatta—

A fever starve, but feed a cold,

the unhappy Vajramukut's fortitude abandoned him; he burst into tears, and exclaimed, "Whosoever enters upon the path of love cannot survive it; and if (by chance) he should live, what is life to him but a prolongation of his misery?"

"Yea," replied the minister's son, "the sage hath said—

The road of love is that which hath no beginning nor end;
Take thou heed of thyself, man! ere thou place foot upon it.

And the wise, knowing that there are three things whose effect upon himself no man can foretell—namely, desire of woman, the dice-box, and the drinking of ardent spirits —find total abstinence from them the best of rules. Yet, after all, if there is no cow, we must milk the bull."

The advice was, of course, excellent, but the hapless lover could not help thinking that on this occasion it came a little too late. However, after a pause he returned to the subject and said, "I have ventured to tread that dangerous way, be its end pain or pleasure, happiness or destruction." He then hung down his head and sighed from the bottom of his heart.

"She is the person who appeared to us at the tank?" asked the pradhan's son, moved to compassion by the state of his master.

The prince assented.

"O great king," resumed the minister's son, "at the time of going away had she said anything to you? or had you said anything to her?"

"Nothing!" replied the other laconically, when he found his friend beginning to take an interest in the affair.

"*Then*," said the minister's son, "it will be exceedingly difficult to get possession of her."

"*Then*," repeated the Raja's son, "I am doomed to death; to an early and melancholy death!"

"Humph!" ejaculated the young statesman rather impatiently, "did she make any sign, or give any hint? Let me know all that happened: half confidences are worse than none."

Upon which the prince related everything that took place by the side of the tank, bewailing the false shame which had made him dumb, and concluding with her pantomime.

The pradhan's son took thought for a while. He thereupon seized the opportunity of representing to his master all the evil effects of bashfulness when women are

concerned, and advised him, as he would be a happy
lover, to brazen his countenance for the next interview.

Which the young Raja faithfully promised to do.

"And, now," said the other, "be comforted, O my
master! I know her name and her dwelling-place.
When she suddenly plucked the lotus flower and worshipped it, she thanked the gods for having blessed her
with a sight of your beauty."

Vajramukut smiled, the first time for the last month.

"When she applied it to her ear, it was as if she
would have explained to thee, 'I am a daughter of the
Carnatic;[1]' and when she bit it with her teeth, she meant
to say that 'My father is Raja Dantawat,[2]' who, by-the-
bye, has been, is, and ever will be, a mortal foe to thy
father."

Vajramukut shuddered.

"When she put it under her foot it meant, 'My name
is Padmavati.[3]'"

Vajramukut uttered a cry of joy.

"And when she placed it in her bosom, 'You are
truly dwelling in my heart' was meant to be understood."

At these words the young Raja started up full of new
life, and after praising with enthusiasm the wondrous
sagacity of his dear friend, begged him by some contrivance to obtain the permission of his parents, and to
conduct him to her city. The minister's son easily got
leave for Vajramukut to travel, under pretext that his
body required change of water, and his mind change of
scene. They both dressed and armed themselves for the
journey, and having taken some jewels, mounted their
horses and followed the road in that direction in which
the princess had gone.

Arrived after some days at the capital of the Carnatic,

---

1 Properly Karnatak; karna in Sanskrit means an ear.

2 Danta in Sanskrit is a tooth.

3 Padma means a foot.

the minister's son having disguised his master and himself in the garb of travelling traders, alighted and pitched
his little tent upon a clear bit of ground in one of the
suburbs.   He then proceeded to inquire for a wise woman,
wanting, he said, to have his fortune told.   When the
prince asked him what this meant, he replied that elderly
dames who professionally predict the future are never
above [ministering to the present, and therefore that, in
such circumstances, they are the properest persons to be
consulted.

"Is this a treatise upon the subject of immorality,
devil?" demanded the King Vikram ferociously.   The
Baital declared that it was not, but that he must tell his
story.

The person addressed pointed to an old woman who,
seated before the door of her hut, was spinning at her
wheel.   Then the young men went up to her with polite
salutations and said, "Mother, we are travelling traders,
and our stock is coming after us; we have come on in
advance for the purpose of finding a place to live in.   If
you will give us a house, we will remain there and pay
you highly."

The old woman, who was a physiognomist as well as
a fortune-teller, looked at the faces of the young men and
liked them, because their brows were wide, and their
mouths denoted generosity.   Having listened to their
words, she took pity upon them and said kindly, "This
hovel is yours, my masters, remain here as long as you
please."   Then she led them into an inner room, again
welcomed them, lamented the poorness of her abode, and
begged them to lie down and rest themselves.

After some interval of time the old woman came to
them once more, and sitting down began to gossip.   The
minister's son upon this asked her, "How is it with thy
family, thy relatives, and connections ; and what are thy
means of subsistence?"   She replied, "My son is a

4

favourite servant in the household of our great king
Dantawat, and your slave is the wet-nurse of the Princess
Padmavati, his eldest child. From the coming on of old
age," she added, "I dwell in this house, but the king pro-
vides for my eating and drinking. I go once a day to see
the girl, who is a miracle of beauty and goodness, wit and
accomplishments, and returning thence, I bear my own
griefs at home.[1]"

In a few days the young Vajramukut had, by his
liberality, soft speech, and good looks, made such progress
in nurse Lakshmi's affections that, by the advice of his
companion, he ventured to broach the subject ever nearest
his heart. He begged his hostess, when she went on the
morrow to visit the charming Padmavati, that she would
be kind enough to slip a bit of paper into the princess's
hand.

"Son," she replied, delighted with the proposal—and
what old woman would not be?—"there is no need for
putting off so urgent an affair till the morrow. Get your
paper ready, and I will immediately give it."

Trembling with pleasure, the prince ran to find his
friend, who was seated in the garden reading, as usual,
and told him what the old nurse had engaged to do. He
then began to debate about how he should write his
letter, to cull sentences and to weigh phrases; whether
"light of my eyes" was not too trite, and "blood of my
liver" rather too forcible. At this the minister's son
smiled, and bade the prince not trouble his head with
composition. He then drew his inkstand from his waist-
shawl, nibbed a reed pen, and choosing a piece of pink and
flowered paper, he wrote upon it a few lines. He then
folded it, gummed it, sketched a lotus flower upon the
outside, and handing it to the young prince, told him to
give it to their hostess, and that all would be well.

---

[1] A common Hindu phrase equivalent to our "I manage to get
on."

4—2

The old woman took her staff in her hand and hobbled straight to the palace. Arrived there, she found the Raja's daughter sitting alone in her apartment. The maiden, seeing her nurse, immediately arose, and making a respectful bow, led her to a seat and began the most affectionate inquiries. After giving her blessing and sitting for some time and chatting about indifferent matters, the nurse said, "O daughter! in infancy I reared and nourished thee, now the Bhagwan (Deity) has rewarded me by giving thee stature, beauty, health, and goodness. My heart only longs to see the happiness of thy womanhood,[1] after which I shall depart in peace. I implore thee read this paper, given to me by the handsomest and the properest young man that my eyes have ever seen."

The princess, glancing at the lotus on the outside of the note, slowly unfolded it and perused its contents, which were as follows:

1.

She was to me the pearl that clings
    To sands all hid from mortal sight,
Yet fit for diadems of kings,
    The pure and lovely light.

2.

She was to me the gleam of sun
    That breaks the gloom of wintry day;
One moment shone my soul upon,
    Then passéd—how soon!—away.

3.

She was to me the dreams of bliss
    That float the dying eyes before,
For one short hour shed happiness,
    And fly to bless no more.

4.

O light, again upon me shine;
    O pearl, again delight my eyes;

---

1 Meaning marriage, maternity, and so forth.

O dreams of bliss, again be mine!—
No! earth may not be Paradise.

I must not forget to remark, parenthetically, that the minister's son, in order to make these lines generally useful, had provided them with a last stanza in triplicate. "For lovers," he said sagely, "are either in the optative mood, the desperative, or the exultative." This time he had used the optative. For the desperative he would substitute:

4

The joys of life lie dead, lie dead,
  The light of day is quenched in gloom;
The spark of hope my heart hath fled—
  What now witholds me from the tomb?

And this was the termination exultative, as he called it:

4

O joy! the pearl is mine again,
  Once more the day is bright and clear,
And now 'tis real, then 'twas vain,
  My dream of bliss—O heaven is here!

The Princess Padmavati having perused this dog- grel with a contemptuous look, tore off the first word of the last line, and said to the nurse, angrily, "Get thee gone, O mother of Yama,[1] O unfortunate creature, and take back this answer"—giving her the scrap of paper— "to the fool who writes such bad verses. I wonder where he studied the humanities. Begone, and never do such an action again!"

The old nurse, distressed at being so treated, rose up and returned home. Vajramukut was too agitated to await her arrival, so he went to meet her on the way. Imagine his disappointment when she gave him the fatal word and repeated to him exactly what happened, not forgetting to describe a single look! He felt tempted to

---

1 Yama is Pluto; 'mother of Yama' is generally applied to an old scold.

plunge his sword into his bosom ; but Fortune interfered, and sent him to consult his confidant.

"Be not so hasty and desperate, my prince," said the pradhan's son, seeing his wild grief ; "you have not understood her meaning. Later in life you will be aware of the fact that, in nine cases out of ten, a woman's 'no' is a distinct 'yes.' This morning's work has been good; the maiden asked where you learnt the humanities, which being interpreted signifies 'Who are you?'"

On the next day the prince disclosed his rank to old Lakshmi, who naturally declared that she had always known it. The trust they reposed in her made her ready to address Padmavati once more on the forbidden subject. So she again went to the palace, and having lovingly greeted her nursling, said to her, "The Raja's son, whose heart thou didst fascinate on the brim of the tank, on the fifth day of the moon, in the light half of the month Yeth, has come to my house, and sends this message to thee: "Perform what you promised; we have now come"; and I also tell thee that this prince is worthy of thee: just as thou art beautiful, so is he endowed with all good qualities of mind and body."

When Padmavati heard this speech she showed great anger, and, rubbing sandal on her beautiful hands, she slapped the old woman's cheeks, and cried, "Wretch, Daina (witch) ! get out of my house; did I not forbid thee to talk such folly in my presence?"

The lover and the nurse were equally distressed at having taken the advice of the young minister, till he explained what the crafty damsel meant. "When she smeared the sandal on her ten fingers," he explained, "and struck the old woman on the face, she signified that when the remaining ten moonlight nights shall have passed away she will meet you in the dark." At the same time he warned his master that to all appearances the lady Padmavati was far too clever to make a comfortable wife. The minister's son especially hated talented, intellectual, and strong-minded women ; he had been heard to describe the torments of Naglok[1] as the compulsory companionship of a polemical divine and a learned authoress, well stricken in years and of forbidding aspect, as such persons mostly are. Amongst womankind he admired—theoretically, as became a philosopher—the small, plump, laughing, chattering, unintellectual, and material-minded. And therefore—excuse the digression, Raja Vikram—he married an old maid, tall, thin, yellow, strictly proper, cold-mannered, a conversationist, and who prided herself upon spirituality. But more wonderful still, after he did marry her, he actually loved her—what an incomprehensible being is man in these matters!

To return, however. The pradhan's son, who detected certain symptoms of strong-mindedness in the Princess Padmavati, advised his lord to be wise whilst wisdom availed him. This sage counsel was, as might be guessed, most ungraciously rejected by him for whose benefit it was intended. Then the sensible young statesman rated himself soundly for having broken his father's rule touching advice, and atoned for it by blindly forwarding the views of his master.

After the ten nights of moonlight had passed, the old nurse was again sent to the palace with the usual message. This time Padmavati put saffron on three of her fingers, and again left their marks on the nurse's cheek. The minister's son explained that this was to crave delay for three days, and that on the fourth the lover would have access to her.

When the time had passed the old woman again went and inquired after her health and well-being. The princess was as usual very wroth, and having personally taken her nurse to the western gate, she called her

---

1 Snake-land ; the infernal region.

" Mother of the elephant's trunk,[1]" and drove her out with threats of the bastinado if she ever came back. This was reported to the young statesman, who, after a few minutes' consideration, said, " The explanation of this matter is, that she has invited you to-morrow, at night-time, to meet her at this very gate."

When brown shadows fell upon the face of earth, and here and there a star spangled the pale heavens, the minister's son called Vajramukut, who had been engaged in adorning himself at least half that day. He had carefully shaved his cheeks and chin: his mustachio was trimmed and curled; he had arched his eyebrows by plucking out with tweezers the fine hairs around them; he had trained his curly musk-coloured love-locks to hang gracefully down his face; he had drawn broad lines of antimony along his eyelids, a most brilliant sectarian mark was affixed to his forehead, the colour of his lips had been heightened by chewing betel-nut——

" One would imagine that you are talking of a silly girl, not of a prince, fiend!" interrupted Vikram, who did not wish his son to hear what he called these fopperies and frivolities.

——and whitened his neck by having it shaved (continued the Baital, speaking quickly, as if determined not to be interrupted), and reddened the tips of his ears by squeezing them, and made his teeth shine by rubbing copper powder into the roots, and set off the delicacy of his fingers by staining the tips with henna. He had not been less careful with his dress: he wore a well-arranged turband, which had taken him at least two hours to bind, and a rich suit of brown stuff chosen for the adventure he was about to attempt, and he hung about his person a number of various weapons, so as to appear a hero— which young damsels admire.

---

1 A form of abuse given to Durga, who was the mother of Ganesha (Janus); the latter had an elephant's head.

Vajramukut asked his friend how he looked, and smiled happily when the other replied " Admirable ! " His happiness was so great that he feared it might not last, and he asked the minister's son how best to conduct himself ?

" As a conqueror, my prince ! " answered that astute young man, " if it so be that you would be one. When you wish to win a woman, always impose upon her. Tell her that you are her master, and she will forthwith believe herself to be your servant. Inform her that she loves you, and forthwith she will adore you. Show her that you care nothing for her, and she will think of nothing but you. Prove to her by your demeanour that you consider her a slave, and she will become your pariah. But above all things—excuse me if I repeat myself too often —beware of the fatal virtue which men call modesty and women sheepishness. Recollect the trouble it has given us, and the danger which we have incurred: all this might have been managed at a tank within fifteen miles of your royal father's palace. And allow me to say that you may still thank your stars : in love a lost opportunity is seldom if ever recovered. The time to woo a woman is the moment you meet her, before she has had time to think; allow her the use of reflection and she may escape the net. And after avoiding the rock of Modesty, fall not, I conjure you, into the gulf of Security. I fear the lady Padmavati, she is too clever and too prudent. When damsels of her age draw the sword of Love, they throw away the scabbard of Precaution. But you yawn —I weary you—it is time for us to move."

Two watches of the night had passed, and there was profound stillness on earth. The young men then walked quietly through the shadows, till they reached the western gate of the palace, and found the wicket ajar. The minister's son peeped in and saw the porter dozing, stately as a Brahman deep in the Vedas, and behind him stood a veiled woman seemingly waiting for somebody. He then returned on tiptoe to the place where he had left his master, and with a parting caution against modesty and security, bade him fearlessly glide through the wicket. Then having stayed a short time at the gate listening with anxious ear, he went back to the old woman's house.

Vajramukut penetrating to the staircase, felt his hand grasped by the veiled figure, who motioning him to tread lightly, led him quickly forwards. They passed under several arches, through dim passages and dark doorways, till at last running up a flight of stone steps they reached the apartments of the princess.

Vajramukut was nearly fainting as the flood of splendour broke upon him. Recovering himself he gazed around the rooms, and presently a tumult of delight invaded his soul, and his body bristled with joy.[1] The scene was that of fairyland. Golden censers exhaled the most costly perfumes, and gemmed vases bore the most beautiful flowers; silver lamps containing fragrant oil illuminated doors whose panels were wonderfully decorated, and walls adorned with pictures in which such figures were formed that on seeing them the beholder was enchanted. On one side of the room stood a bed of flowers and a couch covered with brocade of gold, and strewed with freshly-culled jasmine flowers. On the other side, arranged in proper order, were attar holders, betel-boxes, rose-water bottles, trays, and silver cases with four partitions for essences compounded of rose-leaves, sugar, and spices, prepared sandal wood, saffron, and pods of musk. Scattered about a stuccoed floor white as crystal, were coloured caddies of exquisite confections, and in others sweetmeats of various kinds.[2] Female attendants clothed

---

1 Unexpected pleasure, according to the Hindus, gives a bristly elevation to the down of the body.

2 The Hindus banish "flasks," et hoc genus omne, from these scenes, and perhaps they are right.

in dresses of various colours were standing each according
to her rank, with hands respectfully joined. Some were
reading plays and beautiful poems, others danced and
others performed with glittering fingers and flashing arms
on various instruments—the ivory lute, the ebony pipe,
and the silver kettledrum. In short, all the means and
appliances of pleasure and enjoyment were there ; and
any description of the appearance of the apartments,
which were the wonder of the age, is impossible.

Then another veiled figure, the beautiful Princess
Padmavati, came up and disclosed herself, and dazzled
the eyes of her delighted Vajramukut. She led him into
an alcove, made him sit down, rubbed sandal powder
upon his body, hung a garland of jasmine flowers round
his neck, sprinkled rose-water over his dress, and began
to wave over his head a fan of peacock feathers with a
golden handle.

Said the prince, who despite all efforts could not
entirely shake off his unhappy habit of being modest,
"Those very delicate hands of yours are not fit to ply the
pankha.[1] Why do you take so much trouble? I am
cool and refreshed by the sight of you. Do give the fan
to me and sit down."

"Nay, great king!" replied Padmavati, with the
most fascinating of smiles, "you have taken so much
trouble for my sake in coming here, it is right that I perform service for you."

Upon which her favourite slave, taking the pankha
from the hand of the princess, exclaimed, "This is my
duty. I will perform the service; do you two enjoy yourselves!"

The lovers then began to chew betel, which, by the

---

1 The Pankha, or large common fan, is a leaf of the Corypha
umbraculifera, with the petiole cut to the length of about five feet,
pared round the edges and painted to look pretty. It is waved by
the servant standing behind a chair.

bye, they disposed of in little agate boxes which they drew from their pockets, and they were soon engaged in the tenderest conversation.

Here the Baital paused for a while, probably to take breath. Then he resumed his tale as follows :

In the meantime, it became dawn ; the princess concealed him; and when night returned they again engaged in the same innocent pleasures. Thus day after day sped rapidly by. Imagine, if you can, the youth's felicity; he was of an ardent temperament, deeply enamoured, barely a score of years old, and he had been strictly brought up by serious parents. He therefore resigned himself entirely to the siren for whom he willingly forgot the world, and he wondered at his good fortune, which had thrown in his way a conquest richer than all the mines of Meru.[1] He could not sufficiently admire his Padmavati's grace, beauty, bright wit, and numberless accomplishments. Every morning, for vanity's sake, he learned from her a little useless knowledge in verse as well as prose, for instance, the saying of the poet—

Enjoy the present hour, 'tis thine; be this, O man, thy law; Who e'er resaw the yester? Who the morrow e'er foresaw?

And this highly philosophical axiom—

Eat, drink, and love—the rest's not worth a fillip.

" By means of which he hoped, Raja Vikram !" said the demon, not heeding his royal carrier's "ughs" and "poohs," "to become in course of time almost as clever as his mistress."

Padmavati, being, as you have seen, a maiden of superior mind, was naturally more smitten by her lover's dulness than by any other of his qualities; she adored it, it was such a contrast to herself.[2] At first she did what

1 The fabulous mass of precious stones forming the sacred mountain of Hindu mythology.

2 " I love my love with an ' S,' because he is stupid and not pyschological."

many clever women do—she invested him with the bright-
ness of her own imagination. Still water, she pondered,
runs deep; certainly under this disguise must lurk a
brilliant fancy, a penetrating but a mature and ready
judgment—are they not written by nature's hand on that
broad high brow? With such lovely mustachios can he
be aught but generous, noble-minded, magnanimous?
Can such eyes belong to any but a hero? And she fed
the delusion. She would smile upon him with intense
fondness, when, after wasting hours over a few lines of
poetry, he would misplace all the adjectives and barbar-
ously entreat the metre. She laughed with gratification,
when, excited by the bright sayings that fell from her
lips, the youth put forth some platitude, dim as the lamp
in the expiring fire-fly. When he slipped in grammar she
saw malice under it, when he retailed a borrowed jest she
called it a good one, and when he used—as princes sometimes will—bad language, she discovered in it a charming
simplicity.

At first she suspected that the stratagems which had
won her heart were the results of a deep-laid plot proceeding from her lover. But clever women are apt to be
rarely sharp-sighted in every matter which concerns
themselves. She frequently determined that a third was
in the secret. She therefore made no allusion to it.
Before long the enamoured Vajramukut had told her
everything, beginning with the diatribe against love pronounced by the minister's son, and ending with the solemn
warning that she, the pretty princess, would some day or
other play her husband a foul trick.

"If I do not revenge myself upon *him*," thought the
beautiful Padmavati, smiling like an angel as she listened
to the youth's confidence, "may I become a gardener's
ass in the next birth!"

Having thus registered a vow, she broke silence, and
praised to the skies the young pradhan's wisdom and

sagacity ; professed herself ready from gratitude to become
his slave, and only hoped that one day or other she might
meet that true friend by whose skill her soul had been
gratified in its dearest desire. " Only," she concluded,
" I am convinced that now my Vajramukut knows every
corner of his little Padmavati's heart, he will never expect
her to do anything but love, admire, adore and kiss him !"
Then suiting the action to the word, she convinced him
that the young minister had for once been too crabbed
and cynic in his philosophy.

But after the lapse of a month Vajramukut, who had
eaten and drunk and slept a great deal too much, and who
had not once hunted, became bilious in body and in mind
melancholic. His face turned yellow, and so did the
whites of his eyes; he yawned, as liver patients generally
do, complained occasionally of sick headaches, and lost
his appetite: he became restless and anxious, and once
when alone at night he thus thought aloud : "I have
given up country, throne, home, and everything else, but
the friend by means of whom this happiness was obtained
I have not seen for the long length of thirty days. What
will he say to himself, and how can I know what has
happened to him ?"

In this state of things he was sitting, and in the
meantime the beautiful princess arrived. She saw through
the matter, and lost not a moment in entering upon it.
She began by expressing her astonishment at her lover's
fickleness and fondness for change, and when he was
ready to wax wroth, and quoted the words of the sage,
" A barren wife may be superseded by another in the
eighth year ; she whose children all die, in the tenth ; she
who brings forth only daughters, in the eleventh ; she
who scolds, without delay," thinking that she alluded to
his love, she smoothed his temper by explaining that
she referred to his forgetting his friend. " How is it
possible, O my soul," she asked with the softest of voices,

that thou canst enjoy happiness here whilst thy heart is
wandering there? Why didst thou conceal this from
me, O astute one? Was it for fear of distressing me?
Think better of thy wife than to suppose that she would
ever separate thee from one to whom we both owe so
much!"

After this Padmavati advised, nay ordered, her lover
to go forth that night, and not to return till his mind was
quite at ease, and she begged him to take a few sweetmeats and other trifles as a little token of her admiration
and regard for the clever young man of whom she had
heard so much.

Vajramukut embraced her with a transport of gratitude, which so inflamed her anger, that fearing lest the
cloak of concealment might fall from her countenance,
she went away hurriedly to find the greatest delicacies
which her comfit boxes contained. Presently she
returned, carrying a bag of sweetmeats of every kind for
her lover, and as he rose up to depart, she put into his
hand a little parcel of sugar-plums especially intended for
the friend; they were made up with her own delicate
fingers, and they would please, she flattered herself,
even his discriminating palate.

The young prince, after enduring a number of farewell embraces and hopings for a speedy return, and last
words ever beginning again, passed safely through the
palace gate, and with a relieved aspect walked briskly
to the house of the old nurse. Although it was midnight
his friend was still sitting on his mat.

The two young men fell upon one another's bosoms
and embraced affectionately. They then began to talk of
matters nearest their hearts. The Raja's son wondered
at seeing the jaded and haggard looks of his companion,
who did not disguise that they were caused by his
anxiety as to what might have happened to his friend at
the hand of so talented and so superior a princess. Upon

which Vajramukut, who now thought Padmavati an angel, and his late abode a heaven, remarked with formality— and two blunders to one quotation—that abilities properly directed win for a man the happiness of both worlds.

The pradhan's son rolled his head.

" Again on your hobby-horse, nagging at talent whenever you find it in others!" cried the young prince with a pun, which would have delighted Padmavati. " Surely you are jealous of her!" he resumed, anything but pleased with the dead silence that had received his joke ; " jealous of her cleverness, and of her love for me. She is the very best creature in the world. Even you, woman-hater as you are, would own it if you only knew all the kind messages she sent, and the little pleasant surprise that she has prepared for you. There! take and eat; they are made by her own dear hands!" cried the young Raja, producing the sweetmeats. " As she herself taught me to say—

> Thank God I am a man,
> Not a philosopher!"

" The kind messages she sent me! The pleasant surprise she has prepared for me!" repeated the minister's son in a hard, dry tone. " My lord will be pleased to tell me how she heard of my name?"

" I was sitting one night," replied the prince, "in anxious thought about you, when at that moment the princess coming in and seeing my condition, asked, ' Why are you thus sad? Explain the cause to me.' I then gave her an account of your cleverness, and when she heard it she gave me permission to go and see you, and sent these sweetmeats for you : eat them and I shall be pleased."

" Great king!" rejoined the young statesman, "one thing vouchsafe to hear from me. You have not done well in that you have told my name. You should never let a woman think that your left hand knows the secret which she confided to your right, much less that you have shared it to a third person. Secondly, you did evil in allowing her to see the affection with which you honour your unworthy servant—a woman ever hates her lover's or husband's friend."

"What could I do?" rejoined the young Raja, in a querulous tone of voice. "When I love a woman I like to tell her everything—to have no secrets from her—to consider her another self——"

"Which habit," interrupted the pradhan's son, "you will lose when you are a little older, when you recognize the fact that love is nothing but a bout, a game of skill between two individuals of opposite sexes : the one seeking to gain as much, and the other striving to lose as little as possible; and that the sharper of the twain thus met on the chess-board must, in the long run, win. And reticence is but a habit. Practise it for a year, and you will find it harder to betray than to conceal your thoughts. It hath its joy also. Is there no pleasure, think you, when suppressing an outbreak of tender but fatal confidence in saying to yourself, 'O, if she only knew this?' 'O, if she did but suspect that?' Returning, however, to the sugar-plums, my life to a pariah's that they are poisoned!"

"Impossible!" exclaimed the prince, horror-struck at the thought; "what you say, surely no one ever could do. If a mortal fears not his fellow-mortal, at least he dreads the Deity."

"I never yet knew," rejoined the other, "what a woman in love does fear. However, prince, the trial is easy. Come here, Muti!" cried he to the old woman's dog, "and off with thee to that three-headed kinsman of thine, that attends upon his amiable-looking master.[1]"

Having said this, he threw one of the sweetmeats to

---

[1] Hindu mythology has also its Cerberus, Trisisa, the "three-headed" hound that attends dreadful Yama (Pluto).

the dog; the animal ate it, and presently writhing and falling down, died.

"The wretch! O the wretch!" cried Vajramukut, transported with wonder and anger. "And I loved her! But now it is all over. I dare not associate with such a calamity!"

"What has happened, my lord, has happened!" quoth the minister's son calmly. "I was prepared for something of this kind from so talented a princess. None commit such mistakes, such blunders, such follies as your clever women; they cannot even turn out a crime decently executed. O give me dulness with one idea, one aim, one desire. O thrice blessed dulness that combines with happiness, power."

This time Vajramukut did not defend talent.

"And your slave did his best to warn you against perfidy. But now my heart is at rest. I have tried her strength. She has attempted and failed; the defeat will prevent her attempting again—just yet. But let me ask you to put to yourself one question. Can you be happy without her?"

"Brother!" replied the prince, after a pause, "I cannot"; and he blushed as he made the avowal.

"Well," replied the other, "better confess then conceal that fact; we must now meet her on the battle-field, and beat her at her own weapons—cunning. I do not willingly begin treachery with women, because, in the first place, I don't like it ; and secondly, I know that they will certainly commence practising it upon me, after which I hold myself justified in deceiving them. And probably this will be a good wife; remember that she intended to poison me, not you. During the last month my fear has been lest my prince had run into the tiger's brake. Tell me, my lord, when does the princess expect you to return to her?"

"She bade me," said the young Raja, "not to return

5

till my mind was quite at ease upon the subject of my talented friend."

"This means that she expects you back to-morrow night, as you cannot enter the palace before. And now I will retire to my cot, as it is there that I am wont to ponder over my plans. Before dawn my thought shall mature one which must place the beautiful Padmavati in your power."

"A word before parting," exclaimed the prince: "you know my father has already chosen a spouse for me; what will he say if I bring home a second?"

"In my humble opinion," said the minister's son, rising to retire, "woman is a monogamous, man a polygamous, creature, a fact scarcely established in physiological theory, but very observable in every-day practice. For what said the poet?—

Divorce, friend! Re-wed thee! The spring draweth near,[1]
And a wife's but an almanac—good for the year.

If your royal father say anything to you, refer him to what he himself does."

Reassured by these words, Vajramukut bade his friend a cordial good-night and sought his cot, where he slept soundly, despite the emotions of the last few hours. The next day passed somewhat slowly. In the evening, when accompanying his master to the palace, the minister's son gave him the following directions.

"Our object, dear my lord, is how to obtain possession of the princess. Take, then, this trident, and hide it carefully when you see her show the greatest love and affection. Conceal what has happened, and when she, wondering at your calmness, asks about me, tell her that last night I was weary and out of health, that illness prevented my eating her sweetmeats, but that I shall eat them for supper to-night. When she goes to sleep, then, taking off her jewels and striking her left leg with the

---

[1] Parceque c'est la saison des amours.

trident, instantly come away to me. But should she lie awake, rub upon your thumb a little of this—do not fear, it is only a powder of grubs fed on verdigris—and apply it to her nostrils. It would make an elephant senseless, so be careful how you approach it to your own face."

Vajramukut embraced his friend, and passed safely through the palace gate. He found Padmavati awaiting him; she fell upon his bosom and looked into his eyes, and deceived herself, as clever women will do. Overpowered by her joy and satisfaction, she now felt certain that her lover was hers eternally, and that her treachery had not been discovered; so the beautiful princess fell into a deep sleep.

Then Vajramukut lost no time in doing as the minister's son had advised, and slipped out of the room, carrying off Padmavati's jewels and ornaments. His counsellor having inspected them, took up a sack and made signs to his master to follow him. Leaving the horses and baggage at the nurse's house, they walked to a burning-place outside the city. The minister's son there buried his dress, together with that of the prince, and drew from the sack the costume of a religious ascetic: he assumed this himself, and gave to his companion that of a disciple. Then quoth the guru (spiritual preceptor) to his chela (pupil), "Go, youth, to the bazar, and sell these jewels, remembering to let half the jewellers in the place see the things, and if any one lay hold of thee, bring him to me."

Upon which, as day had dawned, Vajramukut carried the princess's ornaments to the market, and entering the nearest goldsmith's shop, offered to sell them, and asked what they were worth. As your majesty well knows, gardeners, tailors, and goldsmiths are proverbially dishonest, and this man was no exception to the rule. He looked at the pupil's face and wondered, because he had brought articles whose value he did not appear to know.

A thought struck him that he might make a bargain which would fill his coffers, so he offered about a thousandth part of the price. This the pupil rejected, because he wished the affair to go further. Then the goldsmith, seeing him about to depart, sprang up and stood in the doorway, threatening to call the officers of justice if the young man refused to give up the valuables which he said had lately been stolen from his shop. As the pupil only laughed at this, the goldsmith thought seriously of executing his threat, hesitating only because he knew that the officers of justice would gain more than he could by that proceeding. As he was still in doubt a shadow darkened his shop, and in entered the chief jeweller of the city. The moment the ornaments were shown to him he recognized them, and said, "These jewels belong to Raja Dantawat's daughter; I know them well, as I set them only a few months ago!" Then he turned to the disciple, who still held the valuables in his hand, and cried, "Tell me truly whence you received them?"

While they were thus talking, a crowd of ten or twenty persons had collected, and at length the report reached the superintendent of the archers. He sent a soldier to bring before him the pupil, the goldsmith, and the chief jeweller, together with the ornaments. And when all were in the hall of justice, he looked at the jewels and said to the young man, "Tell me truly, whence have you obtained these?"

"My spiritual preceptor," said Vajramukut, pretending great fear, "who is now worshipping in the cemetery outside the town, gave me these white stones, with an order to sell them. How know I whence he obtained them? Dismiss me, my lord, for I am an innocent man."

"Let the ascetic be sent for," commanded the kotwal.[1] Then, having taken both of them, along with the

---

1 The police magistrate, the Catual of Camoens.

jewels, into the presence of King Dantawat, he related the whole circumstances.

"Master," said the king on hearing the statement, "whence have you obtained these jewels?"

The spiritual preceptor, before deigning an answer, pulled from under his arm the hide of a black antelope, which he spread out and smoothed deliberately before using it as an asan.[1] He then began to finger a rosary of beads each as large as an egg, and after spending nearly an hour in mutterings and in rollings of the head, he looked fixedly at the Raja, and replied:

"By Shiva! great king, they are mine own! On the fourteenth of the dark half of the moon at night, I had gone into a place where dead bodies are burned, for the purpose of accomplishing a witch's incantation. After long and toilsome labour she appeared, but her demeanour was so unruly that I was forced to chastise her. I struck her with this, my trident, on the left leg, if memory serves me. As she continued to be refractory, in order to punish her I took off all her jewels and clothes, and told her to go where she pleased. Even this had little effect upon her—never have I looked upon so perverse a witch. In this way the jewels came into my possession."

Raja Dantawat was stunned by these words. He begged the ascetic not to leave the palace for a while, and forthwith walked into the private apartments of the women. Happening first to meet the queen dowager, he said to her, "Go, without losing a minute, O my mother, and look at Padmavati's left leg, and see if there is a mark or not, and what sort of a mark!" Presently she returned, and coming to the king said, "Son, I find thy daughter lying upon her bed, and complaining that she has met with an accident; and indeed Padmavati must be in great pain. I found that some sharp instrument

---

1 The seat of a Hindu ascetic.

with three points had wounded her. The girl says that a
nail hurt her, but I never yet heard of a nail making
three holes. However, we must all hasten, or there will
be erysipelas, tumefaction, gangrene, mortification, amputation, and perhaps death in the house," concluded the
old queen, hurrying away in the pleasing anticipation of
these ghastly consequences.

For a moment King Dantawat's heart was ready to
break. But he was accustomed to master his feelings;
he speedily applied the reins of reflection to the wild steed
of passion. He thought to himself, "the affairs of one's
household, the intentions of one's heart, and whatever
one's losses may be, should not be disclosed to any one.
Since Padmavati is a witch, she is no longer my daughter.
I will verily go forth and consult the spiritual preceptor."

With these words the king went outside, where the
guru was still sitting upon his black hide, making marks
with his trident on the floor. Having requested that the
pupil might be sent away, and having cleared the room,
he said to the jogi, "O holy man! what punishment for
the heinous crime of witchcraft is awarded to a woman
in the Dharma-Shastra[1]?"

"Great king!" replied the devotee, "in the Dharma-
Shastra it is thus written: 'If a Brahman, a cow, a
woman, a child, or any other person whatsoever who
may be dependent on us, should be guilty of a perfidious
act, their punishment is that they be banished the
country.' However much they may deserve death, we
must not spill their blood, as Lakshmi[2] flies in horror
from the deed."

Hearing these words the Raja dismissed the guru
with many thanks and large presents. He waited till
nightfall and then ordered a band of trusty men to seize
Padmavati without alarming the household, and to carry

---

1 The Hindu scriptures.   2 The Goddess of Prosperity.

her into a distant jungle full of fiends, tigers, and bears, and there to abandon her.

In the meantime, the ascetic and his pupil hurrying to the cemetery resumed their proper dresses; they then went to the old nurse's house, rewarded her hospitality till she wept bitterly, girt on their weapons, and mounting their horses, followed the party which issued from the gate of King Dantawat's palace. And it may easily be believed that they found little difficulty in persuading the poor girl to exchange her chance in the wild jungle for the prospect of becoming Vajramukut's wife—lawfully wedded —at Benares. She did not even ask if she was to have a

Mounting their horses, followed the party.

rival in the house,—a question which women, you know, never neglect to put under usual circumstances. After some days the two pilgrims of one love arrived at the house of their fathers, and to all, both great and small, excess in joy came.

" Now, Raja Vikram!" said the Baital, "you have not spoken much; doubtless you are engrossed by the interest of a story wherein a man beats a woman at her own weapon—deceit. But I warn you that you will

assuredly fall into Narak (the infernal regions) if you do
not make up your mind upon and explain this matter.
Who was the most to blame amongst these four? the
lover[1] the lover's friend, the girl, or the father?"

"For my part I think Padmavati was the worst,
she being at the bottom of all their troubles," cried Dharma
Dhwaj. The king said something about young people and
the two senses of seeing and hearing, but his son's sentiment was so sympathetic that he at once pardoned the
interruption. At length, determined to do justice despite
himself, Vikram said, " Raja Dantawat is the person
most at fault."

" In what way was he at fault?" asked the Baital
curiously.

King Vikram gave him this reply: " The Prince
Vajramukut being tempted of the love-god was insane,
and therefore not responsible for his actions. The
minister's son performed his master's business obediently,
without considering causes or asking questions—a very
excellent quality in a dependant who is merely required
to do as he is bid. With respect to the young woman, I
have only to say that she was a young woman, and
thereby of necessity a possible murderess. But the Raja,
a prince, a man of a certain age and experience, a father
of eight! He ought never to have been deceived by so
shallow a trick, nor should he, without reflection, have
banished his daughter from the country."

" Gramercy to you!" cried the Vampire, bursting
into a discordant shout of laughter, " I now return to my
tree. By my tail! I never yet heard a Raja so readily condemn a Raja."

With these words he slipped out of the cloth, leaving
it to hang empty over the great king's shoulder.

---

1 In the original the lover is not blamed; this would be the
Hindu view of the matter; we might be tempted to think of the old
injunction not to seethe a kid in the mother's milk.

Vikram stood for a moment, fixed to the spot with blank dismay. Presently, recovering himself, he retraced his steps, followed by his son, ascended the siras-tree, tore down the Baital, packed him up as before, and again set out upon his way.

Soon afterwards a voice sounded behind the warrior king's back, and began to tell another true story.

THE VAMPIRE'S SECOND STORY.

OF THE RELATIVE VILLANY OF MEN AND WOMEN.

IN the great city of Bhogavati dwelt, once upon a time, a young prince, concerning whom I may say that he strikingly resembled this amiable son of your majesty.

Raja Vikram was silent, nor did he acknowledge the Baital's indirect compliment. He hated flattery, but he liked, when flattered, to be flattered in his own person; a feature in their royal patron's character which the Nine Gems of Science had turned to their own account.

Now the young prince Raja Ram (continued the tale teller) had an old father, concerning whom I may say that he was exceedingly unlike your Rajaship, both as a man and as a parent. He was fond of hunting, dicing, sleeping by day, drinking at night, and eating perpetual tonics, while he delighted in the idleness of watching nautch girls, and the vanity of falling in love. But he was adored by his children because he took the trouble to win their hearts. He did not lay it down as a law of heaven that his offspring would assuredly go to Patala if they neglected the duty of bestowing upon him without cause all their affections, as your moral, virtuous, and highly respectable fathers are only too apt——. Aïe! Aïe!

These sounds issued from the Vampire's lips as the warrior king, speechless with wrath, passed his hand behind his back, and viciously twisted up a piece of the speaker's skin. This caused the Vampire to cry aloud, more however, it would appear, in derision than in real suffering, for he presently proceeded with the same subject.

Fathers, great king, may be divided into three kinds; and be it said aside, that mothers are the same. Firstly, we have the parent of many ideas, amusing, pleasant, of course poor, and the idol of his children. Secondly, there is the parent with one idea and a half. This sort of man would, in your place, say to himself, "That demon fellow speaks a manner of truth. I am not above learning from him, despite his position in life. I will carry out his theory, just to see how far it goes"; and so saying, he wends his way home, and treats his young ones with prodigious kindness for a time, but it is not lasting. Thirdly, there is the real one-idea'd type of parent—yourself, O warrior king Vikram, an admirable example. You learn in youth what you are taught: for instance, the blessed precept that the green stick is of the trees of Paradise; and in age you practise what you have learned. You cannot teach yourselves anything before your beards sprout, and when they grow stiff you cannot be taught by others. If any one attempt to change your opinions you cry,

> What is new is not true,
> What is true is not new.

and you rudely pull his hand from the subject. Yet have you your uses like other things of earth. In life you are good working camels for the mill-track, and when you die your ashes are not worse compost than those of the wise.

Your Rajaship will observe (continued the Vampire, as Vikram began to show symptoms of ungovernable anger) that I have been concise in treating this digression. Had I not been so, it would have led me far indeed from my tale. Now to return.

When the old king became air mixed with air, the

young king, though he found hardly ten pieces of silver in
the paternal treasury and legacies for thousands of golden
ounces, yet mourned his loss with the deepest grief. He
easily explained to himself the reckless emptiness of the
royal coffers as a proof of his dear kind parent's goodness,
because he loved him.

But the old man had left behind him, as he could not
carry it off with him, a treasure more valuable than gold
and silver : one Churaman, a parrot, who knew the world,
and who besides discoursed in the most correct Sanscrit.
By sage counsel and wise guidance this admirable bird
soon repaired his young master's shattered fortunes.

One day the prince said, " Parrot, thou knowest
everything : tell me where there is a mate fit for me.
The shastras inform us, respecting the choice of a wife,
' She who is not descended from his paternal or maternal
ancestors within the sixth degree is eligible by a high
caste man for nuptials. In taking a wife let him
studiously avoid the following families, be they ever so
great, or ever so rich in kine, goats, sheep, gold, or grain :
the family which has omitted prescribed acts of devotion ;
that which has produced no male children ; that in which
the Veda (scripture) has not been read ; that which has
thick hair on the body ; and that in which members have
been subject to hereditary disease. Let a person choose
for his wife a girl whose person has no defect ; who has
an agreeable name ; who walks gracefully, like a young
elephant ; whose hair and teeth are moderate in quantity
and in size ; and whose body is of exquisite softness.' "

" Great king," responded the parrot Churaman,
" there is in the country of Magadh a Raja, Magadhesh-
war by name, and he has a daughter called Chandravati.
You will marry her ; she is very learned, and, what is
better far, very fair. She is of yellow colour, with a nose
like the flower of the sesamum ; her legs are taper, like
the plantain-tree ; her eyes are large, like the principal

leaf of the lotus; her eye-brows stretch towards her ears; her lips are red, like the young leaves of the mango-tree; her face is like the full moon; her voice is like the sound of the cuckoo; her arms reach to her knees; her throat is like the pigeon's; her flanks are thin, like those of the lion; her hair hangs in curls only down to her waist; her teeth are like the seeds of the pomegranate; and her gait is that of the drunken elephant or the goose."

On hearing the parrot's speech, the king sent for an astrologer, and asked him, " Whom shall I marry?" The wise man, having consulted his art, replied, "Chandravati is the name of the maiden, and your marriage with her will certainly take place." Thereupon the young Raja, though he had never seen his future queen, became incontinently enamoured of her. He summoned a Brahman, and sent him to King Magadheshwar, saying, " If you arrange satisfactorily this affair of our marriage we will reward you amply "—a promise which lent wings to the priest.

Now it so happened that this talented and beautiful princess had a jay,[1] whose name was Madan-manjari or Love-garland. She also possessed encyclopædic knowledge after her degree, and, like the parrot, she spoke excellent Sanscrit.

Be it briefly said, O warrior king—for you think that I am talking fables—that in the days of old, men had the art of making birds discourse in human language. The invention is attributed to a great philosopher, who split their tongues, and after many generations produced a selected race born with those members split. He altered the shapes of their skulls by fixing ligatures behind the occiput, which caused the sinciput to protrude, their eyes to become prominent, and their brains to master the art of expressing thoughts in words.

But this wonderful discovery, like those of great

---

[1] In the original a " maina "—the Gracula religiosa.

philosophers generally, had in it a terrible practical flaw. The birds beginning to speak, spoke wisely and so well, they told the truth so persistently, they rebuked their brethren of the featherless skins so openly, they flattered them so little and they counselled them so much, that mankind presently grew tired of hearing them discourse. Thus the art gradually fell into desuetude, and now it is numbered with the things that were.

One day the charming Princess Chandravati was sitting in confidential conversation with her jay. The dialogue was not remarkable, for maidens in all ages seldom consult their confidantes or speculate upon the secrets of futurity, or ask to have dreams interpreted, except upon one subject. At last the princess said, for perhaps the hundredth time that month, "Where, O jay, is there a husband worthy of me?"

"Princess," replied Madan-manjari, "I am happy at length to be able as willing to satisfy your just curiosity. For just it is, though the delicacy of our sex——"

"Now, no preaching!" said the maiden; "or thou shalt have salt instead of sugar for supper."

Jays, your Rajaship, are fond of sugar. So the confidante retained a quantity of good advice which she was about to produce, and replied,

"I now see clearly the ways of Fortune. Raja Ram, king of Bhogavati, is to be thy husband. He shall be happy in thee and thou in him, for he is young and handsome, rich and generous, good-tempered, not too clever, and without a chance of being an invalid."

Thereupon the princess, although she had never seen her future husband, at once began to love him. In fact, though neither had set eyes upon the other, both were mutually in love.

" How can that be, sire?" asked the young Dharma Dhwaj of his father. "I always thought that——"

The great Vikram interrupted his son, and bade him

not to ask silly questions. Thus he expected to neutralize the evil effects of the Baital's doctrine touching the amiability of parents unlike himself.

Now, as both these young people (resumed the Baital) were of princely family and well to do in the world, the course of their love was unusually smooth. When the Brahman sent by Raja Ram had reached Magadh, and had delivered his King's homage to the Raja Magadhesh-war, the latter received him with distinction, and agreed to his proposal. The beautiful princess's father sent for a Brahman of his own, and charging him with nuptial gifts and the customary presents, sent him back to Bhogavati in company with the other envoy, and gave him this order, "Greet Raja Ram, on my behalf, and after placing the tilak or mark upon his forehead, return here with all speed. When you come back I will get all things ready for the marriage."

Raja Ram, on receiving the deputation, was greatly pleased, and after generously rewarding the Brahmans and making all the necessary preparations, he set out in state for the land of Magadha, to claim his betrothed.

In due season the ceremony took place with feasting and bands of music, fireworks and illuminations, rehearsals of scripture, songs, entertainments, processions, and abundant noise. And hardly had the turmeric disappeared from the beautiful hands and feet of the bride, when the bridegroom took an affectionate leave of his new parents —he had not lived long in the house—and receiving the dowry and the bridal gifts, set out for his own country.

Chandravati was dejected by leaving her mother, and therefore she was allowed to carry with her the jay, Madan-manjari. She soon told her husband the wonderful way in which she had first heard his name, and he related to her the advantage which he had derived from confabulation with Churaman, his parrot.

"Then why do we not put these precious creatures

into one cage, after marrying them according to the rites
of the angelic marriage (Gandharva-lagana)?" said the
charming queen.   Like most brides, she was highly
pleased to find an opportunity of making a match.

"Ay! why not, love?   Surely they cannot live happy
in what the world calls single blessedness," replied the
young king.   As bridegrooms sometimes are for a short
time, he was very warm upon the subject of matrimony.

Thereupon, without consulting the parties chiefly
concerned in their scheme, the master and mistress, after
being comfortably settled at the end of their journey,
caused a large cage to be brought, and put into it both
their favourites.

Upon which Churaman the parrot leaned his head on
one side and directed a peculiar look at the jay.   But
Madan-manjari raised her beak high in the air, puffed
through it once or twice, and turned away her face in
extreme disdain.

"Perhaps," quoth the parrot, at length breaking
silence, "you will tell me that you have no desire to be
married?"

"Probably," replied the jay.

"And why?" asked the male bird.

"Because I don't choose," replied the female.

"Truly a feminine form of resolution this," ejaculated
the parrot.   "I will borrow my master's words and call
it a woman's reason, that is to say, no reason at all.
Have you any objection to be more explicit?"

"None whatever," retorted the jay, provoked by the
rude innuendo into telling more plainly than politely
exactly what she thought; "none whatever, sir parrot.
You he-things are all of you sinful, treacherous, deceitful,
selfish, devoid of conscience, and accustomed to sacrifice
us, the weaker sex, to your smallest desire or convenience."

"Of a truth, fair lady," quoth the young Raja Ram
to his bride, "this pet of thine is sufficiently impudent."

"Let her words be as wind in thine ear, master," interrupted the parrot. "And pray, Mistress Jay, what are you she-things but treacherous, false, ignorant, and avaricious beings, whose only wish in this world is to prevent life being as pleasant as it might be?"

"Verily, my love," said the beautiful Chandravati to her bridegroom, "this thy bird has a habit of expressing his opinions in a very free and easy way."

"I can prove what I assert," whispered the jay in the ear of the princess.

"We can confound their feminine minds by an anecdote," whispered the parrot in the ear of the prince.

Briefly, King Vikram, it was settled between the twain that each should establish the truth of what it had advanced by an illustration in the form of a story.

Chandravati claimed, and soon obtained, precedence for the jay. Then the wonderful bird, Madan-manjari, began to speak as follows:—

I have often told thee, O queen, that before coming to thy feet, my mistress was Ratnawati, the daughter of a rich trader, the dearest, the sweetest, the——

Here the jay burst into tears, and the mistress was sympathetically affected. Presently the speaker resumed—

However, I anticipate. In the city of Ilapur there was a wealthy merchant, who was without offspring; on this account he was continually fasting and going on pilgrimage, and when at home he was ever engaged in reading the Puranas and in giving alms to the Brahmans.

At length, by favour of the Deity, a son was born to this merchant, who celebrated his birth with great pomp and rejoicing, and gave large gifts to Brahmans and to bards, and distributed largely to the hungry, the thirsty, and the poor. When the boy was five years old he had him taught to read, and when older he was sent to a guru, who had formerly himself been a student, and who was celebrated as teacher and lecturer.

6

In the course of time the merchant's son grew up. Praise be to Brahma! what a wonderful youth it was, with a face like a monkey's, legs like a stork's, and a back like a camel's. You know the old proverb:—

Expect thirty-two villanies from the limping, and eighty
    from the one-eyed man,
But when the hunchback comes, say "Lord defend us!"

Instead of going to study, he went to gamble with other ne'er-do-weels, to whom he talked loosely, and whom he taught to be bad-hearted as himself. He made love to every woman, and despite his ugliness, he was not unsuccessful. For they are equally fortunate who are very handsome or very ugly, in so far as they are both remarkable and remarked. But the latter bear away the palm. Beautiful men begin well with women, who do all they can to attract them, love them as the apples of their eyes, discover them to be fools, hold them to be their equals, deceive them, and speedily despise them. It is otherwise with the ugly man, who, in consequence of his homeliness, must work his wits and take pains with himself, and become as pleasing as he is capable of being, till women forget his ape's face, bird's legs, and bunchy back.

The hunchback, moreover, became a Tantri, so as to complete his villanies. He was duly initiated by an apostate Brahman, made a declaration that he renounced all the ceremonies of his old religion, and was delivered from their yoke, and proceeded to perform in token of joy an abominable rite. In company with eight men and eight women—a Brahman female, a dancing girl, a weaver's daughter, a woman of ill fame, a washerwoman, a barber's wife, a milkmaid, and the daughter of a landowner—choosing the darkest time of night and the most secret part of the house, he drank with them, was sprinkled and anointed, and went through many ignoble ceremonies, such as sitting nude upon a dead body. The

6—2

teacher informed him that he was not to indulge shame, or aversion to anything, nor to prefer one thing to another, nor to regard caste, ceremonial cleanness or uncleanness, but freely to enjoy all the pleasures of sense—that is, of course, wine and us, since we are the representatives of the wife of Cupid, and wine prevents the senses from going astray. And whereas holy men, holding that the subjugation or annihilation of the passions is essential to final beatitude, accomplish this object by bodily austerities, and by avoiding temptation, he proceeded to blunt the edge of the passions with excessive indulgence. And he jeered at the pious, reminding them that their ascetics are safe only in forests, and while keeping a perpetual fast ; but that he could subdue his passions in the very presence of what they most desired.

Presently this excellent youth's father died, leaving him immense wealth. He blunted his passions so piously and so vigorously, that in very few years his fortune was dissipated. Then he turned towards his neighbour's goods and prospered for a time, till being discovered robbing, he narrowly escaped the stake. At length he exclaimed, " Let the gods perish ! the rascals send me nothing but ill luck ! " and so saying he arose and fled from his own country.

Chance led that villain hunchback to the city of Chandrapur, where, hearing the name of my master Hemgupt, he recollected that one of his father's wealthiest correspondents was so called. Thereupon, with his usual audacity, he presented himself at the house, walked in, and although he was clothed in tatters, introduced himself, told his father's name and circumstances, and wept bitterly.

The good man was much astonished, and not less grieved, to see the son of his old friend in such woful plight. He rose up, however, embraced the youth, and asked the reason of his coming.

"I freighted a vessel," said the false hunchback, "for the purpose of trading to a certain land. Having gone there, I disposed of my merchandise, and, taking another cargo, I was on my voyage home. Suddenly a great storm arose, and the vessel was wrecked, and I escaped on a plank, and after a time arrived here. But I am ashamed, since I have lost all my wealth, and I cannot show my face in this plight in my own city. My excellent father would have consoled me with his pity. But now that I have carried him and my mother to Ganges,[1] every one will turn against me; they will rejoice in my misfortunes, they will accuse me of folly and recklessness —alas! alas! I am truly miserable."

My dear master was deceived by the cunning of the wretch. He offered him hospitality, which was readily enough accepted, and he entertained him for some time as a guest. Then, having reason to be satisfied with his conduct, Hemgupt admitted him to his secrets, and finally made him a partner in his business. Briefly, the villain played his cards so well, that at last the merchant said to himself:

"I have had for years an anxiety and a calamity in my house. My neighbours whisper things to my disadvantage, and those who are bolder speak out with astonishment amongst themselves, saying, 'At seven or eight, people marry their daughters, and this indeed is the appointment of the law: that period is long since gone; she is now thirteen or fourteen years old, and she is very tall and lusty, resembling a married woman of thirty. How can her father eat his rice with comfort and sleep with satisfaction, whilst such a disreputable thing exists in his house? At present he is exposed to shame, and his deceased friends are suffering through his retaining a girl from marriage beyond the period which nature has prescribed.' And now, while I am sitting quietly at

---

1 As we should say, buried them.

home, the Bhagwan (Deity) removes all my uneasiness: by his favour such an opportunity occurs. It is not right to delay. It is best that I shall give my daughter in marriage to him. Whatever can be done to-day is best; who knows what may happen to-morrow ? "

Thus thinking, the old man went to his wife and said to her, " Birth, marriage, and death are all under the direction of the gods ; can anyone say when they will be ours ? We want for our daughter a young man who is of good birth, rich and handsome, clever and honourable. But we do not find him. If the bridegroom be faulty, thou sayest, all will go wrong. I cannot put a string round the neck of our daughter and throw her into the ditch. If, however, thou think well of the merchant's son, now my partner, we will celebrate Ratnawati's marriage with him."

The wife, who had been won over by the hunchback's hypocrisy, was also pleased, and replied, " My lord ! when the Deity so plainly indicates his wish, we should do it ; since, though we have sat quietly at home, the desire of our hearts is accomplished. It is best that no delay be made: and, having quickly summoned the family priest, and having fixed upon a propitious planetary conjunction, that the marriage be celebrated."

Then they called their daughter—ah, me! what a beautiful being she was, and worthy the love of a Gandharva (demigod). Her long hair, purple with the light of youth, was glossy as the bramra's[1] wing ; her brow was pure and clear as the agate ; the ocean-coral looked pale beside her lips, and her teeth were as two chaplets of pearls. Everything in her was formed to be loved. Who could look into her eyes without wishing to do it again ? Who could hear her voice without hoping that such music would sound once more ? And she was good as she was fair. Her father adored her ; her mother,

---

1 A large kind of black bee, common in India.

though a middle-aged woman, was not envious or jealous of her; her relatives doted on her, and her friends could find no fault with her. I should never end were I to tell her precious qualities. Alas, alas! my poor Ratnawati!

So saying, the jay wept abundant tears; then she resumed:

When her parents informed my mistress of their resolution, she replied, " Sadhu—it is well!" She was not like most young women, who hate nothing so much as a man whom their seniors order them to love. She bowed her head and promised obedience, although, as she afterwards told her mother, she could hardly look at her intended, on account of his prodigious ugliness. But presently the hunchback's wit surmounted her disgust. She was grateful to him for his attention to her father and mother; she esteemed him for his moral and religious conduct; she pitied him for his misfortunes, and she fin- ished with forgetting his face, legs, and back in her admir- ation of what she supposed to be his mind.

She had vowed before marriage faithfully to per- form all the duties of a wife, however distasteful to her they might be; but after the nuptials, which were not long deferred, she was not surprised to find that she loved her husband. Not only did she omit to think of his features and figure; I verily believe that she loved him the more for his repulsiveness. Ugly, very ugly men prevail over women for two reasons. Firstly, we begin with repugnance, which in the course of nature turns to affection; and we all like the most that which, when un- accustomed to it, we most disliked. Hence the poet says, with as much truth as is in the male:

> Never despair, O man! when woman's spite
> Detests thy name and sickens at thy sight:
> Sometime her heart shall learn to love thee more
> For the wild hatred which it felt before, &c.

Secondly, the very ugly man appears, deceitfully enough,

to think little of his appearance, and he will give himself
the trouble to pursue a heart because he knows that the
heart will not follow after him. Moreover, we women
(said the jay) are by nature pitiful, and this our enemies
term a " strange perversity." A widow is generally disconsolate if she loses a little, wizen-faced, shrunken-
shanked, ugly, spiteful, distempered thing that scolded
her and quarrelled with her, and beat her and made her
hours bitter; whereas she will follow her husband to
Ganges with exemplary fortitude if he was brave, handsome, generous——

" Either hold your tongue or go on with your story,"
cried the warrior king, in whose mind these remarks
awakened disagreeable family reflections.

" Hi! hi! hi! " laughed the demon; " I will obey
your majesty, and make Madan-manjari, the misanthrop-
ical jay, proceed."

Yes, she loved the hunchback; and how wonderful
is *our* love! quoth the jay. A light from heaven which
rains happiness on this dull, dark earth! A spell falling
upon the spirit, which reminds us of a higher existence!
A memory of bliss! A present delight! An earnest of
future felicity! It makes hideousness beautiful and
stupidity clever, old age young and wickedness good,
moroseness amiable, and low-mindedness magnanimous,
perversity pretty and vulgarity piquant. Truly it is
sovereign alchemy and excellent flux for blending contra-
dictions is *our* love, exclaimed the jay.

And so saying, she cast a triumphant look at the
parrot, who only remarked that he could have desired
a little more originality in her remarks.

For some months (resumed Madan-manjari), the
bride and the bridegroom lived happily together in Hemgupt's house. But it is said:

Never yet did the tiger become a lamb;
and the hunchback felt that the edge of his passions again

wanted blunting. He reflected, "Wisdom is exemption from attachment, and affection for children, wife, and home." Then he thus addressed my poor young mistress :

"I have been now in thy country some years, and I have heard no tidings of my own family, hence my mind is sad, I have told thee everything about myself ; thou must now ask thy mother leave for me to go to my own city, and, if thou wishest, thou mayest go with me."

Ratnawati lost no time in saying to her mother, "My husband wishes to visit his own country ; will you so arrange that he may not be pained about this matter?"

The mother went to her husband, and said, "Your son-in-law desires leave to go to his own country."

Hemgupt replied, "Very well; we will grant him leave. One has no power over another man's son. We will do what he wishes."

The parents then called their daughter, and asked her to tell them her real desire—whether she would go to her father-in-law's house, or would remain in her mother's home. She was abashed at this question, and could not answer ; but she went back to her husband, and said, "As my father and mother have declared that you should do as you like, do not leave me behind."

Presently the merchant summoned his son-in-law, and having bestowed great wealth upon him, allowed him to depart. He also bade his daughter farewell, after giving her a palanquin and a female slave. And the parents took leave of them with wailing and bitter tears ; their hearts were like to break. And so was mine.

For some days the hunchback travelled quietly along with his wife, in deep thought. He could not take her to his city, where she would find out his evil life, and the fraud which he had passed upon her father. Besides which, although he wanted her money, he by no means wanted her company for life. After turning on many

projects in his evil-begotten mind, he hit upon the
following :

He dismissed the palanquin-bearers when halting at
a little shed in the thick jungle through which they were
travelling, and said to his wife, "This is a place of
danger ; give me thy jewels, and I will hide them in my
waist-shawl. When thou reachest the city thou canst
wear them again." She then gave up to him all her ornaments, which were of great value. Thereupon he in-

He dismissed the palanquin-bearers.

veigled the slave girl into the depths of the forest, where
he murdered her, and left her body to be devoured by
wild beasts. Lastly, returning to my poor mistress, he
induced her to leave the hut with him, and pushed her
by force into a dry well, after which exploit he set out
alone with his ill-gotten wealth, walking towards his own
city.

In the meantime, a wayfaring man, who was passing
through that jungle, hearing the sound of weeping, stood
still, and began to say to himself, " How came to my ears

the voice of a mortal's grief in this wild wood?" He then followed the direction of the noise, which led him to a pit, and peeping over the side, he saw a woman crying at the bottom. The traveller at once loosened his girdle cloth, knotted it to his turband, and letting down the line pulled out the poor bride. He asked her who she was, and how she came to fall into that well. She replied, " I am the daughter of Hemgupt, the wealthiest merchant in the city of Chandrapur; and I was journeying with my husband to his own country, when robbers set upon us and surrounded us. They slew my slave girl, they threw me into a well, and having bound my husband they took him away, together with my jewels. I have no tidings of him, nor he of me." And so saying, she burst into tears and lamentations.

The wayfaring man believed her tale, and conducted her to her home, where she gave the same account of the accident which had befallen her, ending with, " Beyond this, I know not if they have killed my husband, or have let him go." The father thus soothed her grief: " Daughter! have no anxiety; thy husband is alive, and by the will of the Deity he will come to thee in a few days. Thieves take men's money, not their lives." Then the parents presented her with ornaments more precious than those which she had lost; and summoning their relations and friends, they comforted her to the best of their power. And so did I.

The wicked hunchback had, meanwhile, returned to his own city, where he was excellently well received, because he brought much wealth with him. His old associates flocked around him rejoicing; and he fell into the same courses which had beggared him before. Gambling and debauchery soon blunted his passions, and emptied his purse. Again his boon companions, finding him without a broken cowrie, drove him from their doors; he stole and was flogged for theft; and lastly, half famished, he fled the city. Then he said to himself, "I must go to my father-in-law, and make the excuse that a grandson has been born to him, and that I have come to offer him congratulations on the event."

Imagine, however, his fears and astonishment, when, as he entered the house, his wife stood before him. At first he thought it was a ghost, and turned to run away, but she went out to him and said, "Husband, be not troubled! I have told my father that thieves came upon us, and killed the slave girl and robbed me and threw me into a well, and bound thee and carried thee off. Tell the same story, and put away all anxious feelings. Come up and change thy tattered garments—alas! some misfortune hath befallen thee. But console thyself; all is now well, since thou art returned to me, and fear not, for the house is thine, and I am thy slave."

The wretch, with all his hardness of heart, could scarcely refrain from tears. He followed his wife to her room, where she washed his feet, caused him to bathe, dressed him in new clothes, and placed food before him. When her parents returned, she presented him to their embrace, saying in a glad way, "Rejoice with me, O my father and mother! the robbers have at length allowed him to come back to us." Of course the parents were deceived; they are mostly a purblind race; and Hemgupt, showing great favour to his worthless son-in-law, exclaimed, "Remain with us, my son, and be happy!"

For two or three months the hunchback lived quietly with his wife, treating her kindly and even affectionately. But this did not last long. He made acquaintance with a band of thieves, and arranged his plans with them.

After a time, his wife one night came to sleep by his side, having put on all her jewels. At midnight, when he saw that she was fast asleep, he struck her with a knife so that she died. Then he admitted his accomplices, who savagely murdered Hemgupt and his wife; and with their assistance he carried off any valuable article upon which he could lay his hands. The ferocious wretch ! As he passed my cage he looked at it, and thought whether he had time to wring my neck. The barking of a dog saved my life ; but my mistress, my poor Ratnawati—ah, me ! ah, me !—

"Queen," said the jay, in deepest grief, "all this have I seen with mine own eyes, and have heard with mine own ears. It affected me in early life, and gave me a dislike for the society of the other sex. With due respect to you, I have resolved to remain an old maid. Let your majesty reflect, what crime had my poor mistress committed ? A male is of the same disposition as a highway robber ; and she who forms friendship with such an one, cradles upon her bosom a black and venomous snake." ,

"Sir Parrot," said the jay, turning to her wooer, " I have spoken. I have nothing more to say, *but* that you he-things are all a treacherous, selfish, wicked race, created for the express purpose of working our worldly woe, and——"

"When a female, O my king, asserts that she has nothing more to say, *but*," broke in Churaman, the parrot, with a loud dogmatical voice, " I know that what she has said merely whets her tongue for what she is about to say. This person has surely spoken long enough and drearily enough."

"Tell me, then, O parrot," said the king, "what faults there may be in the other sex."

" I will relate," quoth Churaman, "an occurrence which in my early youth determined me to live and to die an old bachelor."

When quite a young bird, and before my schooling began, I was caught in the land of Malaya, and was sold to a very rich merchant called Sagardati, a widower with one daughter, the lady Jayashri. As her father spent all his days and half his nights in his counting-house, conning his ledgers and scolding his writers, that young woman had more liberty than is generally allowed to those of her age, and a mighty bad use she made of it.

O king! men commit two capital mistakes in rearing the " domestic calamity," and these are over-vigilance and under-vigilance. Some parents never lose sight of their daughters, suspect them of all evil intentions, and are silly enough to show their suspicions, which is an incentive to evil-doing. For the weak-minded things do naturally say, " I will be wicked at once. What do I now but suffer all the pains and penalties of badness, without enjoying its pleasures ?" And so they are guilty of many evil actions ; for, however vigilant fathers and mothers may be, the daughter can always blind their eyes.

On the other hand, many parents take no trouble whatever with their charges : they allow them to sit in idleness, the origin of badness ; they permit them to communicate with the wicked, and they give them liberty which breeds opportunity. Thus they also, falling into the snares of the unrighteous, who are ever a more painstaking race than the righteous, are guilty of many evil actions.

What, then, must wise parents do? The wise will study the characters of their children, and modify their treatment accordingly. If a daughter be naturally good, she will be treated with a prudent confidence. If she be vicious, an apparent trust will be reposed in her ; but her father and mother will secretly ever be upon their guard. The one-idea'd——

" All this parrot-prate, I suppose, is only intended to vex me," cried the warrior king, who always considered himself, and very naturally, a person of such consequence as ever to be uppermost in the thoughts and minds of others. " If thou must tell a tale, then tell one, Vampire! or else be silent, as I am sick to the death of thy psychics."

"It is well, O warrior king," resumed the Baital. After that Churaman the parrot had given the young Raja Ram a golden mine full of good advice about the management of daughters, he proceeded to describe Jayashri.

She was tall, stout, and well made, of lymphatic temperament, and yet strong passions. Her fine large eyes had heavy and rather full eyelids, which are to be avoided. Her hands were symmetrical without being small, and the palms were ever warm and damp. Though her lips were good, her mouth was somewhat underhung; and her voice was so deep, that at times it sounded like that of a man. Her hair was smooth as the kokila's plume, and her complexion was that of the young jasmine; and these were the points at which most persons looked. Altogether, she was neither handsome nor ugly, which is an excellent thing in woman. Sita the goddess[1] was lovely to excess; therefore she was carried away by a demon. Raja Bali was exceedingly generous, and he emptied his treasury. In this way, exaggeration, even of good, is exceedingly bad.

Yet must I confess, continued the parrot, that, as a rule, the beautiful woman is more virtuous than the ugly. The former is often tempted, but her vanity and conceit enable her to resist, by the self-promise that she shall be tempted again and again. On the other hand, the ugly woman must tempt instead of being tempted, and she must yield, because her vanity and conceit are gratified by yielding, not by resisting.

"Ho, there!" broke in the jay contemptuously. "What woman cannot win the hearts of the silly things called men? Is it not said that a pig-faced female who dwells in Landanpur has a lover?"

I was about to remark, my king! said the parrot,

---

1 The beautiful wife of the demigod Rama Chandra.

somewhat nettled, if the aged virgin had not interrupted me, that as ugly women are more vicious than handsome women, so they are most successful. "We love the pretty, we adore the plain," is a true saying amongst the worldly wise. And why do we adore the plain? Because they seem to think less of themselves than of us—a vital condition of adoration.

Jayashri made some conquests by the portion of good looks which she possessed, more by her impudence, and most by her father's reputation for riches. She was truly shameless, and never allowed herself fewer than half a dozen admirers at the time. Her chief amusement was to appoint interviews with them successively, at intervals so short that she was obliged to hurry away one in order to make room for another. And when a lover happened to be jealous, or ventured in any way to criticize her arrangements, she replied at once by showing him the door. Answer unanswerable!

When Jayashri had reached the ripe age of thirteen, the son of a merchant, who was her father's gossip and neighbour, returned home after a long sojourn in far lands, whither he had travelled in the search of wealth. The poor wretch, whose name, by-the-bye, was Shridat (Gift of Fortune), had loved her in her childhood; and he came back, as men are apt to do after absence from familiar scenes, painfully full of affection for house and home and all belonging to it. From his cross, stingy old uncle to the snarling superannuated beast of a watch-dog, he viewed all with eyes of love and melting heart. He could not see that his idol was greatly changed, and nowise for the better ; that her nose was broader and more club-like, her eyelids fatter and thicker, her under lip more prominent, her voice harsher, and her manner coarser. He did not notice that she was an adept in judging of men's dress, and that she looked with admiration upon all swordsmen, especially upon those who fought upon horses and elephants. The charm of memory, the curious faculty of making past time present, caused all he viewed to be enchanting to him.

Having obtained her father's permission, Shridat applied for betrothal to Jayashri, who with peculiar boldness, had resolved that no suitor should come to her through her parent. And she, after leading him on by all the coquetries of which she was a mistress, refused to marry him, saying that she liked him as a friend, but would hate him as a husband.

You see, my king! there are three several states of feeling with which women regard their masters, and these are love, hate, and indifference. Of all, love is the weakest and the most transient, because the essentially unstable creatures naturally fall out of it as readily as they fall into it. Hate being a sister excitement will easily become, if a man has wit enough to effect the change, love; and hate-love may perhaps last a little longer than love-love. Also, man has the occupation, the excitement, and the pleasure of bringing about the change. As regards the neutral state, that poet was not happy in his ideas who sang—

> Whene'er indifference appears, or scorn,
> Then, man, despair! then, hapless lover, mourn!

For a man versed in the Lila Shastra[1] can soon turn a woman's indifference into hate, which I have shown is as easily permuted to love. In which predicament it is the old thing over again, and it ends in the pure Asat[2] or nonentity.

"Which of these two birds, the jay or the parrot, had dipped deeper into human nature, mighty King Vikram?" asked the demon in a wheedling tone of voice.

The trap was this time set too openly, even for the

[1] The Hindu *Ars Amoris.*

[2] The old philosophers, believing in a "Sat" (τὸ ὄν), postulated an Asat (τὸ μὴ ὄν) and made the latter the root of the former.

royal personage, to fall into it. He hurried on, calling to his son, and not answering a word. The Vampire therefore resumed the thread of his story at the place where he had broken it off.

Shridat was in despair when he heard the resolve of his idol. He thought of drowning himself, of throwing himself down from the summit of Mount Girnar,[1] of becoming a religious beggar; in short, of a multitude of follies. But he refrained from all such heroic remedies for despair, having rightly judged, when he became somewhat calmer, that they would not be likely to further his suit. He discovered that patience is a virtue, and he resolved impatiently enough to practise it. And by perseverance he succeeded. The worse for him! How vain are men to wish! How wise is the Deity, who is deaf to their wishes!

Jayashri, for potent reasons best known to herself, was married to Shridat six months after his return home. He was in raptures. He called himself the happiest man in existence. He thanked and sacrificed to the Bhagwan for listening to his prayers. He recalled to mind with thrilling heart the long years which he had spent in hopeless exile from all that was dear to him, his sadness and anxiety, his hopes and joys, his toils and troubles his loyal love and his vows to Heaven for the happiness of his idol, and for the furtherance of his fondest desires.

For truly he loved her, continued the parrot, and there is something holy in such love. It becomes not only a faith, but the best of faiths—an abnegation of self which emancipates the spirit from its straightest and earthliest bondage, the "I"; the first step in the regions of heaven; a homage rendered through the creature to the Creator; a devotion solid, practical, ardent, not as worship mostly is, a cold and lifeless abstraction; a

---

1 In Western India, a place celebrated for suicides.

merging of human nature into one far nobler and higher, the spiritual existence of the supernal world. For perfect love is perfect happiness, and the only perfection of man; and what is a demon but a being without love? And what makes man's love truly divine, is the fact that it is bestowed upon such a thing as woman.

"And now, Raja Vikram," said the Vampire, speaking in his proper person, " I have given you Madanman-jari the jay's and Churaman the parrot's definitions of the tender passion, or rather their descriptions of its effects. Kindly observe that I am far from accepting either one or the other. Love is, according to me, somewhat akin to mania, a temporary condition of selfishness, a transient confusion of identity. It enables man to predicate of others who are his other selves, that which he is ashamed to say about his real self. I will suppose the beloved object to be ugly, stupid, vicious, perverse, selfish, low-minded, or the reverse; man finds it charming by the same rule that makes his faults and foibles dearer to him than all the virtues and good qualities of his neighbours. Ye call love a spell, an alchemy, a deity. Why? Because it deifies self by gratifying all man's pride, man's vanity, and man's conceit, under the mask of complete unegotism. Who is not in heaven when he is talking of himself? and, prithee, of what else consists all the talk of lovers?"

It is astonishing that the warrior king allowed this speech to last as long as it did. He hated nothing so fiercely, now that he was in middle-age, as any long mention of the "handsome god.[1]" Having vainly endeavoured to stop by angry mutterings the course of the Baital's eloquence, he stepped out so vigorously and so rudely shook that inveterate talker, that the latter once or twice nearly bit off the tip of his tongue. Then the

---

[1] Kama Deva. "Out on thee, foul fiend, talk'st thou of nothing but ladies?"

Vampire became silent, and Vikram relapsed into a walk which allowed the tale to be resumed.

Jayashri immediately conceived a strong dislike for her husband, and simultaneously a fierce affection for a reprobate who before had been indifferent to her. The more lovingly Shridat behaved to her, the more vexed and annoyed she was. When her friends talked to her, she turned up her nose, raising her eyebrows (in token of displeasure), and remained silent. When her husband spoke words of affection to her, she found them dis- agreeable, and turning away her face, reclined on the bed. Then he brought dresses and ornaments of various kinds and presented them to her, saying, "Wear these." Whereupon she would become more angry, knit her brows, turn her face away, and in an audible whisper call him "fool." All day she stayed out of the house, saying to her companions, "Sisters, my youth is passing away, and I have not, up to the present time, tasted any of this world's pleasures." Then she would ascend to the balcony, peep through the lattice, and seeing the repro- bate going along, she would cry to her friend, "Bring that person to me." All night she tossed and turned from side to side, reflecting in her heart, "I am puzzled in my mind what I shall say, and whither I shall go. I have forgotten sleep, hunger, and thirst; neither heat nor cold is refreshing to me."

At last, unable any longer to support the separation from her reprobate paramour, whom she adored, she resolved to fly with him. On one occasion, when she thought that her husband was fast asleep, she rose up quietly, and leaving him, made her way fearlessly in the dark night to her lover's abode. A footpad, who saw her on the way, thought to himself, "Where can this woman, clothed in jewels, be going alone at midnight?" And thus he followed her unseen, and watched her.

When Jayashri reached the intended place, she

went into the house, and found her lover lying at the
door.   He was dead, having been stabbed by the footpad; but she, thinking that he had, according to custom,
drunk intoxicating hemp, sat upon the floor, and raising
his head, placed it tenderly in her lap.   Then, burning
with the fire of separation from him, she began to kiss
his cheeks, and to fondle and caress him with the utmost
freedom and affection.

By chance a Pisach (evil spirit) was seated in a
large fig-tree[1] opposite the house, and it occurred to him,
when beholding this scene, that he might amuse himself
in a characteristic way.   He therefore hopped down
from his branch, vivified the body, and began to return
the woman's caresses.   But as Jayashri bent down to
kiss his lips, he caught the end of her nose in his teeth,
and bit it clean off.   He then issued from the corpse,
and returned to the branch where he had been sitting.

Jayashri was in despair.   She did not, however, lose
her presence of mind, but sat down and proceeded to take
thought; and when she had matured her plan she arose,
dripping with blood, and walked straight home to her
husband's house.   On entering his room she clapped her
hand to her nose, and began to gnash her teeth, and to
shriek so violently, that all the members of the family
were alarmed.   The neighbours also collected in numbers
at the door, and, as it was bolted inside, they broke it
open and rushed in, carrying lights.   There they saw the
wife sitting upon the ground with her face mutilated, and
the husband standing over her, apparently trying to
appease her.

"O ignorant, criminal, shameless, pitiless wretch!"
cried the people, especially the women; "why hast thou
cut off her nose, she not having offended in any way?"

Poor Shridat, seeing at once the trick which had
been played upon him, thought to himself: "One should

---

1 The pipal or *Ficus religiosa*, a favourite roosting-place for fiends.

put no confidence in a changeful mind, a black serpent, or an armed enemy, and one should dread a woman's doings. What cannot a poet describe? What is there that a saint (jogi) does not know? What nonsense will not a drunken man talk? What limit is there to a woman's guile? True it is that the gods know nothing of the defects of a horse, of the thundering of clouds, of a woman's deeds, or of a man's future fortunes. How then can we know?" He could do nothing but weep, and swear by the herb basil, by his cattle, by his grain, by a piece of gold, and by all that is holy, that he had not committed the crime.

In the meanwhile, the old merchant, Jayashri's father, ran off, and laid a complaint before the kotwal, and the footmen of the police magistrate were immediately sent to apprehend the husband, and to carry him bound before the judge. The latter, after due examination, laid the affair before the king. An example happening to be necessary at the time, the king resolved to punish the offence with severity, and he summoned the husband and wife to the court.

When the merchant's daughter was asked to give an account of what had happened, she pointed out the state of her nose, and said, "Maharaj! why inquire of me concerning what is so manifest?" The king then turned to the husband, and bade him state his defence. He said, " I know nothing of it," and in the face of the strongest evidence he persisted in denying his guilt.

Thereupon the king, who had vainly threatened to cut off Shridat's right hand, infuriated by his refusing to confess and to beg for mercy, exclaimed, " How must I punish such a wretch as thou art?" The unfortunate man answered, "Whatever your majesty may consider just, that be pleased to do." Thereupon the king cried, " Away with him, and impale him "; and the people, hearing the command, prepared to obey it.

Before Shridat had left the court, the footpad, who had been looking on, and who saw that an innocent man was about to be unjustly punished, raised a cry for justice, and, pushing through the crowd, resolved to make himself heard. He thus addressed the throne: "Great king, the cherishing of the good, and the punishment of the bad, is the invariable duty of kings." The ruler having caused him to approach, asked him who he was, and he replied boldly, "Maharaj! I am a thief, and this man is innocent, and his blood is about to be shed unjustly. Your majesty has not done what is right in this affair." Thereupon the king charged him to tell the truth according to his religion; and the thief related explicitly the whole circumstances, omitting of course, the murder.

"Go ye," said the king to his messengers, "and look in the mouth of the woman's lover who has fallen dead. If the nose be there found, then has this thief-witness told the truth, and the husband is a guiltless man."

The nose was presently produced in court, and Shridat escaped the stake. The king caused the wicked Jayashri's face to be smeared with oily soot, and her head and eyebrows to be shaved; thus blackened and disfigured, she was mounted upon a little ragged-limbed ass, and was led around the market and the streets, after which she was banished for ever from the city. The husband and the thief were then dismissed with betel and other gifts, together with much sage advice which neither of them wanted.

"My king," resumed the misogyne parrot, "of such excellencies as these are women composed. It is said that 'wet cloth will extinguish fire and bad food will destroy strength; a degenerate son ruins a family, and when a friend is in wrath he takes away life. But a woman is an inflicter of grief in love and in hate; whatever she does turns out to be for our ill. Truly the Deity has created woman a strange being in this world.' And again, 'The beauty of the nightingale is its song, science is the beauty of an ugly man, forgiveness is the beauty of a devotee, and the beauty of a woman is virtue—but where shall we find it?' And again, 'Among the sages, Narudu; among the beasts, the jackal; among the birds, the crow; among men, the barber; and in this world woman—is the most crafty.'

" What I have told thee, my king, I have seen with mine own eyes, and I have heard with mine own ears. At the time I was young, but the event so affected me that I have ever since held female kind to be a walking pest, a two-legged plague, whose mission on earth, like flies and other vermin, is only to prevent our being too happy. O, why do not children and young parrots sprout in crops from the ground—from budding trees or vine-stocks?"

"I was thinking, sire," said the young Dharma Dhwaj to the warrior king his father, " what women would say of us if they could compose Sanskrit verses!"

"Then keep your thoughts to yourself," replied the Raja, nettled at his son daring to say a word in favour of the sex. "You always take the part of wickedness and depravity——"

"Permit me, your majesty," interrupted the Baital, "to conclude my tale."

When Madan-manjari, the jay, and Churaman, the parrot, had given these illustrations of their belief, they began to wrangle, and words ran high. The former insisted that females are the salt of the earth, speaking, 1 presume, figuratively. The latter went so far as to assert that the opposite sex have no souls, and that their brains are in a rudimental and inchoate state of development. Thereupon he was tartly taken to task by his master's bride, the beautiful Chandravati, who told him that those only have a bad opinion of women who have associated with none but the vicious and the low,

and that he should be ashamed to abuse feminine
parrots, because his mother had been one.

This was truly logical.

On the other hand, the jay was sternly reproved for
her mutinous and treasonable assertions by the husband
of her mistress, Raja Ram, who, although still a bridegroom, had not forgotten the gallant rule of his syntax—

The masculine is more worthy than the feminine;
till Madan-manjari burst into tears and declared that her
life was not worth having.   And Raja Ram looked at
her as if he could have wrung her neck.

In short, Raja Vikram, all the four lost their tempers, and with them what little wits they had.   Two of
them were but birds, and the others seem not to have
been much better, being young, ignorant, inexperienced,
and lately married.   How then could they decide so difficult a question as that of the relative wickedness and
villany of men and women?   Had your majesty been
there, the knot of uncertainty would soon have been un-
done by the trenchant edge of your wit and wisdom, your
knowledge and experience.   You have, of course, long since
made up your mind upon the subject?

Dharma Dhwaj would have prevented his father's
reply.   But the youth had been twice reprehended in the
course of this tale, and he thought it wisest to let things
take their own way.

"Women," quoth the Raja, oracularly, "are worse
than we are; a man, however depraved he may be, ever
retains some notion of right and wrong, but a woman
does not.   She has no such regard whatever."

"The beautiful Bangalah Rani for instance?" said
the Baital, with a demoniac sneer.

At the mention of a word, the uttering of which was
punishable by extirpation of the tongue, Raja Vikram's
brain whirled with rage.   He staggered in the violence
of his passion, and putting forth both hands to break

his fall, he dropped the bundle from his back. Then the Baital, disentangling himself and laughing lustily, ran off towards the tree as fast as his thin brown legs would carry him. But his activity availed him little.

The king, puffing with fury, followed him at the top of his speed, and caught him by his tail before he reached the siras-tree, hurled him backwards with force, put foot upon his chest, and after shaking out the cloth, rolled him up in it with extreme violence, bumped his back half a dozen times against the stony ground, and finally, with a jerk, threw him on his shoulder, as he had done before.

The youug prince, afraid to accompany his father whilst he was pursuing the fiend, followed slowly in the rear, and did not join him for some minutes.

But when matters were in their normal state, the Vampire, who had endured with exemplary patience the penalty of his impudence, began in honeyed accents,

"Listen, O warrior king, whilst thy servant recounts unto thee another true tale."

THE VAMPIRE'S THIRD STORY.

OF A HIGH-MINDED FAMILY.

In the venerable city of Bardwan, O warrior king!
(quoth the Vampire) during the reign of the mighty
Rupsen, flourished one Rajeshwar, a Rajput warrior of
distinguished fame. By his valour and conduct he had
risen from the lowest ranks of the army to command it as
its captain. And arrived at that dignity, he did not put
a stop to all improvements, like other chiefs, who rejoice
to rest and return thanks. On the contrary, he became
such a reformer that, to some extent, he remodelled the
art of war.

Instead of attending to rules and regulations, drawn
up in their studies by pandits and Brahmans, he consulted chiefly his own experience and judgment. He
threw aside the systematic plans of campaigns laid down
in the Shastras or books of the ancients, and he acted
upon the spur of the moment. He displayed a skill in
the choice of ground, in the use of light troops, and in
securing his own supplies whilst he cut off those of the
enemy, which Kartikaya himself, God of War, might
have envied. Finding that the bows of his troops were
clumsy and slow to use, he had them all changed before
compelled so to do by defeat; he also gave his attention
to the sword handles, which cramped the men's grasp,
but which having been used for eighteen hundred years,
were considered perfect weapons. And having organized

a special corps of warriors using fire arrows, he soon brought it to such perfection that, by using it against the elephants of his enemies, he gained many a campaign.

One instance of his superior judgment I am about to quote to thee, O Vikram, after which I return to my tale; for thou art truly a warrior king, very likely to imitate the innovations of the great general Rajeshwar.

(A grunt from the monarch was the result of the Vampire's sneer.)

He found his master's armies recruited from Northern Hindustan, and officered by Kshatriya warriors, who grew great only because they grew old and—fat. Thus the energy and talent of the younger men were wasted in troubles and disorders; whilst the seniors were often so ancient that they could not mount their chargers unaided, nor, when they were mounted, could they see anything a dozen yards before them. But they had served in a certain obsolete campaign, and until Rajeshwar gave them pensions and dismissals, they claimed a right to take first part in all campaigns present and future. The commander-in-chief refused to use any captain who could not stand steady on his legs, or endure the sun for a whole day. When a soldier distinguished himself in action, he raised him to the powers and privileges of the warrior caste. And whereas it had been the habit to lavish circles and bars of silver and other metals upon all those who had joined in the war, whether they had sat behind a heap of sand or had been foremost to attack the foe, he broke through the pernicious custom, and he rendered the honour valuable by conferring it only upon the deserving. I need hardly say that, in an inordinately short space of time, his army beat every king and general that opposed it.

One day the great commander-in-chief was seated in a certain room near the threshold of his gate, when the voices of a number of people outside were heard. Rajesh-

war asked, "Who is at the door, and what is the meaning of the noise I hear?"   The porter replied, "It is a
fine thing your honour has asked.   Many persons come
sitting at the door of the rich for the purpose of obtaining a livelihood and wealth.   When they meet together
they talk of various things: it is these very people who
are now making this noise."

   Rajeshwar, on hearing this, remained silent.

   In the meantime a traveller, a Rajput, Birbal by
name, hoping to obtain employment, came from the

In the meantime a traveller, a Rajput, by name Birbal.

southern quarter to the palace of the chief.   The porter
having listened to his story, made the circumstance
known to his master, saying, "O chief! an armed man
has arrived here, hoping to obtain employment, and is
standing at the door.   If I receive a command he shall be
brought into your honour's presence."

   "Bring him in," cried the commander-in-chief.

   The porter brought him in, and Rajeshwar inquired,
"O Rajput, who and what art thou?"

Birbal submitted that he was a person of distinguished fame for the use of weapons, and that his name for fidelity and valour had gone forth to the utmost ends of Bharat-Kandha.[1]

The chief was well accustomed to this style of self-introduction, and its only effect upon his mind was a wish to shame the man by showing him that he had not the least knowledge of weapons. He therefore bade him bare his blade and perform some feat.

Birbal at once drew his good sword. Guessing the thoughts which were hovering about the chief's mind, he put forth his left hand, extending the forefinger upwards, waved his blade like the arm of a demon round his head, and, with a dexterous stroke, so shaved off a bit of nail that it fell to the ground, and not a drop of blood appeared upon the finger-tip.

" Live for ever!" exclaimed Rajeshwar in admiration. He then addressed to the recruit a few questions concerning the art of war, or rather concerning his peculiar views of it. To all of which Birbal answered with a spirit and a judgment which convinced the hearer that he was no common sworder.

Whereupon Rajeshwar bore off the new man at arms to the palace of the king Rupsen, and recommended that he should be engaged without delay.

The king, being a man of few words and many ideas, after hearing his commander-in-chief, asked, "O Rajput, what shall I give thee for thy daily expenditure?"

"Give me a thousand ounces of gold daily," said Birbal, "and then I shall have wherewithal to live on."

"Hast thou an army with thee?" exclaimed the king in the greatest astonishment.

" I have not," responded the Rajput somewhat stiffly. " I have first, a wife; second, a son; third, a

---

[1] India.

daughter; fourth, myself; there is no fifth person with me."

All the people of the court on hearing this turned aside their heads to laugh, and even the women, who were peeping at the scene, covered their mouths with their veils. The Rajput was then dismissed the presence.

It is, however, noticeable amongst you humans, that the world often takes you at your own valuation. Set a high price upon yourselves, and each man shall say to his neighbour, " In this man there must be something." Tell everyone that you are brave, clever, generous, or even handsome, and after a time they will begin to believe you. And when thus you have attained success, it will be harder to unconvince them than it was to convince them. Thus——

" Listen not to him, sirrah," cried Raja Vikram to Dharma Dhwaj, the young prince, who had fallen a little way behind, and was giving ear attentively to the Vampire's ethics. " Listen to him not. And tell me, villain, with these ignoble principles of thine, what will become of modesty, humility, self-sacrifice, and a host of other Guna or good qualities which—which are good qualities ?"

" I know not," rejoined the Baital, " neither do I care. But my habitually inspiriting a succession of human bodies has taught me one fact. The wise man knows himself, and is, therefore, neither unduly humble nor elated, because he had no more to do with making himself than with the cut of his cloak, or with the fitness of his loin-cloth. But the fool either loses his head by comparing himself with still greater fools, or is prostrated when he finds himself inferior to other and lesser fools. This shyness he calls modesty, humility, and so forth. Now, whenever entering a corpse, whether it be of man, woman, or child, I feel peculiarly modest ; I know that my tenement lately belonged to some conceited ass. And——"

"Wouldst thou have me bump thy back against the ground?" asked Raja Vikram angrily.

(The Baital muttered some reply scarcely intelligible about his having this time stumbled upon a metaphysical thread of ideas, and then continued his story.)

Now Rupsen, the king, began by inquiring of himself why the Rajput had rated his services so highly. Then he reflected that if this recruit had asked so much money, it must have been for some reason which would afterwards become apparent. Next, he hoped that if he gave him so much, his generosity might some day turn out to his own advantage. Finally, with this idea in his mind, he summoned Birbal and the steward of his household, and said to the latter, "Give this Rajput a thousand ounces of gold daily from our treasury."

It is related that Birbal made the best possible use of his wealth. He used every morning to divide it into two portions, one of which was distributed to Brahmans and Parohitas.[1] Of the remaining moiety, having made two parts, he gave one as alms to pilgrims, to Bairagis or Vishnu's mendicants, and to Sanyasis or worshippers of Shiva, whose bodies, smeared with ashes, were hardly covered with a narrow cotton cloth and a rope about their loins, and whose heads of artificial hair, clotted like a rope, besieged his gate. With the remaining fourth, having caused food to be prepared, he regaled the poor, while he himself and his family ate what was left. Every evening, arming himself with sword and buckler, he took up his position as guard at the royal bedside, and walked round it all night sword in hand. If the king chanced to wake and asked who was present, Birbal immediately gave reply that " Birbal is here; whatever command you give, that

---

1 The ancient name of a priest by profession, meaning "præpositus" or præses. He was the friend and counsellor of a chief, the minister of a king, and his companion in peace and war. (M. Müller's *Ancient Sanskrit Literature*, p. 485).

he will obey." And oftentimes Rupsen gave him unusual commands, for it is said, "To try thy servant, bid him do things in season and out of season : if he obey thee willingly, know him to be useful ; if he reply, dismiss him at once. Thus is a servant tried, even as a wife by the poverty of her husband, and brethren and friends by asking their aid."

In such manner, through desire of money, Birbal remained on guard all night ; and whether eating, drinking, sleeping, sitting, going or wandering about, during the twenty-four hours, he held his master in watchful remembrance. This, indeed, is the custom ; if a man sell another the latter is sold, but a servant by doing service sells himself, and when a man has become dependent, how can he be happy? Certain it is that however intelligent, clever, or learned a man may be, yet, while he is in his master's presence, he remains silent as a dumb man, and struck with dread. Only while he is away from his lord can he be at ease. Hence, learned men say that to do service aright is harder than any religious study.

On one occasion it is related that there happened to be heard at night-time the wailing of a woman in a neighbouring cemetery. The king on hearing it called out, "Who is in waiting?"

"I am here," replied Birbal; "what command is there?"

"Go," spoke the king, "to the place whence proceeds this sound of woman's wail, and having inquired the cause of her grief, return quickly."

On receiving this order the Rajput went to obey it ; and the king, unseen by him, and attired in a black dress, followed for the purpose of observing his courage.

Presently Birbal arrived at the cemetery. And what sees he there? A beautiful woman of a light yellow colour, loaded with jewels from head to foot, holding a horn in her right and a necklace in her left hand. Sometimes she danced, sometimes she jumped, and sometimes she ran about. There was not a tear in her eye, but beating her head and making lamentable cries, she kept dashing herself on the ground.

Seeing her condition, and not recognizing the goddess born of sea foam, and whom all the host of heaven loved,[1] Birbal inquired, " Why art thou thus beating thyself and crying out ? Who art thou ? And what grief is upon thee ? "

" I am the Royal-Luck," she replied.

" For what reason," asked Birbal, " art thou weeping ? "

The goddess then began to relate her position to the Rajput. She said, with tears, " In the king's palace Shudra (or low caste acts) are done, and hence misfortune will certainly fall upon it, and I shall forsake it. After a month has passed, the king, having endured excessive affliction, will die. In grief for this, I weep. I have brought much happiness to the king's house, and hence I am full of regret that this my prediction cannot in any way prove untrue."

" Is there," asked Birbal, " any remedy for this trouble, so that the king may be preserved and live a hundred years ? "

" Yes," said the goddess, "there is. About eight miles to the east thou wilt find a temple dedicated to my terrible sister Devi. Offer to her thy son's head, cut off with thine own hand, and the reign of thy king shall endure for an age." So saying Raj-Lakshmi disappeared.

Birbal answered not a word, but with hurried steps he turned towards his home. The king, still in black so

---

1 Lakshmi, the Goddess of Prosperity. Raj-Lakshmi would mean the King's Fortune, which we should call tutelary genius. Lakshichara is our "luckless," forming, as Mr. Ward says, an extraordinary coincidence of sound and meaning in languages so different. But the derivations are very distinct.

8

as not to be seen, followed him closely, and observed and listened to everything he did.

The Rajput went straight to his wife, awakened her, and related to her everything that had happened. The wise have said, "she alone deserves the name of wife who always receives her husband with affectionate and submissive words." When she heard the circumstances, she at once aroused her son, and her daughter also awoke. Then Birbal told them all that they must follow him to the temple of Devi in the wood.

On the way the Rajput said to his wife, "If thou wilt give up thy son willingly, I will sacrifice him for our master's sake to Devi the Destroyer."

She replied, "Father and mother, son and daughter, brother and relative, have I now none. You are everything to me. It is written in the scripture that a wife is not made pure by gifts to priests, nor by performing religious rites; her virtue consists in waiting upon her husband, in obeying him and in loving him—yea! though he be lame, maimed in the hands, dumb, deaf, blind, one-eyed, leprous, or humpbacked. It is a true saying that ' a son under one's authority, a body free from sickness, a desire to acquire knowledge, an intelligent friend, and an obedient wife; whoever holds these five will find them bestowers of happiness and dispellers of affliction. An unwilling servant, a parsimonious king, an insincere friend, and a wife not under control; such things are disturbers of ease and givers of trouble.' "

Then the good wife turned to her son and said, " Child by the gift of thy head, the king's life may be spared, and the kingdom remain unshaken."

"Mother," replied that excellent youth, "in my opinion we should hasten this matter. Firstly, I must obey your command; secondly, I must promote the interests of my master; thirdly, if this body be of any use

8—2

to a goddess, nothing better can be done with it in this world."

("Excuse me, Raja Vikram," said the Baital, inter-rupting himself, "if I repeat these fair discourses at full length; it is interesting to hear a young person, whose throat is about to be cut, talk so like a doctor of laws.")

Then the youth thus addressed his sire : "Father, whoever can be of use to his master, the life of that man in this world has been lived to good purpose, and by reason of his usefulness he will be rewarded in other worlds."

His sister, however, exclaimed, "If a mother should give poison to her daughter, and a father sell his son, and a king seize the entire property of his subjects, where then could one look for protection ? " But they heeded her not, and continued talking as they journeyed towards the temple of Devi—the king all the while secretly following them.

Presently they reached the temple, a single room, surrounded by a spacious paved area ; in front was an immense building capable of seating hundreds of people. Before the image there were pools of blood, where victims had lately been slaughtered. In the sanctum was Devi, a large black figure with ten arms. With a spear in one of her right hands she pierced the giant Mahisha ; and with one of her left hands she held the tail of a serpent, and the hair of the giant, whose breast the serpent was biting. Her other arms were all raised above her head, and were filled with different instruments of war ; against her right leg leaned a lion.

Then Birbal joined his hands in prayer, and with Hindu mildness thus addressed the awful goddess : "O mother, let the king's life be prolonged for a thousand years by the sacrifice of my son. O Devi, mother ! destroy, destroy his enemies ! Kill ! kill ! Reduce them to ashes ! Drive them away ! Devour them ! devour them ! Cut them in two ! Drink ! drink their blood ! Destroy them root and branch ! With thy thunderbolt, spear, scymitar, discus, or rope, annihilate them ! Spheng ! Spheng !"

The Rajput, having caused his son to kneel before the goddess, struck him so violent a blow that his head rolled upon the ground. He then threw the sword down, when his daughter, frantic with grief, snatched it up and struck her neck with such force that her head, separated from her body, fell. In her turn the mother, unable to survive the loss of her children, seized the weapon and succeeded in decapitating herself. Birbal, beholding all this slaughter, thus reflected : " My children are dead ; why, now, should I remain in servitude, and upon whom shall I bestow the gold I receive from the king ?" He then gave himself so deep a wound in the neck, that his head also separated from his body.

Rupsen, the king, seeing these four heads on the ground, said in his heart, " For my sake has the family of Birbal been destroyed. Kingly power, for the purpose of upholding which the destruction of a whole household is necessary, is a mere curse, and to carry on government in this manner is not just." He then took up the sword and was about to slay himself, when the Destroying Goddess, probably satisfied with bloodshed, stayed his hand, bidding him at the same time ask any boon he pleased.

The generous monarch begged, thereupon, that his faithful servant might be restored to life, together with all his high-minded family ; and the goddess Devi in the twinkling of an eye fetched from Patala, the regions below the earth, a vase full of Amrita, the water of immortality, sprinkled it upon the dead, and raised them all as before. After which the whole party walked leisurely home, and in due time the king divided his throne with his friend Birbal.

Having stopped for a moment, the Baital proceeded to remark, in a sententious tone, " Happy the servant who grudges not his own life to save that of his master ! And happy, thrice happy the master who can annihilate all greedy longing for existence and worldly prosperity. Raja, I have to ask thee one searching question—Of these five, who was the greatest fool ?"

"Demon ! " exclaimed the great Vikram, all whose cherished feelings about fidelity and family affection, obedience, and high-mindedness, were outraged by this Vampire view of the question ; " if thou meanest by the greatest fool the noblest mind, I reply without hesitating Rupsen, the king."

" Why, prithee?" asked the Baital.

" Because, dull demon," said the king, " Birbal was bound to offer up his life for a master who treated him so generously ; the son could not disobey his father, and the women naturally and instinctively killed themselves, because the example was set to them. But Rupsen the king gave up his throne for the sake of his retainer, and valued not a straw his life and his high inducements to live. For this reason I think him the most meritorious."

"Surely, mighty Vikram," laughed the Vampire, " you will be tired of ever clambering up yon tall tree, even had you the legs and arms of Hanuman[1] himself."

And so saying he disappeared from the cloth, although it had been placed upon the ground.

But the poor Baital had little reason to congratulate himself on the success of his escape. In a short time he was again bundled into the cloth with the ·usual want of ceremony, and he revenged himself by telling another true story.

---

[1] The Monkey God.

THE VAMPIRE'S FOURTH STORY.

OF A WOMAN WHO TOLD THE TRUTH.

" LISTEN, great king!" again began the Baital.

An unimportant Baniya[1] (trader), Hiranyadatt, had a daughter, whose name was Madansena Sundari, the beautiful army of Cupid. Her face was like the moon; her hair like the clouds; her eyes like those of a musk-rat; her eyebrows like a bent bow; her nose like a parrot's bill; her neck like that of a dove; her teeth like pomegranate grains; the red colour of her lips like that of a gourd; her waist lithe and bending like the pards: her hands and feet like softest blossoms; her complexion like the jasmine—in fact, day by day the splendour of her youth increased.

When she had arrived at maturity, her father and mother began often to resolve in their minds the subject of her marriage. And the people of all that country side ruled by Birbar king of Madanpur bruited it abroad that in the house of Hiranyadatt had been born a daughter by whose beauty gods, men, and munis (sages) were fascinated.

Thereupon many, causing their portraits to be painted, sent them by messengers to Hiranyadatt the Baniya, who showed them all to his daughter. But she was capricious, as beauties sometimes are, and when her father said, " Make choice of a husband thyself," she told him

---

1 Generally written " Banyan."

that none pleased her, and moreover she begged of him to find her a husband who possessed good looks, good qualities, and good sense.

At length, when some days had passed, four suitors came from four different countries. The father told them that he must have from each some indication that he possessed the required qualities; that he was pleased with their looks, but that they must satisfy him about their knowledge.

" I have," the first said, "a perfect acquaintance with the Shastras (or Scriptures); in science there is none to rival me. As for my handsome mien, it may plainly be seen by you."

The second exclaimed, " My attainments are unique in the knowledge of archery. I am acquainted with the art of discharging arrows and killing anything which though not seen is heard, and my fine proportions are plainly visible to you."

The third continued, " I understand the language of land and water animals, of birds and of beasts, and I have no equal in strength. Of my comeliness you yourself may judge."

" I have the knowledge," quoth the fourth, " how to make a certain cloth which can be sold for five rubies : having sold it I give the proceeds of one ruby to a Brahman, of the second I make an offering to a deity, a third I wear on my own person, a fourth I keep for my wife ; and, having sold the fifth, I spend it in giving feasts. This is my knowledge, and none other is acquainted with it. My good looks are apparent."

The father hearing these speeches began to reflect, " It is said that excess in anything is not good. Sita[1]

---

1 The daughter of Raja Janaka, married to Ramachandra. The latter placed his wife under the charge of his brother Lakshmana, and went into the forest to worship, when the demon Ravana disguised himself as a beggar, and carried off the prize.

was very lovely, but the demon Ravana carried her away; and Bali king of Mahabahpur gave much alms, but at length he became poor.[1] My daughter is too fair to remain a maiden; to which of these shall I give her?"

So saying, Hiranyadatt went to his daughter, explained the qualities of the four suitors, and asked, "To which shall I give thee?" On hearing these words she was abashed; and, hanging down her head, knew not what to reply.

Then the Baniya, having reflected, said to himself, "He who is acquainted with the Shastras is a Brahman, he who could shoot an arrow at the sound was a Kshatriya or warrior, and he who made the cloth was a Shudra or servile. But the youth who understands the language of birds is of our own caste. To him, therefore, will I marry her." And accordingly he proceeded with the betrothal of his daughter.

Meanwhile Madansena went one day, during the spring season into the garden for a stroll. It happened, just before she came out, that Somdatt, the son of the merchant Dharmdatt, had gone for pleasure into the forest, and was returning through the same garden to his home.

He was fascinated at the sight of the maiden, and said to his friend, "Brother, if I can obtain her my life will be prosperous, and if I do not obtain her my living in the world will be in vain."

Having thus spoken, and becoming restless from the fear of separation, he involuntarily drew near to her, and seizing her hand, said—

"If thou wilt not form an affection for me, I will throw away my life on thy account."

"Be pleased not to do this," she replied; "it will be

---

[1] This great king was tricked by the god Vishnu out of the sway of heaven and earth, but from his exceeding piety he was appointed to reign in Patala, or Hades.

sinful, and it will involve me in the guilt and punishment of shedding blood; hence I shall be miserable in this world and in that to be."

" Thy blandishments," he replied, "have pierced my heart, and the consuming thought of parting from thee has burnt up my body, and memory and understanding have been destroyed by this pain; and from excess of love I have no sense of right or wrong. But if thou wilt make me a promise, I will live again."

She replied, " Truly the Kali Yug (iron age) has commenced, since which time falsehood has increased in the world and truth has diminished; people talk smoothly with their tongues, but nourish deceit in their hearts; religion is destroyed, crime has increased, and the earth has begun to give little fruit. Kings levy fines, Brahmans have waxed covetous, the son obeys not his sire's commands, brother distrusts brother; friendship has departed from amongst friends; sincerity has left masters; servants have given up service; man has abandoned manliness; and woman has abandoned modesty. Five days hence, my marriage is to be; but if thou slay not thyself, I will visit thee first, and after that I will remain with my husband."

Having given this promise, and having sworn by the Ganges, she returned home. The merchant's son also went his way.

Presently the marriage ceremonies came on, and Hiranyadatt the Baniya expended a lakh of rupees in feasts and presents to the bridegroom. The bodies of the twain were anointed with turmeric, the bride was made to hold in her hand the iron box for eye paint, and the youth a pair of betel scissors. During the night before the wedding there was loud and shrill music, the heads and limbs of the young couple were rubbed with an ointment of oil, and the bridegroom's head was duly shaved. The wedding procession was very grand. The streets were a

blaze of flambeaux and torches carried in the hand, fireworks by the ton were discharged as the people passed ;
elephants, oamels, and horses richly caparisoned, were
placed in convenient situations; and before the procession
had reached the house of the bride half a dozen wicked
boys and bad young men were killed or wounded.[1] After
the marriage formulas were repeated, the Baniya gave a
feast or supper, and the food was so excellent that all sat
down quietly, no one uttered a complaint, or brought dishonour on the bride's family, or cut with scissors the
garments of his neighbour.

The ceremony thus happily concluded, the husband
brought Madansena home to his own house.   After some
days the wife of her husband's youngest brother, and also
the wife of his eldest brother, led her at night by force to
her bridegroom, and seated her on a bed ornamented with
flowers.

As her husband proceeded to take her hand, she
jerked it away, and at once openly told him all that she
had promised to Somdatt on condition of his not killing
himself.

"All things," rejoined the bridegroom, hearing her
words, "have their sense ascertained by speech; in speech
they have their basis, and from speech they proceed ; consequently a falsifier of speech falsifies everything.   If
truly you are desirous of going to him, go!"

Receiving her husband's permission, she arose and
went off to the young merchant's house in full dress.
Upon the road a thief saw her, and in high good humour
came up and asked—

"Whither goest thou at midnight in such darkness,
having put on all these fine clothes and ornaments?"

---

1 The procession is fair game, and is often attacked in the dark
with sticks and stones, causing serious disputes.   At the supper the
guests confer the obligation by their presence, and are exceedingly
exacting.

She replied that she was going to the house of her beloved.

"And who here," said the thief, "is thy protector?"

"Kama Deva," she replied, "the beautiful youth who by his fiery arrows wounds with love the hearts of the inhabitants of the three worlds, Ratipati, the husband of Rati,[1] accompanied by the kokila bird,[2] the humming bee and gentle breezes." She then told to the thief the whole story, adding—

"Destroy not my jewels: I give thee a promise before I go, that on my return thou shalt have all these ornaments."

Hearing this the thief thought to himself that it would be useless now to destroy her jewels, when she had promised to give them to him presently of her own good will. He therefore let her go, and sat down and thus soliloquised:

"To me it is astonishing that he who sustained me in my mother's womb should take no care of me now that I have been born and am able to enjoy the good things of this world. I know not whether he is asleep or dead. And I would rather swallow poison than ask man for money or favour. For these six things tend to lower a man:—friendship with the perfidious; causeless laughter; altercation with women; serving an unworthy master; riding an ass, and speaking any language but Sanskrit. And these five things the deity writes on our fate at the hour of birth:—first, age; secondly, action; thirdly, wealth; fourthly, science; fifthly, fame. I have now done a good deed, and as long as a man's virtue is in the ascendant, all people becoming his servants obey

---

1 Rati is the wife of Kama, the God of Desire; and we explain the word by " Spring personified."

2 The Indian Cuckoo (*Cuculus Indicus*). It is supposed to lay its eggs in the nest of the crow.

him. But when virtuous deeds diminish, even his friends become inimical to him."

Meanwhile Madansena had reached the place where Somdatt the young trader had fallen asleep.

She awoke him suddenly, and he springing up in alarm quickly asked her, "Art thou the daughter of a deity? or of a saint? or of a serpent? Tell me truly, who art thou? And whence hast thou come?"

She replied, "I am human—Madansena, the daughter of the Baniya Hiranyadatt. Dost thou not remember taking my hand in that grove, and declaring that thou wouldst slay thyself if I did not swear to visit thee first and after that remain with my husband?"

"Hast thou," he inquired, "told all this to thy husband or not?"

She replied, "I have told him everything; and he, thoroughly understanding the whole affair, gave me permission."

"This matter," exclaimed Somdatt in a melancholy voice, "is like pearls without a suitable dress, or food without clarified butter,[1] or singing without melody; they are all alike unnatural. In the same way, unclean clothes will mar beauty, bad food will undermine strength, a wicked wife will worry her husband to death, a disreputable son will ruin his family, an enraged demon will kill, and a woman, whether she love or hate, will be a source of pain. For there are few things which a woman will not do. She never brings to her tongue what is in her heart, she never speaks out what is on her tongue, and she never tells what she is doing. Truly the Deity has created woman a strange creature in this world." He concluded with these words: "Return thou home; with another man's wife I have no concern."

Madansena rose and departed. On her way she met

---

1 This is the well-known Ghí or Ghee, the one sauce of India, which is as badly off in that matter as England.

the thief, who, hearing her tale, gave her great praise, and let her go unplundered.[1]

She then went to her husband, and related the whole matter to him. But he had ceased to love her, and he said, "Neither a king nor a minister, nor a wife, nor a person's hair nor his nails, look well out of their places. And the beauty of the kokila is its note, of an ugly man knowledge, of a devotee forgiveness, and of a woman her chastity."

The Vampire having narrated thus far, suddenly asked the king, "Of these three, whose virtue was the greatest?"

Vikram, who had been greatly edified by the tale, forgot himself, and ejaculated, "The Thief's."

"And pray why?" asked the Baital.

"Because," the hero explained, "when her husband saw that she loved another man, however purely, he ceased to feel affection for her. Somdatt let her go unharmed, for fear of being punished by the king. But there was no reason why the thief should fear the law and dismiss her; therefore he was the best."

"Hi! hi! hi!" laughed the demon, spitefully. "Here, then, ends my story."

Upon which, escaping as before from the cloth in which he was slung behind the Raja's back, the Baital disappeared through the darkness of the night, leaving father and son looking at each other in dismay.

"Son Dharma Dhwaj," quoth the great Vikram, "the next time when that villain Vampire asks me a question, I allow thee to take the liberty of pinching my arm even before I have had time to answer his questions. In this way we shall never, of a truth, end our task."

"Your words be upon my head, sire," replied the

---

2 The European reader will observe that it is her purity which carries the heroine through all these perils. Moreover, that her virtue is its own reward, as it loses to her the world.

young prince. But he expected no good from his father's new plan, as, arrived under the siras-tree, he heard the Baital laughing with all his might.

"Surely he is laughing at our beards, sire," said the beardless prince, who hated to be laughed at like a young person.

"Let them laugh that win," fiercely cried Raja Vikram, who hated to be laughed at like an elderly person.

*   *   *   *   *   *   *

The Vampire lost no time in opening a fresh story.

THE VAMPIRE'S FIFTH STORY.

OF THE THIEF WHO LAUGHED AND WEPT.

YOUR majesty (quoth the demon, with unusual polite-ness), there is a country called Malaya, on the western coast of the land of Bharat—you see that I am particular in specifying the place—and in it was a city known as Chandrodaya, whose king was named Randhir.

This Raja, like most others of his semi-deified order, had been in youth what is called a Sarva-rasi[1]; that is, he ate and drank and listened to music, and looked at dancers and made love much more than he studied, re-flected, prayed, or conversed with the wise. After the age of thirty he began to reform, and he brought such zeal to the good cause, that in an incredibly short space of time he came to be accounted and quoted as the para-gon of correct Rajas. This was very praiseworthy. Many of Brahma's vicegerents on earth, be it observed, have loved food and drink, and music and dancing, and the worship of Kama, to the end of their days.

Amongst his officers was Gunshankar, a magistrate of police, who, curious to say, was as honest as he was just. He administered equity with as much care before as after dinner; he took no bribes even in the matter of advancing his family; he was rather merciful than other-wise to the poor, and he never punished the rich osten-

---

1 Literally, " one of all tastes "—a wild or gay man, we should say.

tatiously, in order to display his and his law's disrespect for persons. Besides which, when sitting on the carpet of justice, he did not, as some Kotwals do, use rough or angry language to those who cannot reply; nor did he take offence when none was intended.

All the people of the city Chandrodaya, in the province of Malaya, on the western coast of Bharatland, loved and esteemed this excellent magistrate; which did not, however, prevent thefts being committed so frequently and so regularly, that no one felt his property secure. At last the merchants who had suffered most from these depredations went in a body before Gunshankar, and said to him:

"O flower of the law! robbers have exercised great tyranny upon us, so great indeed that we can no longer stay in this city."

Then the magistrate replied, "What has happened, has happened. But in future you shall be free from annoyance. I will make due preparation for these thieves."

Thus saying Gunshankar called together his various delegates, and directed them to increase the number of their people. He pointed out to them how they should keep watch by night; besides which he ordered them to open registers of all arrivals and departures, to make themselves acquainted by means of spies with the movements of every suspected person in the city, and to raise a body of paggis (trackers), who could follow the footprints of thieves even when they wore thieving shoes,[1] till they came up with and arrested them. And lastly, he gave the patrols full power, whenever they might catch a robber in the act, to slay him without asking questions.

People in numbers began to mount guard throughout the city every night, but, notwithstanding this, rob-

---

[1] These shoes are generally made of rags and bits of leather; they have often toes behind the foot, with other similar contrivances, yet they scarcely ever deceive an experienced man.

beries continued to be committed. After a time all the merchants having again met together went before the magistrate, and said, "O incarnation of justice! you have changed your officers, you have hired watchmen, and you have established patrols: nevertheless the thieves have not diminished, and plundering is ever taking place."

Thereupon Gunshankar carried them to the palace, and made them lay their petition at the feet of the king Randhir. That Raja, having consoled them, sent them home, saying, "Be ye of good cheer. I will to-night adopt a new plan, which, with the blessing of the Bhagwan, shall free ye from further anxiety."

Observe, O Vikram, that Randhir was one of those concerning whom the poet sang—

The unwise run from one end to the other.

Not content with becoming highly respectable, correct, and even unimpeachable in point of character, he reformed even his reformation, and he did much more than he was required to do.

When Canopus began to sparkle gaily in the southern skies, the king arose and prepared for a night's work. He disguised his face by smearing it with a certain paint, by twirling his moustachios up to his eyes, by parting his beard upon his chin, and conducting the two ends towards his ears, and by tightly tying a hair from a horse's tail over his nose, so as quite to change its shape. He then wrapped himself in a coarse outer garment, girt his loins, buckled on his sword, drew his shield upon his arm, and without saying a word to those within the palace, he went out into the streets alone, and on foot.

It was dark, and Raja Randhir walked through the silent city for nearly an hour without meeting anyone. As, however, he passed through a back street in the merchants' quarter, he saw what appeared to be a homeless dog, lying at the foot of a house-wall. He approached

9

it, and up leaped a human figure, whilst a loud voice
cried, "Who art thou?"

Randhir replied, "I am a thief; who art thou?"

"And I also am a thief," rejoined the other, much
pleased at hearing this; "come, then, and let us make
together.   But what art thou, a high-toper or a lully-
prigger[1]?"

"A little more ceremony between coves in the lorst,[2]"
whispered the king, speaking as a flash man, "were not
out of place.   But, look sharp, mind old Oliver,[3] or the
lamb-skin man[4] will have the pull of us, and as sure as
eggs is eggs we shall be scragged as soon as lagged.[5]"

"Well, keep your red rag[6] quiet," grumbled the other,
"and let us be working."

Then the pair, king and thief, began work in right
earnest.   The gang seemed to swarm in the street.   They
were drinking spirits, slaying victims, rubbing their bodies
with oil, daubing their eyes with lamp-black, and repeating incantations to enable them to see in the darkness;
others were practising the lessons of the god with the
golden spear,[7] and carrying out the four modes of breach-
ing a house: 1. Picking out burnt bricks.   2. Cutting
through unbaked ones when old, when softened by recent
damp, by exposure to the sun, or by saline exudations.

---

1 The high-toper is a swell-thief, the other is a low dog.

2 Engaged in shoplifting.

3 The moon.

4 The judge.

5 To be lagged is to be taken; scragging is hanging.

6 The tongue.

7 This is the god Kartikeya, a mixture of Mars and Mercury, who
revealed to a certain Yugacharya the scriptures known as "Chauri-
ya-Vidya"— Anglicè, "Thieves' Manual."   The classical robbers of
the Hindu drama always perform according to its precepts.   There
is another work respected by thieves, and called the "Chora-Pancha-
shika," because consisting of fifty lines.

3. Throwing water on a mud wall; and 4. Boring through one of wood. The sons of Skanda were making breaches in the shape of lotus blossoms, the sun, the new moon, the lake, and the water jar, and they seemed to be anointed with magic unguents, so that no eye could behold, no weapon harm them.

At length having filled his bag with costly plunder, the thief said to the king, "Now, my rummy cove, we'll be off to the flash ken, where the lads and the morts are waiting to wet their whistles."

Randhir, who as a king was perfectly familiar with "thieves' Latin," took heart, and resolved to hunt out the secrets of the den. On the way, his companion, perfectly satisfied with the importance which the new cove had attached to a rat-hole,[1] and convinced that he was a true robber, taught him the whistle, the word, and the sign peculiar to the gang, and promised him that he should smack the lit[2] that night before "turning in."

So saying the thief rapped twice at the city gate, which was at once opened to him, and preceding his accomplice led the way to a rock about two kos (four miles) distant from the walls. Before entering the dark forest at the foot of the eminence, the robber stood still for a moment and whistled twice through his fingers with a shrill scream that rang through the silent glades. After a few minutes the signal was answered by the hooting of an owl, which the robber acknowledged by shrieking like a jackal. Thereupon half a dozen armed men arose from their crouching places in the grass, and one advanced towards the new comers to receive the sign. It was given, and they both passed on, whilst the guard sank, as it were, into the bowels of the earth. All these things Randhir carefully remarked: besides which he neglected not to take note of all the distinguishable objects that lay on

---

1 Supposed to be a good omen.
2 Share the booty.

the road, and, when he entered the wood, he scratched
with his dagger all the tree trunks within reach.

After a sharp walk the pair reached a high perpen-
dicular sheet of rock, rising abruptly from a clear space
in the jungle, and profusely printed over with vermilion
hands.   The thief, having walked up to it, and made his
obeisance, stooped to the ground, and removed a bunch

After a few minutes the signal was answered.

of grass.   The two then raised by their united efforts a
heavy trap door, through which poured a stream of light,
whilst a confused hubbub of voices was heard below.

"This is the ken," said the robber, preparing to
descend a thin ladder of bamboo, "follow me!"   And he
disappeared with his bag of valuables.

The king did as he was bid, and the pair entered to-

gether a large hall, or rather a cave, which presented a singular spectacle. It was lighted up by links fixed to the sombre walls, which threw a smoky glare over the place, and the contrast after the deep darkness reminded Randhir of his mother's descriptions of Patal-puri, the infernal city. Carpets of every kind, from the choicest tapestry to the coarsest rug, were spread upon the ground, and were strewed with bags, wallets, weapons, heaps of booty, drinking cups, and all the materials of debauchery.

Passing through this cave the thief led Randhir into another, which was full of thieves, preparing for the pleasures of the night. Some were changing garments, ragged and dirtied by creeping through gaps in the houses : others were washing the blood from their hands and feet ; these combed out their long dishevelled, dusty hair : those anointed their skins with perfumed cocoa-nut oil. There were all manner of murderers present, a villanous collection of Kartikeya's and Bhawani's[1] crew. There were stabbers with their poniards hung to lanyards lashed round their naked waists, Dhaturiya-poisoners[2] distinguished by the little bag slung under the left arm, and Phansigars[3] wearing their fatal kerchiefs round their necks. And Randhir had reason to thank the good deed in the last life that had sent him there in such strict disguise, for amongst the robbers he found, as might be expected, a number of his own people, spies and watchmen, guards and patrols.

The thief, whose importance of manner now showed him to be the chief of the gang, was greeted with applause as he entered the robing room, and he bade all make salám to the new companion. A number of questions

---

1 Bhawani is one of the many forms of the destroying goddess, the wife of Shiva.

2 Wretches who kill with the narcotic seed of the stramonium.

3 Better known as "Thugs," which in India means simply "rascals."

concerning the success of the night's work was quickly put and answered : then the company, having got ready for the revel, flocked into the first cave. There they sat down each in his own place, and began to eat and drink and make merry.

After some hours the flaring torches began to burn out, and drowsiness to overpower the strongest heads. Most of the robbers rolled themselves up in the rugs, and covering their heads, went to sleep. A few still sat with their backs to the wall, nodding drowsily or leaning on one side, and too stupefied with opium and hemp to make any exertion.

At that moment a servant woman, whom the king saw for the first time, came into the cave, and looking at him exclaimed, "O Raja! how came you with these wicked men ? Do you run away as fast as you can, or they will surely kill you when they awake."

" I do not know the way ; in which direction am I to go ?" asked Randhir.

The woman then showed him the road. He threaded the confused mass of snorers, treading with the foot of a tiger-cat, found the ladder, raised the trap-door by exerting all his strength, and breathed once more the open air of heaven. And before plunging into the depths of the wood he again marked the place where the entrance lay, and carefully replaced the bunch of grass.

Hardly had Raja Randhir returned to the palace, and removed the traces of his night's occupation, when he received a second deputation of the merchants, complaining bitterly and with the longest faces about their fresh misfortunes.

"O pearl of equity!" said the men of money, "but yesterday you consoled us with the promise of some contrivance by the blessing of which our houses and coffers would be safe from theft ; whereas our goods have never yet suffered so severely as during the last twelve hours."

Again Randhir dismissed them, swearing that this time he would either die or destroy the wretches who had been guilty of such violence.

Then having mentally prepared his measures, the Raja warned a company of archers to hold themselves in readiness for secret service, and as each one of his own people returned from the robbers' cave he had him privily arrested and put to death—because the deceased, it is said, do not, like Baitals, tell tales. About nightfall, when he thought that the thieves, having finished their work of

Treading with the foot of a tiger cat.

plunder, would meet together as usual for wassail and debauchery, he armed himself, marched out his men, and led them to the rock in the jungle.

But the robbers, aroused by the disappearance of the new companion, had made enquiries and had gained intelligence of the impending danger. They feared to flee during the daytime, lest being tracked they should be discovered and destroyed in detail. When night came they hesitated to disperse, from the certainty that they would be captured in the morning. Then their captain, who throughout had been of one opinion, proposed to

them that they should resist, and promised them success
if they would hear his words. The gang respected him,
for he was known to be brave: they all listened to his
advice, and they promised to be obedient.

As young night began to cast transparent shade upon
the jungle ground, the chief of the thieves mustered his
men, inspected their bows and arrows, gave them en-
couraging words, and led them forth from the cave.
Having placed them in ambush he climbed the rock to
espy the movements of the enemy, whilst others applied
their noses and ears to the level ground. Presently the
moon shone full upon Randhir and his band of archers,
who were advancing quickly and carelessly, for they expected to catch the robbers in their cave. The captain
allowed them to march nearly through the line of ambush.
Then he gave the signal, and at that moment the thieves,
rising suddenly from the bush fell upon the royal troops
and drove them back in confusion.

The king also fled, when the chief of the robbers
shouted out, " Hola ! thou a Rajput and running away
from combat ? " Randhir hearing this halted, and the
two, confronting each other, bared their blades and began
to do battle with prodigious fury.

The king was cunning of fence, and so was the thief.
They opened the duel, as skilful swordsmen should, by
bending almost double, skipping in a circle, each keeping
his eye well fixed upon the other, with frowning brows
and contemptuous lips ; at the same time executing divers
gambados and measured leaps, springing forward like
frogs and backward like monkeys, and beating time with
their sabres upon their shields, which rattled like drums.

Then Randhir suddenly facing his antagonist, cut at
his legs with a loud cry, but the thief sprang in the air,
and the blade whistled harmlessly under him. Next
moment the robber chief's sword, thrice whirled round
his head, descended like lightning in a slanting direction

towards the king's left shoulder : the latter, however, received it upon his target and escaped all hurt, though he staggered with the violence of the blow.

And thus they continued attacking each other, parrying and replying, till their breath failed them and their hands and wrists were numbed and cramped with fatigue. They were so well matched in courage, strength, and address, that neither obtained the least advantage, till the robber's right foot catching a stone slid from under him, and thus he fell to the ground at the mercy of his enemy. The thieves fled, and the Raja, throwing himself on his prize, tied his hands behind him, and brought him back to the city at the point of his good sword.

The next morning Randhir visited his prisoner, whom he caused to be bathed, and washed, and covered with fine clothes. He then had him mounted on a camel and sent him on a circuit of the city, accompanied by a crier proclaiming aloud :

"Who hears ! who hears ! who hears ! the king commands ! This is the thief who has robbed and plundered the city of Chandrodaya. Let all men therefore assemble themselves together this evening in the open space outside the gate leading towards the sea. And let them behold the penalty of evil deeds, and learn to be wise."

Randhir had condemned the thief to be crucified,[1] nailed and tied with his hands and feet stretched out at

---

1 Crucifixion, until late years, was common amongst the Buddhists of the Burmese empire. According to an eye-witness, Mr. F. Carey, the punishment was inflicted in two ways. Sometimes criminals were crucified by their hands and feet being nailed to a scaffold ; others were merely tied up, and fed. In these cases the legs and feet of the patient begin to swell and mortify at the expiration of three or four days ; men are said to have lived in this state for a fortnight, and at last they expired from fatigue and mortification. The sufferings from cramp also must be very severe. In India generally impalement was more common than crucifixion.

full length, in an erect posture until death; everything he wished to eat was ordered to him in order to prolong life and misery. And when death should draw near, melted gold was to be poured down his throat till it should burst from his neck and other parts of his body.

In the evening the thief was led out for execution, and by chance the procession passed close to the house of a wealthy landowner. He had a favourite daughter named Shobhani, who was in the flower of her youth and very lovely; every day she improved, and every moment added to her grace and beauty. The girl had been carefully kept out of sight of mankind, never being allowed outside the high walls of the garden, because her nurse, a wise woman much trusted in the neighbourhood, had at the hour of death given a solemn warning to her parents. The prediction was that the maiden should be the admiration of the city, and should die a Sati-widow[1] before becoming a wife. From that hour Shobhani was kept as a pearl in its casket by her father, who had vowed never to survive her, and had even fixed upon the place and style of his suicide.

But the shaft of Fate[2] strikes down the vulture sailing above the clouds, and follows the worm into the bowels of the earth, and pierces the fish at the bottom of the ocean—how then can mortal man expect to escape it? As the robber chief, mounted upon the camel, was passing to the cross under the old householder's windows, a fire breaking out in the women's apartments, drove the inmates into the rooms looking upon the street.

The hum of many voices arose from the solid pavement of heads: " This is the thief who has been robbing the whole city; let him tremble now, for Randhir will surely crucify him ! "

---

1 Our Suttee. There is an admirable Hindu proverb, which says, " No one knows the ways of woman ; she kills her husband and becomes a Sati."

2 Fate and Destiny are rather Moslem than Hindu fancies.

In beauty and bravery of bearing, as in strength and courage, no man in Chandrodaya surpassed the robber, who, being magnificently dressed, looked, despite his disgraceful cavalcade, like the son of a king. He sat with an unmoved countenance, hardly hearing in his pride the scoffs of the mob ; calm and steady when the whole city was frenzied with anxiety because of him. But as he heard the word " tremble " his lips quivered, his eyes flashed fire, and deep lines gathered between his eyebrows.

Shobhani started with a scream from the casement behind which she had hid herself, gazing with an intense womanly curiosity into the thoroughfare. The robber's face was upon a level with, and not half a dozen feet from, her pale cheeks. She marked his handsome features, and his look of wrath made her quiver as if it had been a flash of lightning. Then she broke away from the fascination of his youth and beauty, and ran breathless to her father, saying :

" Go this moment and get that thief released ! "

The old housekeeper replied : " That thief has been pilfering and plundering the whole city, and by his means the king's archers were defeated; why, then, at my request, should our most gracious Raja Randhir release him ? "

Shobhani, almost beside herself, exclaimed : " If by giving up your whole property, you can induce the Raja to release him, then instantly so do ; if he does not come to me, I must give up my life ! "

The maiden then covered her head with her veil, and sat down in the deepest despair, whilst her father, hearing her words, burst into a cry of grief, and hastened to present himself before the Raja. He cried out :

" O great king, be pleased to receive four lakhs of rupees, and to release this thief."

But the king replied : " He has been robbing the

whole city, and by reason of him my guards have been destroyed. I cannot by any means release him."

Then the old householder finding, as he had expected, the Raja inexorable, and not to be moved, either by tears or bribes, or by the cruel fate of the girl, returned home with fire in his heart, and addressed her :

" Daughter, I have said and done all that is possible ; but it avails me nought with the king. Now, then, we die."

In the mean time, the guards having led the thief all round the city, took him outside the gates, and made him stand near the cross. Then the messengers of death arrived from the palace, and the executioners began to nail his limbs. He bore the agony with the fortitude of the brave ; but when he heard what had been done by the old householder's daughter, he raised his voice and wept bitterly, as though his heart had been bursting, and almost with the same breath he laughed heartily as at a feast. All were startled by his merriment ; coming as it did at a time when the iron was piercing his flesh, no man could see any reason for it.

When he died, Shobhani, who was married to him in the spirit, recited to herself these sayings :

" There are thirty-five millions of hairs on the human body. The woman who ascends the pile with her husband will remain so many years in heaven. As the snake-catcher draws the serpent from his hole, so she, rescuing her husband from hell, rejoices with him ; aye, though he may have sunk to a region of torment, be restrained in dreadful bonds, have reached the place of anguish, be exhausted of strength, and afflicted and tortured for his crimes. No other effectual duty is known for virtuous women at any time after the death of their lords, except casting themselves into the same fire. As long as a woman in her successive transmigrations, shall decline burning herself, like a faithful wife, in the same fire with her deceased lord, so long shall she not be exempted from springing again to life in the body of some female animal."

Therefore the beautiful Shobhani, virgin and wife, resolved to burn herself, and to make the next life of the thief certain. She showed her courage by thrusting her finger into a torch flame till it became a cinder, and she solemnly bathed in the nearest stream.

A hole was dug in the ground, and upon a bed of green tree-trunks were heaped hemp, pitch, faggots, and clarified butter, to form the funeral pyre. The dead body, anointed, bathed, and dressed in new clothes, was then laid upon the heap, which was some two feet high. Shobhani prayed that as long as fourteen Indras reign, or as many years as there are hairs in her head, she might abide in heaven with her husband, and be waited upon by the heavenly dancers. She then presented her ornaments and little gifts of corn to her friends, tied some cotton round both wrists, put two new combs in her hair, painted her forehead, and tied up in the end of her body-cloth clean parched rice[1] and cowrie-shells. These she gave to the bystanders, as she walked seven times round the funeral pyre, upon which lay the body. She then ascended the heap of wood, sat down upon it, and taking the thief's head in her lap, without cords or levers or upper layer or faggots, she ordered the pile to be lighted. The crowd standing around set fire to it in several places, drummed their drums, blew their conchs, and raised a loud cry of " Hari bol ! Hari bol ![2] " Straw was thrown on, and pitch and clarified butter were freely poured out.

---

1 Properly speaking, the husbandman should plough with not fewer than four bullocks ; but few can afford this. If he plough with a cow or a bullock, and not with a bull, the rice produced by his ground is unclean, and may not be used in any religious ceremony.

2 A shout of triumph, like our " Huzza " or " Hurrah !" of late degraded into " Hooray." " Hari bol " is of course religious, meaning " Call upon Hari ! " *i.e.* Krishna, *i.e.* Vishnu.

But Shobhani's was a Sahamaran, a blessed easy death : no part of her body was seen to move after the pyre was lighted—in fact, she seemed to die before the flame touched her.

By the blessing of his daughter's decease, the old householder beheaded himself.[1] He caused an instrument to be made in the shape of a half-moon with an edge like a razor, and fitting the back of his neck. At both ends of it, as at the beam of a balance, chains were fastened. He sat down with eyes closed; he was rubbed with the purifying clay of the holy river, Vaiturani[2]; and he repeated the proper incantations. Then placing his feet upon the extremities of the chains, he suddenly jerked up his neck, and his severed head rolled from his body upon the ground. What a happy death was this !

The Baital was silent, as if meditating on the fortunate transmigration which the old householder had thus secured.

"But what could the thief have been laughing at, sire ? " asked the young prince Dharma Dhwaj of his father.

"At the prodigious folly of the girl, my son," replied the warrior king, thoughtlessly.

"I am indebted once more to your majesty," burst out the Baital, "for releasing me from this unpleasant position, but the Raja's penetration is again at fault. Not to leave your royal son and heir labouring under a false impression, before going I will explain why the brave thief burst into tears, and why he laughed at such a moment.

"He wept when he reflected that he could not re-

---

1 This form of suicide is one of those recognized in India. So in Europe we read of fanatics who, with a suicidal ingenuity, have succeeded in crucifying themselves.

2 The river of Jaganath in Orissa ; it shares the honours of sanctity with some twenty-nine others, and in the lower regions it represents the classical Styx.

quite her kindness in being willing to give up everything she had in the world to save his life; and this thought deeply grieved him.

Then it struck him as being passing strange that she had begun to love him when the last sand of his life was well nigh run out; that wondrous are the ways of the revolving heavens which bestow wealth upon the niggard that cannot use it, wisdom upon the bad man who will misuse it, a beautiful wife upon the fool who cannot protect her, and fertilizing showers upon the stony hills. And thinking over these things, the gallant and beautiful thief laughed aloud.

Presently the Demon was trussed up as usual.

" Before returning to my siras-tree," continued the Vampire, " as I am about to do in virtue of your majesty's unintelligent reply, I may remark that men may laugh and cry, or may cry and laugh, about everything in this world, from their neighbours' deaths, which, as a general rule, in no wise concern them, to their own latter ends, which do concern them exceedingly. For my part, I am in the habit of laughing at everything, because it animates the brain, stimulates the lungs, beautifies the countenance, and—for the moment, good-bye, Raja Vikram!

The warrior king, being forewarned this time, shifted the bundle containing the Baital from his back to under his arm, where he pressed it with all his might.

This proceeding, however, did not prevent the Vampire from slipping back to his tree, and leaving an empty cloth with the Raja.

Presently the demon was trussed up as usual; a voice sounded behind Vikram, and the loquacious thing again began to talk.

THE VAMPIRE'S SIXTH STORY.

IN WHICH THREE MEN DISPUTE ABOUT A WOMAN.

ON the lovely banks of Jumna's stream there was a city known as Dharmasthal—the Place of Duty; and therein dwelt a certain Brahman called Keshav. He was a very pious man, in the constant habit of performing penance and worship upon the river Sidi. He modelled his own clay images instead of buying them from others; he painted holy stones red at the top, and made to them offerings of flowers, fruit, water, sweetmeats, and fried peas. He had become a learned man somewhat late in life, having, until twenty years old, neglected his reading, and addicted himself to worshipping the beautiful youth Kama-Deva[1] and Rati his wife, accompanied by the cuckoo, the humming-bee, and sweet breezes.

One day his parents having rebuked him sharply for his ungovernable conduct, Keshav wandered to a neighbouring hamlet, and hid himself in the tall fig-tree which shadowed a celebrated image of Panchánan.[2] Presently an evil thought arose in his head: he defiled the god, and threw him into the nearest tank.

---

1 Cupid. His wife Rati is the spring personified. The Hindu poets always unite love and spring, and perhaps physiologically they are correct.

2 An incarnation of the third person of the Hindu Triad, or Triumvirate, Shiva the God of Destruction, the Indian Bacchus. The image has five faces, and each face has three eyes. In Bengal it is found in many villages, and the women warn their children not to touch it on pain of being killed.

The next morning, when the person arrived whose livelihood depended on the image, he discovered that his god was gone. He returned into the village distracted, and all was soon in an uproar about the lost deity.

In the midst of this confusion the parents of Keshav arrived, seeking for their son; and a man in the crowd declared that he had seen a young man sitting in Panchánan's tree, but what had become of the god he knew not.

The runaway at length appeared, and the suspicions of the villagers fell upon him as the stealer of Panchánan. He confessed the fact, pointed out the place where he had thrown the stone, and added that he had polluted the god. All hands and eyes were raised in amazement at this atrocious crime, and every one present declared that Panchánan would certainly punish the daring insult by immediate death. Keshav was dreadfully frightened; he began to obey his parents from that very hour, and applied to his studies so sedulously that he soon became the most learned man of his country.

Now Keshav the Brahman had a daughter whose name was the Madhumalati or Sweet Jasmine. She was very beautiful. Whence did the gods procure the materials to form so exquisite a face? They took a portion of the most excellent part of the moon to form that beautiful face? Does any one seek a proof of this? Let him look at the empty places left in the moon. Her eyes resembled the full-blown blue nymphæa; her arms the charming stalk of the lotus; her flowing tresses the thick darkness of night.

When this lovely person arrived at a marriageable age, her mother, father, and brother, all three became very anxious about her. For the wise have said, "A daughter nubile but without a husband is ever a calamity hanging over a house." And, "Kings, women, and climbing plants love those who are near them." Also,

10—2

"Who is there that has not suffered from the sex? for a woman cannot be kept in due subjection, either by gifts or kindness, or correct conduct, or the greatest services, or the laws of morality, or by the terror of punishment, for she cannot discriminate between good and evil."

It so happened that one day Keshav the Brahman went to the marriage of a certain customer of his,[1] and his son repaired to the house of a spiritual preceptor in order to read. During their absence, a young man came to the house, when the Sweet Jasmine's mother, inferring his good qualities from his good looks, said to him, "I will give to thee my daughter in marriage." The father also had promised his daughter to a Brahman youth whom he had met at the house of his employer; and the brother likewise had betrothed his sister to a fellow student at the place where he had gone to read.

After some days father and son came home, accompanied by these two suitors, and in the house a third was already seated. The name of the first was Tribikram, of the second Baman, and of the third Madhusadan. The three were equal in mind and body, in knowledge, and in age.

Then the father, looking upon them, said to himself, "Ho! there is one bride and three bridegrooms; to whom shall I give, and to whom shall I not give? We three have pledged our word to these three. A strange circumstance has occurred; what must we do?"

He then proposed to them a trial of wisdom, and made them agree that he who should quote the most excellent saying of the wise should become his daughter's husband.

Quoth Tribikram: "Courage is tried in war; integrity in the payment of debt and interest; friendship

---

1 A village Brahman on stated occasions receives fees from all the villagers.

in distress; and the faithfulness of a wife in the day of poverty."

Baman proceeded: "That woman is destitute of virtue who in her father's house is not in subjection, who wanders to feasts and amusements, who throws off her veil in the presence of men, who remains as a guest in the houses of strangers, who is much devoted to sleep, who drinks inebriating beverages, and who delights in distance from her husband."

"Let none," pursued Madhusadan, "confide in the sea, nor in whatever has claws or horns, or who carries deadly weapons; neither in a woman, nor in a king."

Whilst the Brahman was doubting which to prefer, and rather inclining to the latter sentiment, a serpent bit the beautiful girl, and in a few hours she died.

Stunned by this awful sudden death, the father and the three suitors sat for a time motionless. They then arose, used great exertions, and brought all kinds of sorcerers, wise men and women who charm away poisons by incantations. These having seen the girl said, "She cannot return to life." The first declared, "A person always dies who has been bitten by a snake on the fifth, sixth, eighth, ninth, and fourteenth days of the lunar month." The second asserted, "One who has been bitten on a Saturday or a Tuesday does not survive." The third opined, "Poison infused during certain six lunar mansions cannot be got under." Quoth the fourth, "One who has been bitten in any organ of sense, the lower lip, the cheek, the neck, or the stomach, cannot escape death." The fifth said, "In this case even Brahma, the Creator, could not restore life—of what account, then, are we? Do you perform the funeral rites; we will depart."

Thus saying, the sorcerers went their way. The mourning father took up his daughter's corpse and caused it to be burnt, in the place where dead bodies are usually burnt, and returned to his house.

After that the three young men said to one another, "We must now seek happiness elsewhere. And what better can we do than obey the words of Indra, the God of Air, who spake thus?—

"'For a man who does not travel about there is no felicity, and a good man who stays at home is a bad man. Indra is the friend of him who travels. Travel!

"'A traveller's legs are like blossoming branches, and he himself grows and gathers the fruit. All his wrongs vanish, destroyed by his exertion on the roadside. Travel!

"'The fortune of a man who sits, sits also; it rises when he rises; it sleeps when he sleeps; it moves well when he moves. Travel!

"'A man who sleeps is like the Iron Age. A man who awakes is like the Bronze Age. A man who rises up is like the Silver Age. A man who travels is like the Golden Age. Travel!

"'A traveller finds honey; a traveller finds sweet figs. Look at the happiness of the sun, who travelling never tires. Travel!'"

Before parting they divided the relics of the beloved one, and then they went their way.

Tribikram, having separated and tied up the burnt bones, became one of the Vaisheshikas, in those days a powerful sect. He solemnly forswore the eight great crimes, namely: feeding at night; slaying any animal; eating the fruit of trees that give milk, or pumpkins or young bamboos: tasting honey or flesh; plundering the wealth of others; taking by force a married woman; eating flowers, butter, or cheese; and worshipping the gods of other religions. He learned that the highest act of virtue is to abstain from doing injury to sentient creatures; that crime does not justify the destruction of life; and that kings, as the administrators of criminal justice, are the greatest of sinners. He professed the five vows of total abstinence from falsehood, eating flesh or fish, theft, drinking spirits, and marriage. He bound himself to possess nothing beyond a white loin-cloth, a towel to wipe the mouth, a beggar's dish, and a brush of woollen threads to sweep the ground for fear of treading on insects. And he was ordered to fear secular affairs; the miseries of a future state; the receiving from others more than the food of a day at once; all accidents; provisions, if connected with the destruction of animal life; death and disgrace; also to please all, and to obtain compassion from all.

He attempted to banish his love. He said to himself, "Surely it was owing only to my pride and selfishness that I ever looked upon a woman as capable of affording happiness; and I thought, 'Ah! ah! thine eyes roll about like the tail of the water-wagtail, thy lips resemble the ripe fruit, thy bosom is like the lotus bud, thy form is resplendent as gold melted in a crucible, the moon wanes through desire to imitate the shadow of thy face, thou resemblest the pleasure-house of Cupid; the happiness of all time is concentrated in thee; a touch from thee would surely give life to a dead image; at thy approach a living admirer would be changed by joy into a lifeless stone; obtaining thee I can face all the horrors of war; and were I pierced by showers of arrows, one glance of thee would heal all my wounds.'

"My mind is now averted from the world. Seeing her I say, 'Is this the form by which men are bewitched? This is a basket covered with skin; it contains bones, flesh, blood, and impurities. The stupid creature who is captivated by this—is there a cannibal feeding in Currim a greater cannibal than he? These persons call a thing made up of impure matter a face, and drink its charms as a drunkard swallows the inebriating liquor from his cup.

The blind, infatuated beings! Why should I be pleased or displeased with this body, composed of flesh and blood? It is my duty to seek Him who is the Lord of this body, and to disregard everything which gives rise either to pleasure or to pain.'"

Baman, the second suitor, tied up a bundle of his beloved one's ashes, and followed—somewhat prematurely —the precepts of the great lawgiver Manu. "When the father of a family perceives his muscles becoming flaccid, and his hair grey, and sees the child of his child, let him then take refuge in a forest. Let him take up his conse-

Baman, the second suitor, tied up a bundle and followed

crated fire and all his domestic implements for making oblations to it, and, departing from the town to the lonely wood, let him dwell in it with complete power over his organs of sense and of action. With many sorts of pure food, such as holy sages used to eat, with green herbs, roots, and fruit, let him perform the five great sacraments, introducing them with due ceremonies. Let him wear a black antelope-hide, or a vesture of bark; let him bathe evening and morning; let him suffer the hair of his head, his beard and his nails to grow continually. Let him

slide backwards and forwards on the ground; or let him
stand a whole day on tiptoe; or let him continue in mo-
tion, rising and sitting alternately; but at sunrise, at
noon, and at sunset, let him go to the waters and bathe.
In the hot season let him sit exposed to five fires, four
blazing around him, with the sun above; in the rains,
let him stand uncovered, without even a mantle, where
the clouds pour the heaviest showers; in the cold season
let him wear damp clothes, and let him increase by degrees
the austerity of his devotions. Then, having reposited
his holy fires, as the law directs, in his mind, let him live
without external fire, without a mansion, wholly silent,
feeding on roots and fruit."

Meanwhile Madhusadan the third, having taken a
wallet and neckband, became a Jogi, and began to wander
far and wide, living on nothing but chaff, and practising
his devotions. In order to see Brahma he attended to
the following duties; 1. Hearing; 2. Meditation; 3. Fixing the Mind; 4. Absorbing the Mind. He combated
the three evils, restlessness, injuriousness, voluptuousness,
by settling the Deity in his spirit, by subjecting his
senses, and by destroying desire. Thus he would do
away with the illusion (Maya) which conceals all true
knowledge. He repeated the name of the Deity till it
appeared to him in the form of a Dry Light or glory.
Though connected with the affairs of life, that is, with
affairs belonging to a body containing blood, bones, and
impurities; to organs which are blind, palsied, and full
of weakness and error; to a mind filled with thirst, hunger,
sorrow, infatuation; to confirmed habits, and to the fruits
of former births: still he strove not to view these things
as realities. He made a companion of a dog, honouring
it with his own food, so as the better to think on spirit.
He practised all the five operations connected with the
vital air, or air collected in the body. He attended much
to Pranayama, or the gradual suppression of breathing,

and he secured fixedness of mind as follows. By placing his sight and thoughts on the tip of his nose he perceived smell; on the tip of his tongue he realized taste, on the root of his tongue he knew sound, and so forth. He practised the eighty-four Asana or postures, raising his hand to the wonders of the heavens, till he felt no longer the inconveniences of heat or cold, hunger or thirst. He particularly preferred the Padma or lotus-posture, which consists of bringing the feet to the sides, holding the right in the left hand and the left in the right. In the

Meanwhile Madhusadan, the third, became a Jogi.

work of suppressing his breath he permitted its respiration to reach at furthest twelve fingers' breadth, and gradually diminished the distance from his nostrils till he could confine it to the length of twelve fingers from his nose, and even after restraining it for some time he would draw it from no greater distance than from his heart. As respects time, he began by retaining inspiration for twenty-six seconds, and he enlarged this period gradually till he became perfect. He sat cross-legged, closing with his fingers all the avenues of inspiration, and he practised

Prityahara, or the power of restraining the members of
the body and mind, with meditation and concentration, to
which there are four enemies, viz., a sleepy heart, human
passions, a confused mind, and attachment to anything
but the one Brahma. He also cultivated Yama, that is,
inoffensiveness, truth, honesty, the forsaking of all evil in
the world, and the refusal of gifts except for sacrifice,
and Nihama, *i.e.*, purity relative to the use of water after
defilement, pleasure in everything whether in prosperity
or adversity, renouncing food when hungry, and keeping
down the body. Thus delivered from these four enemies
of the flesh, he resembled the unruffled flame of the lamp,
and by Brahmagnana, or meditating on the Deity, placing his mind on the sun, moon, fire, or any other luminous body, or within his heart, or at the bottom of his
throat, or in the centre of his skull, he was enabled to
ascend from gross images of omnipotence to the works
and the divine wisdom of the glorious original.

One day Madhusadan, the Jogi, went to a certain
house for food, and the householder having seen him
began to say, "Be so good as to take your food here this
day!"   The visitor sat down, and when the victuals
were ready, the host caused his feet and hands to be
washed, and leading him to the Chauka, or square place
upon which meals are served, seated him and sat by him.
And he quoted the scripture: "No guest must be dismissed in the evening by a housekeeper: he is sent by
the returning sun, and whether he come in fit season or
unseasonably, he must not sojourn in the house without
entertainment: let me not eat any delicate food, without
asking my guest to partake of it: the satisfaction of a
guest will assuredly bring the housekeeper wealth, reputation, long life, and a place in heaven."

The householder's wife then came to serve up the
food, rice and split peas, oil, and spices, all cooked in a
new earthen pot with pure firewood. Part of the

meal was served and the rest remained to be served, when the woman's little child began to cry aloud and to catch hold of its mother's dress. She endeavoured to release herself, but the boy would not let go, and the more she coaxed the more he cried, and was obstinate. On this the mother became angry, took up the boy and threw him upon the fire, which instantly burnt him to ashes.

Madhusadan, the Jogi, seeing this, rose up without eating. The master of the house said to him, "Why eatest thou not?" He replied, "I am 'Atithi,' that is to say, to be entertained at your house, but how can one eat under the roof of a person who has committed such a Rakshasa-like (devilish) deed? Is it not said, 'He who does not govern his passions, lives in vain'? 'A foolish king, a person puffed up with riches, and a weak child, desire that which cannot be procured'? Also, 'A king destroys his enemies, even when flying; and the touch of an elephant, as well as the breath of a serpent, are fatal; but the wicked destroy even while laughing'?"

Hearing this, the householder smiled; presently he arose and went to another part of the tenement, and brought back with him a book, treating on Sanjivnividya, or the science of restoring the dead to life. This he had taken from its hidden place, two beams almost touching one another with the ends in the opposite wall. The precious volume was in single leaves, some six inches broad by treble that length, and the paper was stained with yellow orpiment and the juice of tamarind seeds to keep away insects.

The householder opened the cloth containing the book, untied the flat boards at the top and bottom, and took out from it a charm. Having repeated this Mantra, with many ceremonies, he at once restored the child to life, saying, "Of all precious things, knowledge is the most valuable; other riches may be stolen, or diminished by expenditure, but knowledge is immortal, and the greater the expenditure the greater the increase; it can be shared with none, and it defies the power of the thief."

The Jogi, seeing this marvel, took thought in his heart, "If I could obtain that book, I would restore my beloved to life, and give up this course of uncomfortable postures and difficulty of breathing." With this resolution he sat down to his food, and remained in the house.

At length night came, and after a time, all, having eaten supper, and gone to their sleeping-places, lay down. The Jogi also went to rest in one part of the house, but did not allow sleep to close his eyes. When he thought that a fourth part of the hours of darkness had sped, and that all were deep in slumber, then he got up very quietly, and going into the room of the master of the house, he took down the book from the beam-ends and went his ways.

Madhusadan, the Jogi, went straight to the place where the beautiful Sweet Jasmine had been burned. There he found his two rivals sitting talking together and comparing experiences. They recognized him at once, and cried aloud to him, "Brother! thou also hast been wandering over the world; tell us this—hast thou learned anything which can profit us?" He replied, "I have learned the science of restoring the dead to life"; upon which they both exclaimed, "If thou hast really learned such knowledge, restore our beloved to life."

Madhusadan proceeded to make his incantations, despite terrible sights in the air, the cries of jackals, owls, crows, cats, asses, vultures, dogs, and lizards, and the wrath of innumerable invisible beings, such as messengers of Yama (Pluto), ghosts, devils, demons, imps, fiends, devas, succubi, and others. All the three lovers drawing blood from their own bodies, offered it to the goddess Chandi, repeating the following incantation, "Hail! supreme delusion! Hail! goddess of the universe! Hail!

thou who fulfillest the desires of all. May I presume to offer thee the blood of my body; and wilt thou deign to accept it, and be propitious towards me!"

They then made a burnt-offering of their flesh, and each one prayed, "Grant me, O goddess! to see the maiden alive again, in proportion to the fervency with which I present thee with mine own flesh, invoking thee to be propitious to me. Salutation to thee again and again, under the mysterious syllables ang! ang!"

Then they made a heap of the bones and the ashes, which had been carefully kept by Tribikram and Baman. As the Jogi Madhusadan proceeded with his incantation, a white vapour arose from the ground, and, gradually condensing, assumed a perispiritual form—the fluid envelope of the soul. The three spectators felt their blood freeze as the bones and the ashes were gradually absorbed into the before shadowy shape, and they were restored to themselves only when the maiden Madhuvati begged to be taken home to her mother.

Then Kama, God of Love, blinded them, and they began fiercely to quarrel about who should have the beautiful maid. Each wanted to be her sole master. Tribikram declared the bones to be the great fact of the incantation; Baman swore by the ashes; and Madhusadan laughed them both to scorn. No one could decide the dispute; the wisest doctors were all nonplussed; and as for the Raja—well! we do not go for wit or wisdom to kings. I wonder if the great Raja Vikram could decide which person the woman belonged to?

"To Baman, the man who kept her ashes, fellow!" exclaimed the hero, not a little offended by the free remarks of the fiend.

"Yet," rejoined the Baital impudently, "if Tribikram had not preserved her bones how could she have been restored to life? And if Madhusadan had not learned the science of restoring the dead to life how could she have been revivified? At least, so it seems to me. But perhaps your royal wisdom may explain."

"Devil!" said the king angrily, "Tribikram, who preserved her bones, by that act placed himself in the position of her son; therefore he could not marry her. Madhusadan, who, restoring her to life, gave her life, was evidently a father to her; he could not, then, become her husband. Therefore she was the wife of Baman, who had collected her ashes."

"I am happy to see, O king," exclaimed the Vampire, "that in spite of my presentiments, we are not to part company just yet. These little trips I hold to be, like lovers' quarrels, the prelude to closer union. With your leave we will still practise a little suspension."

And so saying, the Baital again ascended the tree, and was suspended there.

"Would it not be better," thought the monarch, after recapturing and shouldering the fugitive, "for me to sit down this time and listen to the fellow's story? Perhaps the double exercise of walking and thinking confuses me."

With this idea Vikram placed his bundle upon the ground, well tied up with turband and waistband; then he seated himself cross-legged before it, and bade his son do the same.

The Vampire strongly objected to this measure, as it was contrary, he asserted, to the covenant between him and the Raja. Vikram replied by citing the very words of the agreement, proving that there was no allusion to walking or sitting.

Then the Baital became sulky, and swore that he would not utter another word. But he, too, was bound by the chain of destiny. Presently he opened his lips, with the normal prelude that he was about to tell a true tale.

THE VAMPIRE'S SEVENTH STORY.

SHOWING THE EXCEEDING FOLLY OF MANY WISE FOOLS.

THE Baital resumed.

Of all the learned Brahmans in the learnedest university of Gaur (Bengal) none was so celebrated as Vishnu Swami. He could write verse as well as prose in dead languages, not very correctly, but still, better than all his fellows—which constituted him a distinguished writer. He had history, theosophy, and the four Vedas of Scriptures at his fingers' ends, he was skilled in the argute science of Nyasa or Disputation, his mind was a mine of Pauranic or cosmogonico-traditional lore, handed down from the ancient fathers to the modern fathers: and he had written bulky commentaries, exhausting all that tongue of man has to say, upon the obscure text of some old philosopher whose works upon ethics, poetry, and rhetoric were supposed by the sages of Gaur to contain the germs of everything knowable. His fame went over all the country; yea, from country to country. He was a sea of excellent qualities, the father and mother of Brahmans, cows, and women, and the horror of loose persons, cut-throats, courtiers, and courtesans. As a benefactor he was equal to Karna, most liberal of heroes. In regard to truth he was equal to the veracious king Yudhishtira.

True, he was sometimes at a loss to spell a common word in his mother tongue, and whilst he knew to a finger-breadth how many palms and paces the sun, the moon, and all the stars are distant from the earth, he would have been puzzled to tell you where the region called Yavana[1] lies. Whilst he could enumerate, in strict chronological succession, every important event that happened five or six million years before he was born, he was profoundly ignorant of those that occurred in his own day. And once he asked a friend seriously, if a cat let loose in the jungle would not in time become a tiger.

Yet did all the members of alma mater Kasi, Pandits[2] as well as students, look with awe upon Vishnu Swami's livid cheeks, and lack-lustre eyes, grimed hands and soiled cottons.

Now it so happened that this wise and pious Brahmanic peer had four sons, whom he brought up in the strictest and most serious way. They were taught to repeat their prayers long before they understood a word of them, and when they reached the age of four[3] they had read a variety of hymns and spiritual songs. Then they were set to learn by heart precepts that inculcate sacred duties, and arguments relating to theology, abstract and concrete.

Their father, who was also their tutor, sedulously cultivated, as all the best works upon education advise, their implicit obedience, humble respect, warm attachment, and the virtues and sentiments generally. He praised them secretly and reprehended them openly, to exercise their humility. He derided their looks, and dressed them coarsely, to preserve them from vanity and conceit. Whenever they anticipated a " treat," he

---

1 The land of Greece.

2 Savans, professors. So in the old saying, "Hanta, Pandit Sansara"—Alas! the world is learned! This a little antedates the well-known schoolmaster.

3 Children are commonly sent to school at the age of five. Girls are not taught to read, under the common idea that they will become widows if they do.

punctually disappointed them, to teach them self-denial. Often when he had promised them a present, he would revoke, not break his word, in order that discipline might have a name and habitat in his household. And knowing by experience how much stronger than love is fear, he frequently threatened, browbeat, and overawed them with the rod and the tongue, with the terrors of this world, and with the horrors of the next, that they might be kept in the right way by dread of falling into the bottomless pits that bound it on both sides.

At the age of six they were transferred to the Chatushpati[1] or school. Every morning the teacher and his pupils assembled in the hut where the different classes were called up by turns. They laboured till noon, and were allowed only two hours, a moiety of the usual time, for bathing, eating, sleep, and worship, which took up half the period. At 3 P.M. they resumed their labours, repeating to the tutor what they had learned by heart, and listening to the meaning of it: this lasted till twilight. They then worshipped, ate and drank for an hour: after which came a return of study, repeating the day's lessons, till 10 P.M.

In their rare days of ease—for the learned priest, mindful of the words of the wise, did not wish to dull them by everlasting work—they were enjoined to disport themselves with the gravity and the decorum that befit young Samditats, not to engage in night frolics, not to use free jests or light expressions, not to draw pictures on the walls, not to eat honey, flesh, and sweet substances turned acid, not to talk to little girls at the well-side, on no account to wear sandals, carry an umbrella, or handle a die even for love, and by no means to steal their neighbours' mangoes.

As they advanced in years their attention during

---

1 Meaning the place of reading the four Shastras.

work time was unremittingly directed to the Vedas.
Wordly studies were almost excluded, or to speak more
correctly, whenever wordly studies were brought upon the
carpet, they were so evil entreated, that they well nigh
lost all form and feature. History became " The Annals
of India on Brahminical Principles," opposed to the Bud-
dhistical; geography " The Lands of the Vedas," none
other being deemed worthy of notice; and law, " The
Institutes of Manu," then almost obsolete, despite their
exceeding sanctity.

But Jatu-harini[1] had evidently changed these children
before they were born ; and Shani[2] must have been in the
ninth mansion when they came to light.

Each youth as he attained the mature age of twelve
was formally entered at the University of Kasi, where,
without loss of time, the first became a gambler, the
second a confirmed libertine, the third a thief, and the
fourth a high Buddhist, or in other words an utter atheist.

Here King Vikram frowned at his son, a hint that he
had better not behave himself as the children of highly
moral and religious parents usually do. The young prince
understood him, and briefly remarking that such things
were common in distinguished Brahman families, asked
the Baital what he meant by the word " Atheist."

Of a truth (answered the Vampire) it is most difficult
to explain. The sages assign to it three or four several
meanings: first, one who denies that the gods exist ;
secondly, one who owns that the gods exist but denies that
they busy themselves with human affairs ; and thirdly,
one who believes in the gods and in their providence, but
also believes that they are easily to be set aside. Similarly

---

1 A certain goddess who plays tricks with mankind. If a son when
grown up act differently from what his parents did, people say that
he has been changed in the womb.

2 Shani is the planet Saturn, which has an exceedingly baleful
influence in India as elsewhere.

some atheists derive all things from dead and unintelligent matter; others from matter living and energetic but without sense or will: others from matter with forms and qualities generable and conceptible; and others from a plastic and methodical nature. Thus the Vishnu Swamis of the world have invested the subject with some confusion. The simple, that is to say, the mass of mortality, have confounded that confusion by reproachfully applying the word atheist to those whose opinions differ materially from their own.

But I being at present, perhaps happily for myself, a Vampire, and having, just now, none of these human or inhuman ideas, meant simply to say that the pious priest's fourth son being great at second and small in the matter of first causes, adopted to their fullest extent the doctrines of the philosophical Buddhas.[1] Nothing according to him exists but the five elements, earth, water, fire, air (or wind), and vacuum, and from the last proceeded the penultimate, and so forth. With the sage Patanjali, he held the universe to have the power of perpetual progression.[2] He called that Matra (matter), which is an eternal and infinite principle, beginningless and endless. Organization, intelligence, and design, he opined, are inherent in matter as growth is in a tree. He did not believe in soul or spirit, because it could not be detected in the body, and because it was a departure from physiological analogy. The idea "I am," according to him, was not the identification of spirit with matter, but a product of the mutation of matter in this cloud-like, error-formed world. He believed in Substance (Sat) and scoffed at Unsubstance (Asat). He asserted the subtlety and glo-

---

1 The Eleatic or Materialistic school of Hindu philosophy, which agrees to explode an intelligent separate First Cause.

2 The writings of this school give an excellent view of the "progressive system," which has popularly been asserted to be a modern idea. But Hindu philosophy seems to have exhausted every fancy that can spring from the brain of man.

bularity of atoms which are uncreate. He made mind
and intellect a mere secretion of the brain, or rather words
expressing not a thing, but a state of things. Reason
was to him developed instinct, and life an element of the
atmosphere affecting certain organisms. He held good
and evil to be merely geographical and chronological expressions, and he opined that what is called Evil is mostly
an active and transitive form of Good. Law was his
great Creator of all things, but he refused a creator of
law, because such a creator would require another creator, and so on in a quasi-interminable series up to absurd-
ity. This reduced his law to a manner of haphazard.
To those who, arguing against it, asked him their favourite question, How often might a man after he had jumbled
a set of letters in a bag fling them out upon the ground
before they would fall into an exact poem? he replied
that the calculation was beyond his arithmetic, but that
the man had only to jumble and fling long enough inevit-
ably to arrive at that end. He rejected the necessity as
well as the existence of revelation, and he did not credit
the miracles of Krishna, because, according to him, nature
never suspends her laws, and, moreover, he had never
seen aught supernatural. He ridiculed the idea of Maha-
pralaya, or the great destruction, for as the world had no
beginning, so it will have no end. He objected to absorption, facetiously observing with the sage Jamadagni, that
it was pleasant to eat sweetmeats, but that for his part
he did not wish to become the sweetmeat itself. He
would not believe that Vishnu had formed the universe
out of the wax in his ears. He positively asserted that
trees are not bodies in which the consequences of merit
and demerit are received. Nor would he conclude that
to men were attached rewards and punishments from all
eternity. He made light of the Sanskara, or sacrament.
He admitted Satwa, Raja, and Tama,[1] but only as pro-

---

1 Tama is the natural state of matter, Raja is passion acting

perties of matter. He acknowledged gross matter (Sthula-sharir), and atomic matter (Shukshma-sharir), but not Linga-sharir, or the archetype of bodies. To doubt all things was the foundation of his theory, and to scoff at all who would not doubt was the corner-stone of his practice. In debate he preferred logical and mathematical grounds, requiring a categorical "because" in answer to his "why?" He was full of morality and natural religion, which some say is no religion at all. He gained the name of atheist by declaring with Gotama that there are innumerable worlds, that the earth has nothing beneath it but the circumambient air, and that the core of the globe is incandescent. And he was called a practical atheist—a worse form apparently—for supporting the following dogma: "that though creation may attest that a creator has been, it supplies no evidence to prove that a creator still exists." On which occasion, Shiromani, a nonplussed theologian, asked him, "By whom and for what purpose wast thou sent on earth?" The youth scoffed at the word "sent," and replied, "Not being thy Supreme Intelligence, or Infinite Nihility, I am unable to explain the phenomenon." Upon which he quoted—

How sunk in darkness Gaur must be
Whose guide is blind Shiromani!

At length it so happened that the four young men, having frequently been surprised in flagrant delict, were summoned to the dread presence of the university Gurus,[1] who addressed them as follows:—

"There are four different characters in the world: he who perfectly obeys the commands; he who practises the commands, but follows evil; he who does neither good nor evil; and he who does nothing but evil. The third character, it is observed, is also an offender, for he neglects that which he ought to observe. But ye all belong to the fourth category."

upon nature, and Satwa is excellence. These are the three gunas or qualities of matter.

1 Spiritual preceptors and learned men.

Then turning to the elder they said :

" In works written upon the subject of government it
is advised, 'Cut off the gambler's nose and ears, hold up
his name to public contempt, and drive him out of the
country, that he may thus become an example to others.
For they who play must more often lose than win; and
losing, they must either pay or not pay. In the latter
case they forfeit caste, in the former they utterly reduce
themselves. And though a gambler's wife and children
are in the house, do not consider them to be so, since it
is not known when they will be lost.[1] Thus he is left in
a state of perfect not-twoness (solitude), and he will be
reborn in hell.' O young man! thou hast set a bad example to others, therefore shalt thou immediately exchange this university for a country life."

Then they spoke to the second offender thus :—

" The wise shun woman, who can fascinate a man in
the twinkling of an eye; but the foolish, conceiving an
affection for her, forfeit in the pursuit of pleasure their
truthfulness, reputation, and good disposition, their way of
life and mode of thought, their vows and their religion.
And to such the advice of their spiritual teachers comes
amiss, whilst they make others as bad as themselves. For
it is said, ' He who has lost all sense of shame, fears not
to disgrace another ; ' and there is the proverb, 'A wild
cat that devours its own young is not likely to let a rat
escape ; ' therefore must thou too, O young man! quit
this seat of learning with all possible expedition."

The young man proceeded to justify himself by
quotations from the Lila-shastra, his text-book, by citing
such lines as—

Fortune favours folly and force,

and by advising the elderly professors to improve their

---

[1] Under certain limitations, gambling is allowed by Hindu law,
and the winner has power over the person and property of the loser.
No "debts of honour" in Hindustan !

skill in the peace and war of love. But they drove him out with execrations.

As sagely and as solemnly did the Pandits and the Gurus reprove the thief and the atheist, but they did not dispense the words of wisdom in equal proportions. They warned the former that petty larceny is punishable with fine, theft on a larger scale with mutilation of the hand, and robbery, when detected in the act, with loss of life[1]; that for cutting purses, or for snatching them out of a man's waistcloth,[2] the first penalty is chopping off the fingers, the second is the loss of the hand, and the third is death. Then they call him a dishonour to the college, and they said, "Thou art as a woman, the greatest of plunderers; other robbers purloin property which is worthless, thou stealest the best; they plunder in the night, thou in the day," and so forth. They told him that he was a fellow who had read his Chauriya Vidya to more purpose than his ritual.[3] And they drove him from the door as he in his shamelessness began to quote texts about the four approved ways of housebreaking, namely, picking out burnt bricks, cutting through unbaked bricks, throwing water on a mud wall, and boring one of wood with a centre-bit.

But they spent six mortal hours in convicting the atheist, whose abominations they refuted by every possible argumentation: by inference, by comparison, and by sounds, by Sruti and Smriti, *i.e.*, revelational and traditional, rational and evidential, physical and metaphysical, analytical and synthetical, philosophical and philological, historical, and so forth. But they found all their endeavours

---

1 Quotations from standard works on Hindu criminal law, which in some points at least is almost as absurd as our civilized codes.

2 Hindus carry their money tied up in a kind of sheet, which is wound round the waist and thrown over the shoulder.

3 A thieves' manual in the Sanskrit tongue; it aspires to the dignity of a "Scripture."

vain. " For," it is said, " a man who has lost all shame,
who can talk without sense, and who tries to cheat his
opponent, will never get tired, and will never be put
down." He declared that a non-ad was far more
probable than a monad (the active principle), or the duad
(the passive principle or matter.) He compared their
faith with a bubble in the water, of which we can never
predicate that it does exist or it does not. It is, he said,
unreal, as when the thirsty mistakes the meadow mist for
a pool of water. He proved the eternity of sound.[1] He
impudently recounted and justified all the villanies
of the Vamachari or left-handed sects. He told them
that they had taken up an ass's load of religion, and had
better apply to honest industry. He fell foul of the gods;
accused Yama of kicking his own mother, Indra of tempt-
ing the wife of his spiritual guide, and Shiva of associating
with low women. Thus, he said, no one can respect
them. Do not we say when it thunders awfully, " the
rascally gods are dying ! " And when it is too wet,
" these villain gods are sending too much rain " ? Briefly,
the young Brahman replied to and harangued them all so
impertinently, if not pertinently, that they, waxing angry,
fell upon him with their staves, and drove him out of
assembly.

Then the four thriftless youths returned home to
their father, who in his just indignation had urged their
disgrace upon the Pandits and Gurus, otherwise these
dignitaries would never have resorted to such extreme
measures with so distinguished a house. He took the
opportunity of turning them out upon the world, until
such time as they might be able to show substantial signs
of reform. "For," he said, "those who have read science
in their boyhood, and who in youth, agitated by evil pas-

---

[1] All sounds, say the Hindus, are of similar origin, and they do
not die ; if they did, they could not be remembered

sions, have remained in the insolence of ignorance, feel regret in their old age, and are consumed by the fire of avarice." In order to supply them with a motive for the task proposed, he stopped their monthly allowance. But he added, if they would repair to the neighbouring university of Jayasthal, and there show themselves something better than a disgrace to their family, he would direct their maternal uncle to supply them with all the necessaries of food and raiment.

In vain the youths attempted, with sighs and tears and threats of suicide, to soften the paternal heart. He was inexorable, for two reasons. In the first place, after wondering away the wonder with which he regarded his own failure, he felt that a stigma now attached to the name of the pious and learned Vishnu Swami, whose lectures upon " Management during Teens," and whose "Brahman Young Man's Own Book," had become standard works. Secondly, from a sense of duty, he determined to omit nothing that might tend to reclaim the reprobates. As regards the monthly allowance being stopped, the reverend man had become every year a little fonder of his purse; he had hoped that his sons would have qualified themselves to take pupils, and thus achieve for themselves, as he phrased it, "A genteel independence"; whilst they openly derided the career, calling it "an admirable provision for the more indigent members of the middle classes." For which reason he referred them to their maternal uncle, a man of known and remarkable penuriousness.

The four ne'er-do-weels, foreseeing what awaited them at Jayasthal, deferred it as a last resource; determining first to see a little life, and to push their way in the world, before condemning themselves to the tribulations of reform.

They tried to live without a monthly allowance, and notably they failed; it was squeezing, as men say, oil from

sand. The gambler, having no capital, and, worse still,
no credit, lost two or three suvernas[1] at play, and could
not pay them; in consequence of which he was soundly
beaten with iron-shod staves, and was nearly compelled
by the keeper of the hell to sell himself into slavery.
Thus he became disgusted; and telling his brethren that
they would find him at Jayasthal, he departed, with the
intention of studying wisdom.

A month afterwards came the libertine's turn to be
disappointed. He could no longer afford fine new clothes;
even a well-washed coat was beyond his means. He had

They tried to live without a monthly allowance, and notably they failed.

reckoned upon his handsome face, and he had matured a
plan for laying various elderly conquests under contribu-
tion. Judge, therefore, his disgust when all the women—
high and low, rich and poor, old and young, ugly and
beautiful—seeing the end of his waistcloth thrown empty
over his shoulder, passed him in the streets without even
deigning a look. The very shopkeepers' wives, who once
had adored his mustachio and had never ceased talking
of his "elegant" gait, despised him; and the wealthy old
person who formerly supplied his small feet with the

---

1 Gold pieces.

choicest slippers, left him to starve. Upon which he also in a state of repentance, followed his brother to acquire knowledge.

"Am I not," quoth the thief to himself, "a cat in climbing, a deer in running, a snake in twisting, a hawk in pouncing, a dog in scenting ?—keen as a hare, tenacious as a wolf, strong as a lion ?—a lamp in the night, a horse on a plain, a mule on a stony path, a boat in the water, a rock on land[1] ?" The reply to his own questions was of course affirmative. But despite all these fine qualities, and notwithstanding his scrupulous strictness in invocating the house-breaking tool and in devoting a due portion of his gains to the gods of plunder,[2] he was caught in a store-room by the proprietor, who inexorably handed him over to justice. As he belonged to the priestly caste,[3] the fine imposed upon him was heavy. He could not pay it, and therefore he was thrown into a dungeon, where he remained for some time. But at last he escaped from jail, when he made his parting bow to Kartikeya,[4] stole a blanket from one of the guards, and set out for Jayasthal, cursing his old profession.

The atheist also found himself in a position that deprived him of all his pleasures. He delighted in after-dinner controversies, and in bringing the light troops of his wit to bear upon the unwieldy masses of lore and

1 These are the qualifications specified by Hindu classical authorities as necessary to make a distinguished thief.

2 Every Hindu is in a manner born to a certain line of life, virtuous or vicious, honest or dishonest ; and his Dharma, or religious duty, consists in conforming to the practice and the worship of his profession. The "Thug," for instance, worships Bhawani, who enables him to murder successfully ; and his remorse would arise from neglecting to murder.

3 Hindu law sensibly punishes, in theory at least, for the same offence the priest more severely than the layman—a hint for him to practise what he preaches.

4 The Hindu Mercury, god of rascals.

logic opposed to him by polemical Brahmans who, out
of respect for his father, did not lay an action against
him for overpowering them in theological disputation.[1]
In the strange city to which he had removed no one knew
the son of Vishnu Swami, and no one cared to invite him
to the house.   Once he attempted his usual trick upon a
knot of sages who, sitting round a tank, were recreating
themselves with quoting mystical Sanskrit shlokas[2] of
abominable long-windedness.   The result was his being
obliged to ply his heels vigorously in flight from the justly
incensed *literati*, to whom he had said "tush" and "pish,"
at least a dozen times in as many minutes.   He therefore
also followed the example of his brethren, and started for
Jayasthal with all possible expedition.

Arrived at the house of their maternal uncle, the
young men, as by one assent, began to attempt the un-
loosening of his purse-strings.   Signally failing in this
and in other notable schemes, they determined to lay in
that stock of facts and useful knowledge which might
reconcile them with their father, and restore them to that
happy life at Gaur which they then despised, and which
now brought tears into their eyes.

Then they debated with one another what they
should study.

*   *   *   *   *   *   *

That branch of the preternatural, popularly called
"white magic," found with them favour.

*   *   *   *   *   *   *

They chose a Guru or teacher strictly according to
the orders of their faith, a wise man of honourable family

---

1 A penal offence in India.   How is it that we English have
omitted to codify it ?   The laws of Manu also punish severely all
disdainful expressions, such as "tush" or "pish," addressed
during argument to a priest.

2 Stanzas, generally speaking, on serious subjects.

and affable demeanour, who was not a glutton nor leprous, nor blind of one eye, nor blind of both eyes, nor very short, nor suffering from whitlows,[1] asthma, or other disease, nor noisy and talkative, nor with any defect about the fingers and toes, nor subject to his wife.

* * * * * * *

A grand discovery had been lately made by a certain physiologico-philosophico-psychologico-materialist, a Jayasthalian. In investigating the vestiges of creation, the cause of causes, the effect of effects, and the original origin of that Matra (matter) which some regard as an entity, others as a non-entity, others self-existent, others merely specious and therefore unexistent, he became convinced that the fundamental form of organic being is a globule having another globule within itself. After inhabiting a garret and diving into the depths of his self-consciousness for a few score years, he was able to produce such complex globule in triturated and roasted flint by means of—I will not say what. Happily for creation in general, the discovery died a natural death some centuries ago. An edifying spectacle, indeed, for the world to see ; a cross old man sitting amongst his gallipots and crucibles, creating animalculæ, providing the corpses of birds, beasts, and fishes with what is vulgarly called life, and supplying to epigenesis all the latest improvements !

In those days the invention, being a novelty, engrossed the thoughts of the universal learned, who were in a fever of excitement about it. Some believed in it so implicitly that they saw in every experiment a hundred things which they did not see. Others were so sceptical and contradictory that they would not preceive what they did see. Those blended with each fact their own deduc-

---

1 Whitlows on the nails show that the sufferer, in the last life, stole gold from a Brahman.

tions, whilst these span round every reality the web of their own prejudices. Curious to say, the Jayasthalians, amongst whom the luminous science arose, hailed it with delight, whilst the Gaurians derided its claim to be considered an important addition to human knowledge.

Let me try to remember a few of their words.

" Unfortunate human nature," wrote the wise of Gaur against the wise of Jayasthal, " wanted no crowning indignity but this! You had already proved that the body is made of the basest element—earth. You had argued away the immovability, the ubiquity, the permanency, the eternity, and the divinity of the soul, for is not your favourite axiom, ' It is the nature of limbs which thinketh in man'? The immortal mind is, according to you, an ignoble viscus; the god-like gift of reason is the instinct of a dog somewhat highly developed. Still you left us something to hope. Still you allowed us one boast. Still life was a thread connecting us with the Giver of Life. But now, with an impious hand, in blasphemous rage ye have rent asunder that last frail tie." And so forth.

" Welcome! thrice welcome! this latest and most admirable development of human wisdom," wrote the sage Jayasthalians against the sage Gaurians, " which has assigned to man his proper state and status and station in the magnificent scale of being. We have not created the facts which we have investigated, and which we now proudly publish. We have proved materialism to be nature's own system. But our philosophy of matter cannot overturn any truth, because, if erroneous, it will necessarily sink into oblivion; if real, it will tend only to instruct and to enlighten the world. Wise are ye in your generation, O ye sages of Gaur, yet withal wondrous illogical." And much of this kind.

Concerning all which, mighty king! I, as a Vampire, have only to remark that those two learned bodies, like your Rajaship's Nine Gems of Science, were in the habit of talking most about what they least understood.

The four young men applied the whole force of their talents to mastering the difficulties of the life-giving process; and in due time, their industry obtained its reward.

  * * * * * * *

The bone thereupon stood upright, and hopped about.

Then they determined to return home. As with beating hearts they approached the old city, their birthplace, and gazed with moistened eyes upon its tall spires and grim pagodas, its verdant meads and venerable groves, they saw a Kanjar,[1] who, having tied up in a bundle the skin and bones of a tiger which he had found dead, was about to go on his way. Then said the thief to the gambler, "Take we these remains with us, and by means of them prove the truth of our science before the people of Gaur, to the offence of their noses.[2]" Being

---

1 A low caste Hindu, who catches and exhibits snakes and performs other such mean offices.

2 Meaning, in spite of themselves.

now possessed of knowledge, they resolved to apply it to its proper purpose, namely, power over the property of others. Accordingly, the wencher, the gambler, and the atheist kept the Kanjar in conversation whilst the thief vivified a shank bone; and the bone thereupon stood upright, and hopped about in so grotesque and wonderful a way that the man, being frightened, fled as if I had been close behind him.

Vishnu Swami had lately written a very learned commentary on the mystical words of Lokakshi:

"The Scriptures are at variance—the tradition is at variance. He who gives a meaning of his own, quoting the Vedas, is no philosopher.

"True philosophy, through ignorance, is concealed as in the fissures of a rock.

"But the way of the Great One—that is to be followed."

And the success of his book had quite effaced from the Brahman mind the holy man's failure in bringing up his children. He followed up this by adding to his essay on education a twentieth tome, containing recipes for the "Reformation of Prodigals."

The learned and reverend father received his sons with open arms. He had heard from his brother-in-law that the youths were qualified to support themselves, and when informed that they wished to make a public experiment of their science, he exerted himself, despite his disbelief in it, to forward their views.

The Pandits and Gurus were long before they would consent to attend what they considered dealings with Yama (the Devil). In consequence, however, of Vishnu Swami's name and importunity, at length, on a certain day, all the pious, learned, and reverend tutors, teachers, professors, prolocutors, pastors, spiritual fathers, poets, philosophers, mathematicians, schoolmasters, pedagogues, bear-leaders, institutors, gerund-grinders, preceptors, dominies, brushers, coryphæi, dry-nurses, coaches, mentors, monitors, lecturers, prelectors, fellows, and heads of houses at the university at Gaur, met together in a large garden, where they usually diverted themselves out of hours with ball-tossing, pigeon-tumbling, and kite-flying.

Presently the four young men, carrying their bundle of bones and the other requisites, stepped forward, walking slowly with eyes downcast, like shrinking cattle : for it is said, the Brahman must not run, even when it rains.

After pronouncing an impromptu speech, composed for them by their father, and so stuffed with erudition that even the writer hardly understood it, they announced their wish to prove, by ocular demonstration, the truth of a science upon which their short-sighted rivals of Jayasthal had cast cold water, but which, they remarked in the eloquent peroration of their discourse, the sages of Gaur had welcomed with that wise and catholic spirit of inquiry which had ever characterized their distinguished body.

Huge words, involved sentences, and the high-flown compliment, exceedingly undeserved, obscured, I suppose, the bright wits of the intellectual convocation, which really began to think that their liberality of opinion deserved all praise.

None objected to what was being prepared, except one of the heads of houses ; his appeal was generally scouted, because his Sanskrit style was vulgarly intelligible, and he had the bad name of being a practical man. The metaphysician Rashik Lall sneered to Vaiswata the poet, who passed on the look to the theo-philosopher Vardhaman. Haridatt the antiquarian whispered the metaphysician Vasudeva, who burst into a loud laugh; whilst Narayan, Jagasharma, and Devaswami, all very learned in the Vedas, opened their eyes and stared at him with well-simulated astonishment. So he, being offended, said nothing more, but arose and walked home.

A great crowd gathered round the four young men and their father, as opening the bundle that contained the tiger's remains, they prepared for their task.

One of the operators spread the bones upon the ground and fixed each one into its proper socket, not forgetting even the teeth and tusks.

The second connected, by means of a marvellous unguent, the skeleton with the muscles and heart of an elephant, which he had procured for the purpose.

The third drew from his pouch the brain and eyes of

They prepared for their task.

a large tom-cat, which he carefully fitted into the animal's skull, and then covered the body with the hide of a young rhinoceros.

Then the fourth—the atheist—who had been directing the operation, produced a globule having another globule within itself. And as the crowd pressed on them, craning their necks, breathless with anxiety, he placed the Principle of Organic Life in the tiger's body with such effect that the monster immediately heaved its chest, breathed, agitated its limbs, opened its eyes, jumped to its feet, shook itself, glared around, and began to gnash

12—2

its teeth and lick its chops, lashing the while its ribs with its tail.

The sages sprang back, and the beast sprang forward. With a roar like thunder during Elephanta-time,[1] it flew at the nearest of the spectators, flung Vishnu Swami to the ground and clawed his four sons. Then, not even stopping to drink their blood, it hurried after the flying herd of wise men. Jostling and tumbling, stumbling and catching at one another's long robes, they rushed in hottest haste towards the garden gate. But the beast, having the muscles of an elephant as well as the bones of a tiger, made a few bounds of eighty or ninety feet each, easily distanced them, and took away all chance of escape. To be brief: as the monster was frightfully hungry after its long fast, and as the imprudent young men had furnished it with admirable implements of destruction, it did not cease its work till one hundred and twenty-one learned and highly distinguished Pandits and Gurus lay upon the ground chawed, clawed, sucked dry, and in most cases stone-dead. Amongst them, I need hardly say, were the sage Vishnu Swami and his four sons.

Having told this story the Vampire hung silent for a time. Presently he resumed—

"Now, heed my words, Raja Vikram! I am about to ask thee, Which of all those learned men was the most finished fool ? The answer is easily found, yet it must be distasteful to thee. Therefore mortify thy vanity, as soon as possible, or I shall be talking, and thou wilt be walking through this livelong night, to scanty purpose. Remember ! science without understanding is of little use ; indeed, understanding is superior to science, and those devoid of understanding perish as did the persons who revivified the tiger. Before this, I warned thee to beware of thyself, and of thine own conceit. Here, then,

---

1 When the moon is in a certain lunar mansion, at the conclusion of the wet season.

is an opportunity for self-discipline—which of all those learned men was the greatest fool ? "

The warrior king mistook the kind of mortification imposed upon him, and pondered over the uncomfortable nature of the reply—in the presence of his son.

Again the Baital taunted him.

"The greatest fool of all," at last said Vikram, in slow and by no means willing accents, "was the father. Is it not said, 'There is no fool like an old fool'? "

"Gramercy!" cried the Vampire, bursting out into a discordant laugh, "I now return to my tree. By this head! I never before heard a father so readily condemn a father." With these words he disappeared, slipping out of the bundle.

The Raja scolded his son a little for want of obedience, and said that he had always thought more highly of his acuteness—never could have believed that he would have been taken in by so shallow a trick. Dharma Dhwaj answered not a word to this, but promised to be wiser another time.

Then they returned to the tree, and did what they had so often done before.

And, as before, the Baital held his tongue for a time. Presently he began as follows.

THE VAMPIRE'S EIGHTH STORY.

OF THE USE AND MISUSE OF MAGIC PILLS.

THE lady Chandraprabha, daughter of the Raja Subichar, was a particularly beautiful girl, and marriageable withal. One day as Vasanta, the Spring, began to assert its reign over the world, animate and inanimate, she went accompanied by her young friends and companions to stroll about her father's pleasure-garden.

The fair troop wandered through sombre groves, where the dark tamala-tree entwined its branches with the pale green foliage of the nim, and the pippal's domes of quivering leaves contrasted with the columnar aisles of the banyan fig. They admired the old monarchs of the forest, bearded to the waist with hangings of moss, the flowing creepers delicately climbing from the lower branches to the topmost shoots, and the cordage of llianas stretching from trunk to trunk like bridges for the monkeys to pass over. Then they issued into a clear space dotted with asokas bearing rich crimson flowers, cliterias of azure blue, madhavis exhibiting petals virgin white as the snows on Himalaya, and jasmines raining showers of perfumed blossoms upon the grateful earth. They could not sufficiently praise the tall and graceful stem of the arrowy areca, contrasting with the solid pyramid of the cypress, and the more masculine stature of the palm. Now they lingered in the trellised walks closely covered over with vines and creepers; then they stopped to gather the golden bloom weighing down the mango boughs, and to smell the highly-scented flowers that hung from the green fretwork of the chambela.

It was spring, I have said. The air was still except when broken by the hum of the large black bramra bee, as he plied his task amidst the red and orange flowers of the dak, and by the gushings of many waters that made music as they coursed down their stuccoed channels between borders of many coloured poppies and beds of various flowers. From time to time the dulcet note of the kokila bird, and the hoarse plaint of the turtle-dove deep hid in her leafy bower, attracted every ear and thrilled every heart. The south wind—"breeze of the south,[1] the friend of love and spring" blew with a voluptuous warmth, for rain clouds canopied the earth, and the breath of the narcissus, the rose, and the citron, teemed with a languid fragrance.

The charms of the season affected all the damsels. They amused themselves in their privacy with pelting blossoms at one another, running races down the smooth broad alleys, mounting the silken swings that hung between the orange trees, embracing one another, and at times trying to push the butt of the party into the fish-pond. Perhaps the liveliest of all was the lady Chandra-prabha, who on account of her rank could pelt and push all the others, without fear of being pelted and pushed in return.

It so happened, before the attendants had had time to secure privacy for the princess and her women, that Manaswi, a very handsome youth, a Brahman's son, had wandered without malicious intention into the garden. Fatigued with walking, and finding a cool shady place beneath a tree, he had lain down there, and had gone to sleep, and had not been observed by any of the king's

---

1 In Hindustan, it is the prevailing wind of the hot weather.

people. He was still sleeping when the princess and her companions were playing together.

Presently Chandraprabha, weary of sport, left her friends, and singing a lively air, tripped up the stairs leading to the summer-house. Aroused by the sound of her advancing footsteps, Manaswi sat up; and the princess, seeing a strange man, started. But their eyes had met, and both were subdued by love—love vulgarly called "love at first sight."

"Nonsense!" exclaimed the warrior king, testily, "I can never believe in that freak of Kama Deva." He

But their eyes had met.

spoke feelingly, for the thing had happened to himself more than once, and on no occasion had it turned out well.

"But there is such a thing, O Raja, as love at first sight," objected the Baital, speaking dogmatically.

"Then perhaps thou canst account for it, dead one," growled the monarch surlily.

"I have no reason to do so, O Vikram," retorted the

Vampire, "when you men have already done it.   Listen,
then, to the words of the wise.   In the olden time, one of
your great philosophers invented a fluid pervading all
matter, strongly self-repulsive like the steam of a brass
pot, and widely spreading like the breath of scandal.
The repulsiveness, however, according to that wise man,
is greatly modified by its second property, namely, an
energetic attraction or adhesion to all material bodies.
Thus every substance contains a part, more or less, of
this fluid, pervading it throughout, and strongly bound to
each component atom.   He called it 'Ambericity,' for the
best of reasons, as it has no connection with amber, and
he described it as an imponderable, which, meaning that
it could not be weighed, gives a very accurate and satis-
factory idea of its nature.

"Now, said that philosopher, whenever two bodies
containing that unweighable substance in unequal proportions happen to meet, a current of imponderable passes from
one to the other, producing a kind of attraction, and tending to adhere.   The operation takes place instantaneously
when the force is strong and much condensed.   Thus the
vulgar who call things after their effects and not from
their causes, term the action of this imponderable love at
first sight; the wise define it to be a phenomenon of
ambericity.   As regards my own opinion about the
matter, I have long ago told it to you, O Vikram !   Silli-
ness—"

"Either hold your tongue, fellow, or go on with your
story," cried the Raja, wearied out by so many words that
had no manner of sense.

Well! the effect of the first glance was that Manaswi,
the Brahman's son, fell back in a swoon and remained
senseless upon the ground where he had been sitting; and
the Raja's daughter began to tremble upon her feet, and
presently dropped unconscious upon the floor of the
summer-house.   Shortly after this she was found by her

companions and attendants, who, quickly taking her up in
their arms and supporting her into a litter, conveyed her
home.

Manaswi, the Brahman's son, was so completely
overcome, that he lay there dead to everything. Just
then the learned, deeply read, and purblind Pandits
Muldev and Shashi by name, strayed into the garden, and
stumbled upon the body.

"Friend," said Muldev, "how came this youth thus
to fall senseless on the ground?"

"Man," replied Shashi, "doubtless some damsel has
shot forth the arrows of her glances from the bow of her
eyebrows, and thence he has become insensible!"

"We must lift him up then," said Muldev the
benevolent.

"What need is there to raise him?" asked Shashi
the misanthrope by way of reply.

Muldev, however, would not listen to these words.
He ran to the pond hard by, soaked the end of his waistcloth in water, sprinkled it over the young Brahman,
raised him from the ground, and placed him sitting against
the wall. And perceiving, when he came to himself, that
his sickness was rather of the soul than of the body, the old
men asked him how he came to be in that plight.

"We should tell our griefs," answered Manaswi, "only
to those who will relieve us! What is the use of communicating them to those who, when they have heard,
cannot help us? What is to be gained by the empty
pity or by the useless condolence of men in general?"

The Pandits, however, by friendly looks and words,
presently persuaded him to break silence, when he said,
"A certain princess entered this summer-house, and from
the sight of her I have fallen into this state. If I can
obtain her, I shall live; if not, I must die."

"Come with me, young man!" said Muldev the
benevolent; " I will use every endeavour to obtain her, and

if I do not succeed I will make thee wealthy and independent of the world."

Manaswi rejoined : " The Deity in his beneficence has created many jewels in this world, but the pearl, woman, is chiefest of all ; and for her sake only does man desire wealth. What are riches to one who has abandoned his wife ? What are they who do not possess beautiful wives ? they are but beings inferior to the beasts ! wealth is the fruit of virtue ; ease, of wealth ; a wife, of ease. And where no wife is, how can there be happiness ? " And the enamoured youth rambled on in this way, curious to us, Raja Vikram, but perhaps natural enough in a Brahman's son suffering under that endemic malady—determination to marry.

" Whatever thou mayest desire," said Muldev, " shall by the blessing of heaven be given to thee."

Manaswi implored him, saying most pathetically, " O Pandit, bestow then that damsel upon me ! "

Muldev promised to do so, and having comforted the youth, led him to his own house. Then he welcomed him politely, seated him upon the carpet, and left him for a few minutes, promising him to return. When he reappeared, he held in his hand two little balls or pills, and showing them to Manaswi, he explained their virtues as follows :

" There is in our house an hereditary secret, by means of which I try to promote the weal of humanity. But in all cases my success depends mainly upon the purity and the heartwholeness of those that seek my aid. If thou place this in thy mouth, thou shalt be changed into a damsel twelve years old, and when thou withdrawest it again, thou shalt again recover thine original form. Beware, however, that thou use the power for none but a good purpose; otherwise some great calamity will befall thee. Therefore, take counsel of thyself before undertaking this trial ! "

What lover, O warrior king Vikram, would have hesitated, under such circumstances, to assure the Pandit that he was the most innocent, earnest, and well-intentioned being in the Three Worlds?

The Brahman's son, at least, lost no time in so doing. Hence the simple-minded philosopher put one of the pills into the young man's mouth, warning him on no account to swallow it, and took the other into his own mouth. Upon which Manaswi became a sprightly young maid, and Muldev was changed to a reverend and decrepid senior, not fewer than eighty years old.

Thus transformed, the twain walked up to the palace of the Raja Subichar, and stood for a while to admire the gate. Then passing through seven courts, beautiful as the Paradise of Indra, they entered, unannounced, as became the priestly dignity, a hall where, surrounded by his courtiers, sat the ruler. The latter, seeing the Holy Brahman under his roof, rose up, made the customary humble salutation, and taking their right hands, led what appeared to be the father and daughter to appropriate seats. Upon which Muldev, having recited a verse, bestowed upon the Raja a blessing whose beauty has been diffused over all creation.

"May that Deity[1] who as a mannikin deceived the great king Bali; who as a hero, with a monkey-host, bridged the Salt Sea; who as a shepherd lifted up the mountain Gobarddhan in the palm of his hand, and by it saved the cowherds and cowherdesses from the thunders of heaven—may that Deity be thy protector!"

Having heard and marvelled at this display of elo-

---

1 Vishnu, as a dwarf, sank down into and secured in the lower regions the Raja Bali, who by his piety and prayerfulness was subverting the reign of the lesser gods; as Ramachandra he built a bridge between Lanka (Ceylon) and the main land; and as Krishna he defended, by holding up a hill as an umbrella for them, his friends the shepherds and shepherdesses from the thunders of Indra, whose worship they had neglected.

quence, the Raja inquired, " Whence hath your holiness
come ? "

" My country," replied Muldev, " is on the northern
side of the great mother Ganges, and there too my dwelling is.   I travelled to a distant land, and having found in
this maiden a worthy wife for my son, I straightway
returned homewards.   Meanwhile a famine had laid waste
our village, and my wife and my son have fled I know not
where.   Encumbered with this damsel, how can I wander
about seeking them ?   Hearing the name of a pious and
generous ruler, I said to myself, ' I will leave her under
his charge until my return.'   Be pleased to take great
care of her."

For a minute the Raja sat thoughtful and silent.   He
was highly pleased with the Brahman's perfect compliment.   But he could not hide from himself that he was
placed between two difficulties : one, the charge of a
beautiful young girl, with pouting lips, soft speech, and
roguish eyes ; the other, a priestly curse upon himself and
his kingdom.   He thought, however, refusal the more
dangerous : so he raised his face and exclaimed, " O produce of Brahma's head,[1] I will do what your highness has
desired of me."

Upon which the Brahman, after delivering a benediction of adieu almost as beautiful and spirit-stirring as
that with which he had presented himself, took the betel[2]
and went his ways.

Then the Raja sent for his daughter Chandraprabha
and said to her, " This is the affianced bride of a young
Brahman, and she has been trusted to my protection for
a time by her father-in-law.   Take her therefore into the
inner rooms, treat her with the utmost regard, and never

---

1 The priestly caste sprang, as has been said, from the noblest
part of the Demiurgus ; the three others from lower members.

2 A chew of betel leaf and spices is offered by the master of the
house when dismissing a visitor.

allow her to be separated from thee, day or night, asleep or awake, eating or drinking, at home or abroad."

Chandraprabha took the hand of Sita—as Manaswi had pleased to call himself—and led the way to her own apartment. Once the seat of joy and pleasure, the rooms now wore a desolate and melancholy look. The windows were darkened, the attendants moved noiselessly over the carpets, as if their footsteps would cause headache, and there was a faint scent of some drug much used in cases of deliquium. The apartments were handsome, but the only ornament in the room where they sat was a large bunch of withered flowers in an arched recess, and these, though possibly interesting to some one, were not likely to find favour as a decoration in the eyes of everybody.

The Raja's daughter paid the greatest attention and talked with unusual vivacity to the Brahman's daughter-in-law, either because she had roguish eyes, or from some presentiment of what was to occur, whichever you please, Raja Vikram, and it is no matter which. Still Sita could not help perceiving that there was a shade of sorrow upon the forehead of her fair new friend, and so when they retired to rest she asked the cause of it.

Then Chandraprabha related to her the sad tale : "One day in the spring season, as I was strolling in the garden along with my companions, I beheld a very handsome Brahman, and our eyes having met, he became unconscious, and I also was insensible. My companions seeing my condition, brought me home, and therefore I know neither his name nor his abode. His beautiful form is impressed upon my memory. I have now no desire to eat or to drink, and from this distress my colour has become pale and my body is thus emaciated." And the beautiful princess sighed a sigh that was musical and melancholy, and concluded by predicting for herself—as persons similarly placed often do—a sudden and untimely end about the beginning of the next month.

"What wilt thou give me," asked the Brahman's daughter-in-law demurely, "if I show thee thy beloved at this very moment?"

The Raja's daughter answered, "I will ever be the lowest of thy slaves, standing before thee with joined hands."

Upon which Sita removed the pill from her mouth, and instantly having become Manaswi, put it carefully away in a little bag hung round his neck. At this sight Chandraprabha felt abashed, and hung down her head in beautiful confusion. To describe—

"I will have no descriptions, Vampire!" cried the great Vikram, jerking the bag up and down as if he were sweating gold in it. "The fewer of thy descriptions the better for us all."

Briefly (resumed the demon), Manaswi reflected upon the eight forms of marriage—viz., Bramhalagan, when a girl is given to a Brahman, or man of superior caste, without reward; Daiva, when she is presented as a gift or fee to the officiating priest at the close of a sacrifice; Arsha, when two cows are received by the girl's father in exchange for the bride[1]; Prajapatya, when the girl is given at the request of a Brahman, and the father says to his daughter and her to betrothed, "Go, fulfil the duties of religion"; Asura, when money is received by the father in exchange for the bride; Rakshasha, when she is captured in war, or when her bridegroom overcomes his rival; Paisacha, when the girl is taken away from her father's house by craft; and eighthly, Gandharva-lagan, or the marriage that takes place by mutual consent.[2]

---

[1] Respectable Hindus say that receiving a fee for a daughter is like selling flesh.

[2] A modern custom amongst the low caste is for the bride and bridegroom, in the presence of friends, to place a flower garland on each other's necks, and thus declare themselves man and wife. The old classical Gandharva-lagan has been before explained.

Manaswi preferred the latter, especially as by her rank and age the princess was entitled to call upon her father for the Lakshmi Swayambara wedding, in which she would have chosen her own husband. And thus it is that Rama, Arjuna, Krishna, Nala, and others, were proposed to by the princesses whom they married.

For five months after these nuptials, Manaswi never stirred out of the palace, but remained there by day a woman, and a man by night. The consequence was that he—I call him " he," for whether Manaswi or Sita, his mind ever remained masculine—presently found himself in a fair way to become a father.

Now, one would imagine that a change of sex every twenty-four hours would be variety enough to satisfy even a man. Manaswi, however, was not contented. He began to pine for more liberty, and to find fault with his wife for not taking him out into the world. And you might have supposed that a young person who, from love at first sight, had fallen senseless upon the steps of a summer-house, and who had devoted herself to a sudden and untimely end because she was separated from her lover, would have repressed her yawns and little irritable words even for a year after having converted him into a husband. But no ! Chandraprabha soon felt as tired of seeing Manaswi and nothing but Manaswi, as Manaswi was weary of seeing Chandraprabha and nothing but Chandraprabha. Often she had been on the point of proposing visits and out-of-door excursions. But when at last the idea was first suggested by her husband, she at once became an injured woman. She hinted how foolish it was for married people to imprison themselves and to quarrel all day. When Manaswi remonstrated, saying that he wanted nothing better than to appear before the world with her as his wife, but that he really did not know what her father might do to him, she threw out a cutting sarcasm upon his effeminate appearance during the hours

of light.   She then told him of an unfortunate young
woman in an old nursery tale who had unconsciously
married a fiend that became a fine handsome man at night
when no eye could see him, and utter ugliness by day
when good looks show to advantage.   And lastly, when
inveighing against the changeableness, fickleness, and
infidelity of mankind, she quoted the words of the poet—

> Out upon change! it tires the heart
>   And weighs the noble spirit down;
> A vain, vain world indeed thou art
>   That can such vile condition own;
> The veil hath fallen from my eyes,
> I cannot love where I despise. . . .

You can easily, O King Vikram, continue for yourself and
conclude this lecture, which I leave unfinished on account
of its length.

Chandraprabha and Sita, who called each other the
Zodiacal Twins and Laughter Light,[1] and All-consenters,
easily persuaded the old Raja that their health would be
further improved by air, exercise, and distractions.   Subichar, being delighted with the change that had taken
place in a daughter whom he loved, and whom he had
feared to lose, told them to do as they pleased.   They
began a new life, in which short trips and visits, baths
and dances, music parties, drives in bullock chariots, and
water excursions succeeded one another.

It so happened that one day the Raja went with his
whole family to a wedding feast in the house of his grand
treasurer, where the latter's son saw Manaswi in the
beautiful shape of Sita.   This was a third case of love at
first sight, for the young man immediately said to a particular friend, "If I obtain that girl, I shall live; if not, I
shall abandon life."

---

[1] Meaning that the sight of each other will cause a smile, and that
what one purposes the other will consent to.

In the meantime the king, having enjoyed the feast, came back to his palace with his whole family. The condition of the treasurer's son, however, became very distressing; and through separation from his beloved, he gave up eating and drinking. The particular friend had kept the secret for some days, though burning to tell it. At length he found an excuse for himself in the sad state of his friend, and he immediately went and divulged all that he knew to the treasurer. After this he felt relieved.

The minister repaired to the court, and laid his case before the king, saying, "Great Raja! through the love of that Brahman's daughter-in-law, my son's state is very bad; he has given up eating and drinking; in fact he is consumed by the fire of separation. If now your majesty could show compassion, and bestow the girl upon him, his life would be saved. If not——"

"Fool!" cried the Raja, who, hearing these words, had waxed very wroth; "it is not right for kings to do injustice. Listen! when a person puts any one in charge of a protector, how can the latter give away his trust without consulting the person that trusted him? And yet this is what you wish me to do."

The treasurer knew that the Raja could not govern his realm without him, and he was well acquainted with his master's character. He said to himself, "This will not last long;" but he remained dumb, simulating hopelessness, and hanging down his head, whilst Subichar alternately scolded and coaxed, abused and flattered him, in order to open his lips. Then, with tears in his eyes, he muttered a request to take leave; and as he passed through the palace gates, he said aloud, with a resolute air, "It will cost me but ten days of fasting!"

The treasurer, having returned home, collected all his attendants, and went straightway to his son's room. Seeing the youth still stretched upon his sleeping-mat, and very yellow for the want of food, he took his hand,

13

and said in a whisper, meant to be audible, "Alas! poor
son, I can do nothing but perish with thee."

The servants, hearing this threat, slipped one by one
out of the room, and each went to tell his friend that the
grand treasurer had resolved to live no longer. After
which, they went back to the house to see if their master
intended to keep his word, and curious to know, if he did
intend to die, how, where, and when it was to be. And
they were not disappointed: I do not mean that they
wished their lord to die, as he was a good master to them,
but still there was an excitement in the thing——

(Raja Vikram could not refrain from showing his
anger at the insult thus cast by the Baital upon human
nature; the wretch, however, pretending not to notice it,
went on without interrupting himself.)

——which somehow or other pleased them.

When the treasurer had spent three days without
touching bread or water, all the cabinet council met and
determined to retire from business unless the Raja yielded
to their solicitations. The treasurer was their working
man. "Besides which," said the cabinet council, "if a
certain person gets into the habit of refusing us, what is
to be the end of it, and what is the use of being cabinet
councillors any longer?"

Early on the next morning, the ministers went in a
body before the Raja, and humbly represented that "the
treasurer's son is at the point of death, the effect of a full
heart and an empty stomach. Should he die, the father,
who has not eaten or drunk during the last three days"
(the Raja trembled to hear the intelligence, though he
knew it), "his father, we say, cannot be saved. If the
father dies the affairs of the kingdom come to ruin,—is he
not the grand treasurer? It is already said that half the
accounts have been gnawed by white ants, and that some
pernicious substance in the ink has eaten jagged holes
through the paper, so that the other half of the accounts

13—2

is illegible. It were best, sire, that you agree to what
we represent."

The white ants and corrosive ink were too strong for
the Raja's determination. Still, wishing to save appearances, he replied, with much firmness, that he knew
the value of the treasurer and his son, that he would
do much to save them, but that he had passed his royal
word, and had undertaken a trust. That he would rather
die a dozen deaths than break his promise, or not discharge his duty faithfully. That man's condition in this
world is to depart from it, none remaining in it; that one
comes and that one goes, none knowing when or where;
but that eternity is eternity for happiness or misery. And
much of the same nature, not very novel, and not perhaps
quite to the purpose, but edifying to those who knew
what lay behind the speaker's words.

The ministers did not know their lord's character so
well as the grand treasurer, and they were more impressed
by his firm demeanour and the number of his words than
he wished them to be. After allowing his speech to settle
in their minds, he did away with a great part of its effect
by declaring that such were the sentiments and the principles—when a man talks of his principles, O Vikram!
ask thyself the reason why—instilled into his youthful
mind by the most honourable of fathers and the most virtuous of mothers. At the same time that he was by no
means obstinate or proof against conviction. In token
whereof he graciously permitted the councillors to convince him that it was his royal duty to break his word
and betray his trust, and to give away another man's
wife.

Pray do not lose your temper, O warrior king! Subichar, although a Raja, was a weak man; and you know,
or you ought to know, that the wicked may be wise in
their generation, but the weak never can.

Well, the ministers hearing their lord's last words,

took courage, and proceeded to work upon his mind by
the figure of speech popularly called "rigmarole." They
said: "Great king! that old Brahman has been gone
many days, and has not returned; he is probably dead
and burnt. It is therefore right that by giving to the
grand treasurer's son his daughter-in-law, who is only
affianced, not fairly married, you should establish your
government firmly. And even if he should return, bestow villages and wealth upon him; and if he be not then
content, provide another and a more beautiful wife for his
son, and dismiss him. A person should be sacrificed for
the sake of a family, a family for a city, a city for a
country, and a country for a king!"

Subichar having heard them, dismissed them with
the remark that as so much was to be said on both sides,
he must employ the night in thinking over the matter,
and that he would on the next day favour them with his
decision. The cabinet councillors knew by this that he
meant that he would go and consult his wives. They
retired contented, convinced that every voice would be in
favour of a wedding, and that the young girl, with so good
an offer, would not sacrifice the present to the future.

That evening the treasurer and his son supped together.

The first words uttered by Raja Subichar, when he
entered his daughter's apartment, were an order addressed
to Sita: "Go thou at once to the house of my treasurer's
son."

Now, as Chandraprabha and Manaswi were generally scolding each other, Chandraprabha and Sita were
hardly on speaking terms. When they heard the Raja's
order for their separation they were —

— "Delighted?" cried Dharma Dhwaj, who for some
reason took the greatest interest in the narrative.

"Overwhelmed with grief, thou most guileless Yuva
Raja (young prince)!" ejaculated the Vampire.

Raja Vikram reproved his son for talking about things of which he knew nothing, and the Baital resumed.

They turned pale and wept, and they wrung their hands, and they begged and argued and refused obedience. In fact they did everything to make the king revoke his order.

"The virtue of a woman," quoth Sita, "is destroyed through too much beauty; the religion of a Brahman is impaired by serving kings; a cow is spoiled by distant pasturage, wealth is lost by committing injustice, and prosperity departs from the house where promises are not kept."

The Raja highly applauded the sentiment, but was firm as a rock upon the subject of Sita marrying the treasurer's son.

Chandraprabha observed that her royal father, usually so conscientious, must now be acting from interested motives, and that when selfishness sways a man, right becomes left and left becomes right, as in the reflection of a mirror.

Subichar approved of the comparison; he was not quite so resolved, but he showed no symptoms of changing his mind.

Then the Brahman's daughter-in-law, with the view of gaining time—a famous stratagem amongst feminines —said to the Raja: "Great king, if you are determined upon giving me to the grand treasurer's son, exact from him the promise that he will do what I bid him. Only on this condition will I ever enter his house!"

"Speak, then," asked the king; "what will he have to do?"

She replied, "I am of the Brahman or priestly caste, he is the son of a Kshatriya or warrior: the law directs that before we twain can wed, he should perform Yatra (pilgrimage) to all the holy places."

" Thou hast spoken Veda-truth, girl," answered the

Raja, not sorry to have found so good a pretext for tem-
porizing, and at the same time to preserve his character
for firmness, resolution, determination.

That night Manaswi and Chandraprabha, instead of
scolding each other, congratulated themselves upon
having escaped an imminent danger—which they did
not escape.

In the morning Subichar sent for his ministers, in-
cluding his grand treasurer and his love-sick son, and told
them how well and wisely the Brahman's daughter-in-
law had spoken upon the subject of the marriage. All of
them approved of the condition; but the young man ventured to suggest, that while he was a-pilgrimaging the
maiden should reside under his father's roof. As he and
his father showed a disposition to continue their fasts in
case of the small favour not being granted, the Raja,
though very loath to separate his beloved daughter and
her dear friend, was driven to do it. And Sita was carried off, weeping bitterly, to the treasurer's palace. That
dignitary solemnly committed her to the charge of his
third and youngest wife, the lady Subhagya-Sundari,
who was about her own age, and said, "You must both
live together, without any kind of wrangling or conten-
tion, and do not go into other people's houses." And
the grand treasurer's son went off to perform his pil-
grimages.

It is no less sad than true, Raja Vikram, that in less
than six days the disconsolate Sita waxed weary of being
Sita, took the ball out of her mouth, and became Manaswi.
Alas for the infidelity of mankind! But it is gratifying
to reflect that he met with the punishment with which
the Pandit Muldev had threatened him. One night the
magic pill slipped down his throat. When morning
dawned, being unable to change himself into Sita, Manaswi
was obliged to escape through a window from the lady
Subhagya-Sundari's room. He sprained his ankle with

the leap, and he lay for a time upon the ground—where I leave him whilst convenient to me.

When Muldev quitted the presence of Subichar, he resumed his old shape, and returning to his brother Pandit Shashi, told him what he had done. Whereupon Shashi, the misanthrope, looked black, and used hard words and told his friend that good nature and soft-heartedness had caused him to commit a very bad action—a grievous sin. Incensed at this charge, the philanthropic Muldev became angry, and said, "I have warned the youth about his purity; what harm can come of it?"

"Thou hast," retorted Shashi, with irritating coolness, "placed a sharp weapon in a fool's hand."

"I have not," cried Muldev, indignantly.

"Therefore," drawled the malevolent, "you are answerable for all the mischief he does with it, and mischief assuredly he will do."

"He will not, by Brahma!" exclaimed Muldev.

"He will, by Vishnu!" said Shashi, with an amiability produced by having completely upset his friend's temper; "and if within the coming six months he does not disgrace himself, thou shalt have the whole of my book-case; but if he does, the philanthropic Muldev will use all his skill and ingenuity in procuring the daughter of Raja Subichar as a wife for his faithful friend Shashi."

Having made this covenant, they both agreed not to speak of the matter till the autumn.

The appointed time drawing near, the Pandits began to make inquiries about the effect of the magic pills. Presently they found out that Sita, alias Manaswi, had one night mysteriously disappeared from the grand treasurer's house, and had not been heard of since that time. This, together with certain other things that transpired presently, convinced Muldev, who had cooled down in six months, that his friend had won the wager. He prepared to make honourable payment by handing a pill to old Shashi, who at once became a stout, handsome young Brahman, some twenty years old. Next putting a pill into his own mouth, he resumed the shape and form under which he had first appeared before Raja Subichar; and, leaning upon his staff, he led the way to the palace.

The king, in great confusion, at once recognized the old priest, and guessed the errand upon which he and the youth were come. However, he saluted them, and offered them seats, and receiving their blessings, he began to make inquiries about their health and welfare. At last he mustered courage to ask the old Brahman where he had been living for so long a time.

"Great king," replied the priest, "I went to seek after my son, and having found him, I bring him to your majesty. Give him his wife, and I will take them both home with me."

Raja Subichar prevaricated not a little; but presently, being hard pushed, he related everything that had happened.

"What is this that you have done?" cried Muldev, simulating excessive anger and astonishment. "Why have you given my son's wife in marriage to another man? You have done what you wished, and now, therefore, receive my Shrap (curse)!"

The poor Raja, in great trepidation, said, "O Divinity! be not thus angry! I will do whatever you bid me."

Said Muldev, "If through dread of my excommunication you will freely give whatever I demand of you, then marry your daughter, Chandraprabha, to this my son. On this condition I forgive you. To me, now a necklace of pearls and a venomous krishna (cobra capella); the most powerful enemy and the kindest friend; the most precious gem and a clod of earth; the softest bed and the hardest stone; a blade of grass and the loveliest woman—are precisely the same. All I desire is that in some holy place, repeating the name of God, I may soon end my days."

Subichar, terrified by this additional show of sanctity, at once summoned an astrologer, and fixed upon the auspicious moment and lunar influence. He did not consult the princess, and had he done so she would not have resisted his wishes. Chandraprabha had heard of Sita's escape from the treasurer's house, and she had on the subject her own suspicions. Besides which she looked forward to a certain event, and she was by no means sure that her royal father approved of the Gandharba form of marriage—at least for his daughter. Thus the Brahman's son receiving in due time the princess and her dowry, took leave of the king and returned to his own village.

Hardly, however, had Chandraprabha been married to Shashi the Pandit, when Manaswi went to him, and began to wrangle, and said, "Give me my wife!" He had recovered from the effects of his fall, and having lost her he therefore loved her—very dearly.

But Shashi proved by reference to the astrologers, priests, and ten persons as witnesses, that he had duly wedded her, and brought her to his home; "therefore," said he, "she is *my* spouse."

Manaswi swore by all holy things that he had been legally married to her, and that he was the father of her child that was about to be. "How then," continued he, "can she be *thy* spouse?" He would have summoned Muldev as a witness, but that worthy, after remonstrating with him, disappeared. He called upon Chandraprabha to confirm his statement, but she put on an innocent face, and indignantly denied ever having seen the man.

Still, continued the Baital, many people believed Manaswi's story, as it was marvellous and incredible. Even to the present day, there are many who decidedly think him legally married to the daughter of Raja Subichar.

"Then they are pestilent fellows!" cried the warrior king Vikram, who hated nothing more than clandestine and runaway matches. "No one knew that the villain, Manaswi, was the father of her child; whereas, the Pandit Shashi married her lawfully, before witnesses, and with all the ceremonies.[1] She therefore remains his wife, and the child will perform the funeral obsequies for him, and offer water to the manes of his pitris (ancestors). At least, so say law and justice."

"Which justice is often unjust enough!" cried the Vampire; "and ply thy legs, mighty Raja; let me see if thou canst reach the siras-tree before I do."

*　　　*　　　*　　　*　　　*　　　*

"The next story, O Raja Vikram, is remarkably interesting."

---

1 This would be the verdict of a Hindu jury.

THE VAMPIRE'S NINTH STORY.

SHOWING THAT A MAN'S WIFE BELONGS NOT TO HIS BODY
BUT TO HIS HEAD.

FAR and wide through the lovely land overrun by
the Arya from the Western Highlands spread the fame
of Unmadini, the beautiful daughter of Haridas the Brahman.   In the numberless odes, sonnets, and acrostics
addressed to her by a hundred Pandits and poets her
charms were sung with prodigious triteness.   Her presence was compared to light shining in a dark house;
her face to the full moon; her complexion to the yellow
champaka flower; her curls to female snakes; her eyes
to those of the deer; her eyebrows to bent bows; her
teeth to strings of little opals; her feet to rubies and red
gems,[1] and her gait to that of the wild goose.   And none
forgot to say that her voice affected the author like the
song of the kokila bird, sounding from the shadowy brake,
when the breeze blows coolly, or that the fairy beings of
Indra's heaven would have shrunk away abashed at her
loveliness.

But, Raja Vikram! all the poets failed to win the
fair Unmadini's love.   To praise the beauty of a beauty
is not to praise her.   Extol her wit and talents, which
has the zest of novelty, then you may succeed.   For the
same reason, read inversely, the plainer and cleverer is the

---

[1] Because stained with the powder of Mhendi, or the *Lawsonia
inermis* shrub.

bosom you would fire, the more personal you must be
upon the subject of its grace and loveliness. Flattery,
you know, is ever the match which kindles the flame of
love. True it is that some by roughness of demeanour
and bluntness in speech, contrasting with those whom
they call the "herd," have the art to succeed in the service of the bodyless god.[1] But even they must——

The young prince Dharma Dhwaj could not help
laughing at the thought of how this must sound in his
father's ear. And the Raja hearing the ill-timed merriment, sternly ordered the Baital to cease his immoralities
and to continue his story.

Thus the lovely Unmadini, conceiving an extreme
contempt for poets and literati, one day told her father,
who greatly loved her, that her husband must be a fine
young man who never wrote verses. Withal she insisted
strongly on mental qualities and science, being a person
of moderate mind and an adorer of talent—when not
perverted to poetry.

As you may imagine, Raja Vikram, all the beauty's
bosom friends, seeing her refuse so many good offers,
confidently predicted that she would pass through the
jungle and content herself with a bad stick, or that she
would lead ring-tailed apes in Patala.

At length when some time had elapsed, four suitors
appeared from four different countries, all of them claim-
ing equal excellence in youth and beauty, strength and
understanding. And after paying their respects to Haridas, and telling him their wishes, they were directed to
come early on the next morning and to enter upon the
first ordeal—an intellectual conversation.

This they did.

" Foolish the man," quoth the young Mahasani,

---

1 Kansa's son ; so called because the god Shiva, when struck by
his shafts, destroyed him with a fiery glance.

"that seeks permanence in this world—frail as the stem of the plantain-tree, transient as the ocean foam.

"All that is high shall presently fall; all that is low must finally perish.

"Unwillingly do the manes of the dead taste the tears shed by their kinsmen: then wail not, but perform the funeral obsequies with diligence."

"What ill-omened fellow is this?" quoth the fair Unmadini, who was sitting behind her curtain; "besides, he has dared to quote poetry!" There was little chance of success for that suitor.

"She is called a good woman, and a woman of pure descent," quoth the second suitor, "who serves him to whom her father and mother have given her; and it is written in the scriptures that a woman who in the life-time of her husband, becoming a devotee, engages in fasting, and in austere devotion, shortens his days, and hereafter falls into the fire. For it is said—

> " A woman's bliss is found not in the smile
> Of father, mother, friend, nor in herself;
> Her husband is her only portion here,
> Her heaven *hereafter*."

The word "serve," which might mean "obey," was peculiarly disagreeable to the fair one's ears, and she did not admire the check so soon placed upon her devotion, or the decided language and manner of the youth. She therefore mentally resolved never again to see that person, whom she determined to be stupid as an elephant.

"A mother," said Gunakar, the third candidate, "protects her son in babyhood, and a father when his offspring is growing up. But the man of warrior descent defends his brethren at all times. Such is the custom of the world, and such is my state. I dwell on the heads of the strong!"

Therefore those assembled together looked with great respect upon the man of valour.

Devasharma, the fourth suitor, contented himself with listening to the others, who fancied that he was overawed by their cleverness. And when it came to his turn he simply remarked, "Silence is better than speech." Being further pressed, he said, " A wise man will not proclaim his age, nor a deception practised upon himself, nor his riches, nor the loss of riches, nor family faults, nor incantations, nor conjugal love, nor medicinal prescriptions, nor religious duties, nor gifts, nor reproach, nor the infidelity of his wife."

Thus ended the first trial. The master of the house dismissed the two former speakers, with many polite expressions and some trifling presents. Then having given betel to them, scented their garments with attar, and sprinkled rose-water over their heads, he accompanied them to the door, showing much regret. The two latter speakers he begged to come on the next day.

Gunakar and Devasharma did not fail. When they entered the assembly-room and took the seats pointed out to them, the father said, " Be ye pleased to explain and make manifest the effects of your mental qualities. So shall I judge of them."

" I have made," said Gunakar, "a four-wheeled carriage, in which the power resides to carry you in a moment wherever you may purpose to go."

" I have such power over the angel of death," said Devasharma, " that I can at all times raise a corpse, and enable my friends to do the same."

Now tell me by thy brains, O warrior King Vikram, which of these two youths was the fitter husband for the maid?

Either the Raja could not answer the question, or perhaps he would not, being determined to break the spell which had already kept him walking to and fro for so many hours. Then the Baital, who had paused to let his royal carrier commit himself, seeing that the attempt had failed, proceeded without making any further comment.

The beautiful Unmadini was brought out, but she hung down her head and made no reply. Yet she took care to move both her eyes in the direction of Devasharma. Whereupon Haridas, quoting the proverb that "pearls string with pearls," formally betrothed to him his daughter.

The soldier suitor twisted the ends of his mustachios into his eyes, which were red with wrath, and fumbled with his fingers about the hilt of his sword. But he was a man of noble birth, and presently his anger passed away.

Mahasani the poet, however, being a shameless person—and when can we be safe from such?—forced himself into the assembly and began to rage and to storm, and to quote proverbs in a loud tone of voice. He remarked that in this world women are a mine of grief, a poisonous root, the abode of solicitude, the destroyers of resolution, the occasioners of fascination, and the plunderers of all virtuous qualities. From the daughter he passed to the father, and after saying hard things of him as a " Maha-Brahman,[1]" who took cows and gold and worshipped a monkey, he fell with a sweeping censure upon all priests and sons of priests, more especially Devasharma. As the bystanders remonstrated with him, he

---

1 " Great Brahman "; used contemptuously to priests who officiate for servile men. Brahmans lose their honour by the following things: By becoming servants to the king; by pursuing any secular business; by acting priests to Shudras (serviles); by officiating as priests for a whole village; and by neglecting any part of the three daily services. Many violate these rules; yet to kill a Brahman is still one of the five great Hindu sins. In the present age of the world, the Brahman may not accept a gift of cows or of gold; of course he despises the law. As regards monkey worship, a certain Rajah of Nadiya is said to have expended £10,000 in marrying two monkeys with all the parade and splendour of the Hindu rite.

became more violent, and when Haridas, who was a weak man, appeared terrified by his voice, look, and gesture, he swore a solemn oath that despite all the betrothals in the world, unless Unmadini became his wife he would commit suicide, and as a demon haunt the house and injure the inmates.

Gunakar the soldier exhorted this shameless poet to slay himself at once, and to go where he pleased. But as Haridas reproved the warrior for inhumanity, Mahasani nerved by spite, love, rage, and perversity to an heroic death, drew a noose from his bosom, rushed out of the house, and suspended himself to the nearest tree.

And, true enough, as the midnight gong struck, he appeared in the form of a gigantic and malignant Rakshasa (fiend), dreadfully frightened the household of Haridas, and carried off the lovely Unmadini, leaving word that she was to be found on the topmost peak of Himalaya.

The unhappy father hastened to the house where Devasharma lived. There, weeping bitterly and wringing his hands in despair, he told the terrible tale, and besought his intended son-in-law to be up and doing.

The young Brahman at once sought his late rival, and asked his aid. This the soldier granted at once, although he had been nettled at being conquered in love by a priestling.

The carriage was at once made ready, and the suitors set out, bidding the father be of good cheer, and that before sunset he should embrace his daughter. They then entered the vehicle ; Gunakar with cabalistic words caused it to rise high in the air, and Devasharma put to flight the demon by reciting the sacred verse,[1] " Let us meditate on the supreme splendour (or adorable light) of that Divine Ruler (the sun) who may illuminate our under-

---

[1] The celebrated Gayatri, the Moslem Kalmah.

standings. Venerable men, guided by the intelligence, salute the divine sun (Sarvitri) with oblations and praise. Om ! "

Then they returned with the girl to the house, and Haridas blessed them, praising the sun aloud in the joy of his heart. Lest other accidents might happen, he chose an auspicious planetary conjunction, and at a fortunate moment rubbed turmeric upon his daughter's hands.

The wedding was splendid, and broke the hearts of twenty-four rivals. In due time Devasharma asked leave from his father-in-law to revisit his home, and to carry with him his bride. This request being granted, he set out accompanied by Gunakar the soldier, who swore not to leave the couple before seeing them safe under their own roof-tree.

It so happened that their road lay over the summits of the wild Vindhya hills, where dangers of all kinds are as thick as shells upon the shore of the deep. Here were rocks and jagged precipices making the traveller's brain whirl when he looked into them. There impetuous torrents roared and flashed down their beds of black stone, threatening destruction to those who would cross them. Now the path was lost in the matted thorny underwood and the pitchy shades of the jungle, deep and dark as the valley of death. Then the thunder-cloud licked the earth with its fiery tongue, and its voice shook the crags and filled their hollow caves. At times, the sun was so hot, that wild birds fell dead from the air. And at every moment the wayfarers heard the trumpeting of giant elephants, the fierce howling of the tiger, the grisly laugh of the foul hyæna, and the whimpering of the wild dogs as they coursed by on the tracks of their prey.

Yet, sustained by the five-armed god[1] the little party passed safely through all these dangers. They had al-

---

1 Kama again.

most emerged from the damp glooms of the forest into the open plains which skirt the southern base of the hills, when one night the fair Unmadini saw a terrible vision.

She beheld herself wading through a sluggish pool of muddy water, which rippled, curdling as she stepped into it, and which, as she advanced, darkened with the slime raised by her feet. She was bearing in her arms the semblance of a sick child, which struggled convulsively and filled the air with dismal wails. These cries seemed to be answered by a multitude of other children, some bloated like toads, others mere skeletons lying upon the bank, or floating upon the thick brown waters of the pond. And all seemed to address their cries to her, as if she were the cause of their weeping; nor could all her efforts quiet or console them for a moment.

When the bride awoke, she related all the particulars of her ill-omened vision to her husband; and the latter, after a short pause, informed her and his friend that a terrible calamity was about to befall them. He then drew from his travelling wallet a skein of thread. This he divided into three parts, one for each, and told his companions that in case of grievous bodily injury, the bit of thread wound round the wounded part would instantly make it whole. After which he taught them the Mantra,[1] or mystical word by which the lives of men are restored to their bodies, even when they have taken their allotted places amongst the stars, and which for evident reasons I do not want to repeat. It concluded, however, with the three Vyahritis, or sacred syllables—Bhuh, Bhuvah, Svar!

Raja Vikram was perhaps a little disappointed by this declaration. He made no remark, however, and the Baital thus pursued :

As Devasharma foretold, an accident of a terrible

---

[1] From " Man," to think; primarily meaning, what makes man think.

14—2

nature did occur. On the evening of that day, as they emerged upon the plain, they were attacked by the Kiratas, or savage tribes of the mountain.[1] A small, black, wiry figure, armed with a bow and little cane arrows, stood in their way, signifying by gestures that they must halt and lay down their arms. As they continued to advance, he began to speak with a shrill chattering, like the note of an affrighted bird, his restless red eyes glared with rage, and he waved his weapon furiously round his head. Then from the rocks and thickets on both sides of the path poured a shower of shafts upon the three strangers.

The unequal combat did not last long. Gunakar, the soldier, wielded his strong right arm with fatal effect and struck down some threescore of the foes. But new swarms came on like angry hornets buzzing round the destroyer of their nests. And when he fell, Devasharma, who had left him for a moment to hide his beautiful wife in the hollow of a tree, returned, and stood fighting over the body of his friend till he also, overpowered by numbers, was thrown to the ground. Then the wild men, drawing their knives, cut off the heads of their helpless enemies, stripped their bodies of all their ornaments, and departed, leaving the woman unharmed for good luck.

When Unmadini, who had been more dead than alive during the affray, found silence succeed to the horrid din of shrieks and shouts, she ventured to creep out of her refuge in the hollow tree. And what does she behold? her husband and his friend are lying upon the ground, with their heads at a short distance from their bodies. She sat down and wept bitterly.

Presently, remembering the lesson which she had learned that very morning, she drew forth from her bosom the bit of thread and proceeded to use it. She approached

---

1 The Cirrhadæ of classical writers.

the heads to the bodies, and tied some of the magic string round each neck. But the shades of evening were fast deepening, and in her agitation, confusion and terror, she made a curious mistake by applying the heads to the wrong trunks. After which, she again sat down, and having recited her prayers, she pronounced, as her husband had taught her, the life-giving incantation.

In a moment the dead men were made alive. They opened their eyes, shook themselves, sat up and handled their limbs as if to feel that all was right. But something or other appeared to them all wrong. They placed their palms upon their foreheads, and looked downwards, and started to their feet and began to stare at their hands and legs. Upon which they scrutinized the very scanty articles of dress which the wild men had left upon them, and lastly one began to eye the other with curious puzzled looks.

The wife, attributing their gestures to the confusion which one might expect to find in the brains of men who have just undergone so great a trial as amputation of the head must be, stood before them for a moment or two. She then with a cry of gladness flew to the bosom of the individual who was, as she supposed, her husband. He repulsed her, telling her that she was mistaken. Then, blushing deeply in spite of her other emotions, she threw both her beautiful arms round the neck of the person who must be, she naturally concluded, the right man. To her utter confusion, he also shrank back from her embrace.

Then a horrid thought flashed across her mind: she perceived her fatal mistake, and her heart almost ceased to beat.

"This is *thy* wife!" cried the Brahman's head that had been fastened to the soldier's body.

"No; she is *thy* wife!" replied the soldier's head which had been placed upon the Brahman's body.

"Then she is *my* wife!" rejoined the first compound creature.

"By no means! she is *my* wife," cried the second.

"What then am I?" asked Devasharma-Gunakar.

"What do you think I am?" answered Gunakar-Devasharma, with another question.

"Unmadini shall be *mine*," quoth the head.

"You lie, she shall be *mine*," shouted the body.

"Holy Yama,[1] hear the villain," exclaimed both of them at the same moment.

  * * * * * *

In short, having thus begun, they continued to quarrel violently, each one declaring that the beautiful Unmadini belonged to him, and to him only. How to settle their dispute Brahma the Lord of creatures only knows. I do not, except by cutting off their heads once more, and by putting them in their proper places. And I am quite sure, O Raja Vikram! that thy wits are quite unfit to answer the question, To which of these two is the beautiful Unmadini wife? It is even said—amongst us Baitals —that when this pair of half-husbands appeared in the presence of the Just King, a terrible confusion arose, each head declaiming all the sins and peccadilloes which its body had committed, and that Yama the holy ruler himself hit his forefinger with vexation.[2]

Here the young prince Dharma Dhwaj burst out laughing at the ridiculous idea of the wrong heads. And the warrior king, who, like single-minded fathers in

---

1 The Hindu Pluto; also called the Just King.

2 Yama judges the dead, whose souls go to him in four hours and forty minntes; therefore a corpse cannot be burned till after that time. His residence is Yamálaya, and it is on the south side of the earth; down South, as we say. (I, Sam. xxv. 1, and xxx. 15). The Hebrews, like the Hindus, held the northern parts of the world to be higher than the southern. Hindus often joke a man who is seen walking in that direction, and ask him where he is going.

general, was ever in the idea that his son had a velleity
for deriding and otherwise vexing him, began a severe
course of reproof. He reminded the prince of the common saying that merriment without cause degrades a man
in the opinion of his fellows, and indulged him with a
quotation extensively used by grave fathers, namely, that
the loud laugh bespeaks a vacant mind. After which he
proceeded with much pompousness to pronounce the following opinion:

"It is said in the Shastras ——"

"Your majesty need hardly display so much erudition! Doubtless it comes from the lips of Jayudeva or
some other one of your Nine Gems of Science, who know
much more about their songs and their stanzas than they
do about their scriptures," insolently interrupted the
Baital, who never lost an opportunity of carping at those
reverend men.

"It is said in the Shastras," continued Raja Vikram
sternly, after hesitating whether he should or should not
administer a corporeal correction to the Vampire, "that
Mother Ganga[1] is the queen amongst rivers, and the
mountain Sumeru[2] is the monarch among mountains, and
the tree Kalpavriksha[3] is the king of all trees, and the
head of man is the best and most excellent of limbs.
And thus, according to this reason, the wife belonged to
him whose noblest position claimed her."

"The next thing your majesty will do, I suppose,"
continued the Baital, with a sneer, "is to support the
opinions of the Digambara, who maintains that the soul

---

1 The "Ganges," in heaven called Mandakini. I have no idea
why we still adhere to our venerable corruption of the word.

2 The fabulous mountain supposed by Hindu geographers to
occupy the centre of the universe.

3 The all-bestowing tree in Indra's Paradise, which grants
everything asked of it. It is the Tuba of Al-Islam, and is not un-
known to the Apocryphal New Testament.

is exceedingly rarefied, confined to one place, and of equal dimensions with the body, or the fancies of that worthy philosopher Jaimani, who, conceiving soul and mind and matter to be things purely synonymous, asserts outwardly and writes in his books that the brain is the organ of the mind which is acted upon by the immortal soul, but who inwardly and verily believes that the brain is the mind, and consequently that the brain is the soul or spirit or whatever you please to call it; in fact, that soul is a natural faculty of the body. A pretty doctrine, indeed, for a Brahman to hold. You might as well agree with me at once that the soul of man resides, when at home, either in a vein in the breast, or in the pit of his stomach, or that half of it is in a man's brain and the other or reasoning half is in his heart, an organ of his body."

"What has all this string of words to do with the matter, Vampire?" asked Raja Vikram angrily.

"Only," said the demon laughing, "that in my opinion, as opposed to the Shastras and to Raja Vikram, that the beautiful Unmadini belonged, not to the head part but to the body part. Because the latter has an immortal soul in the pit of its stomach, whereas the former is a box of bone, more or less thick, and contains brains which are of much the same consistence as those of a calf."

" Villain !" exclaimed the Raja, " does not the soul or conscious life enter the body through the sagittal suture and lodge in the brain, thence to contemplate, through the same opening, the divine perfections ? "

" I must, however, bid you farewell for the moment, O warrior king, Sakadhipati-Vikramaditya[1]! I feel a sudden and ardent desire to change this cramped position for one more natural to me."

---

1 " Vikramaditya, Lord of the Saka." This is *prévoyance* on the part of the Vampire ; the king had not acquired the title.

The warrior monarch had so far committed himself that he could not prevent the Vampire from flitting. But he lost no more time in following him than a grain of mustard, in its fall, stays on a cow's horn. And when he had thrown him over his shoulder, the king desired him of his own accord to begin a new tale.

" O my left eyelid flutters," exclaimed the Baital in despair, " my heart throbs, my sight is dim : surely now beginneth the end. It is as Vidhata hath written on my forehead—how can it be otherwise [1] ? Still listen, O mighty Raja, whilst I recount to you a true story, and Saraswati [2] sit on my tongue."

---

[1] On the sixth day after the child's birth, the god Vidhata writes all its fate upon its forehead. The Moslems have a similar idea,.and probably it passed to the Hindus.

[2] Goddess of eloquence. " The waters of the Saraswati" is the classical Hindu phrase for the mirage.

THE VAMPIRE'S TENTH STORY.[1]

OF THE MARVELLOUS DELICACY OF THREE QUEENS.

THE Baital said, O king, in the Gaur country, Vardh-man by name, there is a city, and one called Gunshekhar was the Raja of that land. His minister was one Abhaich-and, a Jain, by whose teachings the king also came into the Jain faith.

The worship of Shiva and of Vishnu, gifts of cows, gifts of lands, gifts of rice balls, gaming and spirit-drink-ing, all these he prohibited. In the city no man could get leave to do them, and as for bones, into the Ganges no man was allowed to throw them, and in these matters the minister, having taken orders from the king, caused a proclamation to be made about the city, saying, " Who-ever these acts shall do, the Raja having confiscated, will punish him and banish him from the city."

Now one day the Díwán[2] began to say to the Raja, " O great king, to the decisions of the Faith be pleased to

[1] This story is perhaps the least interesting in the collection. I have translated it literally, in order to give an idea of the original. The reader will remark in it the source of our own nursery tale about the princess who was so high born and delicately bred, that she could discover the three peas laid beneath a straw mattress and four feather beds. The Hindus, however, believe that Sybaritism can be carried so far; I remember my Pandit asserting the truth of the story.

[2] A minister. The word, as is the case with many in this col-lection, is quite modern Moslem, and anachronistic.

give ear. Whosoever takes the life of another, his life also in the future birth is taken : this very sin causes him to be born again and again upon earth and to die.   And thus he ever continues to be born again and to die. Hence for one who has found entrance into this world to cultivate religion is right and proper.   Be pleased to behold !   By love, by wrath, by pain, by desire, and by fascination overpowered, the gods Brahma, Vishnu, and Mahadeva (Shiva) in various ways upon the earth are ever becoming incarnate.   Far better than they is the Cow, who is free from passion, enmity, drunkenness, anger, covetousness, and inordinate affection, who supports mankind, and whose progeny in many ways give ease and solace to the creatures of the world.   These deities and sages (munis) believe in the Cow.[1]

" For such reason to believe in the gods is not good. Upon this earth be pleased to believe in the Cow.   It is our duty to protect the life of everyone, beginning from the elephant, through ants, beasts, and birds, up to man. In the world righteousness equal to that there is none. Those who, eating the flesh of other creatures, increase

---

1 The cow is called the mother of the gods, and is declared by Brahma, the first person of the triad, Vishnu and Shiva being the second and the third, to be a proper object of worship. "If a European speak to the Hindu about eating the flesh of cows," says an old missionary, " they immediately raise their hands to their ears ; yet milkmen, carmen, and farmers beat the cow as unmercifully as a carrier of coals beats his ass in England." The Jains or Jainas (from ji, to conquer ; as subduing the passions) are one of the atheistical sects with whom the Brahmans have of old carried on the fiercest religious controversies, ending in many a sanguinary fight.   Their tenets are consequently exaggerated and ridiculed, as in the text.   They believe that there is no such God as the common notions on the subject point out, and they hold that the highest act of virtue is to abstain from injuring sentient creatures.   Man does not possess an immortal spirit : death is the same to Brahma and to a fly.   Therefore there is no heaven or hell separate from present pleasure or pain.   Hindu Epicureans !—" Epicuri de grege porci."

their own flesh, shall in the fulness of time assuredly obtain the fruition of Narak [1] ; hence for a man it is proper to attend to the conversation of life. They who understand not the pain of other creatures, and who continue to slay and to devour them, last but few days in the land, and return to mundane existence, maimed, limping, one-eyed, blind, dwarfed, hunchbacked, and imperfect in such wise. Just as they consume the bodies of beasts and of birds, even so they end by spoiling their own bodies. From drinking spirits also the great sin arises, hence the consuming of spirits and flesh is not advisable."

The minister having in this manner explained to the king the sentiments of his own mind, so brought him over to the Jain faith, that whatever he said, so the king did. Thus in Brahmans, in Jogis, in Janganis, in Sevras, in Sannyasis,[2] and in religious mendicants, no man believed, and according to this creed the rule was carried on.

---

1 Narak is one of the multitudinous places of Hindu punishment, said to adjoin the residence of Ajarna. The less cultivated Jains believe in a region of torment. The illuminati, however, have a sovereign contempt for the Creator, for a future state, and for all religious ceremonies. As Hindus, however, they believe in future births of mankind, somewhat influenced by present actions. The "next birth" in the mouth of a Hindu, we are told, is the same as "to-morrow" in the mouth of a Christian. The metempsychosis is on an extensive scale : according to some, a person who loses human birth must pass through eight millions of successive incarnations—fish, insects, worms, birds, and beasts—before he can reappear as a man.

2 Jogi, or Yogi, properly applies to followers of the Yoga or Patanjala school, who by ascetic practices acquire power over the elements. Vulgarly, it is a general term for mountebank vagrants, worshippers of Shiva. The Janganis adore the same deity, and carry about a Linga. The Sevras are Jain beggars, who regard their chiefs as superior to the gods of other sects. The Sannyasis are mendicant followers of Shiva ; they never touch metals or fire, and, in religious parlance, they take up the staff. They are opposed to the Viragis, worshippers of Vishnu, who contend as strongly against the worshippers of gods who receive bloody offerings, as a Christian could do against idolatry.

Now one day, being in the power of Death, Raja Gunshekhar died. Then his son Dharmadhwaj sat upon the carpet (throne), and began to rule. Presently he caused the minister Abhaichand to be seized, had his head shaved all but seven locks of hair, ordered his face to be blackened, and mounting him on an ass, with drums beaten, had him led all about the city, and drove him from the kingdom. From that time he carried on his rule free from all anxiety.

It so happened that in the season of spring, the king Dharmadhwaj, taking his queens with him, went for a stroll in the garden, where there was a large tank with lotuses blooming within it. The Raja admiring its beauty, took off his clothes and went down to bathe.

After plucking a flower and coming to the bank, he was going to give it into the hands of one of his queens, when it slipped from his fingers, fell upon her foot, and broke it with the blow. Then the Raja being alarmed, at once came out of the tank, and began to apply remedies to her.

Hereupon night came on, and the moon shone brightly : the falling of its rays on the body of the second queen formed blisters. And suddenly from a distance the sound of a wooden pestle came out of a householder's dwelling, when the third queen fainted away with a severe pain in the head.

Having spoken thus much the Baital said "O my king! of these three which is the most delicate ?" The Raja answered, " She indeed is the most delicate who fainted in consequence of the headache." The Baital hearing this speech, went and hung himself from the very same tree, and the Raja, having gone there and taken him down and fastened him in the bundle and placed him on his shoulder, carried him away.

THE VAMPIRE'S ELEVENTH STORY.

WHICH PUZZLES RAJA VIKRAM.

THERE is a queer time coming, O Raja Vikram!—a queer time coming (said the Vampire), a queer time coming. Elderly people like you talk abundantly about the good old days that were, and about the degeneracy of the days that are. I wonder what you would say if you could but look forward a few hundred years.

Brahmans shall disgrace themselves by becoming soldiers and being killed, and Serviles (Shudras) shall dishonour themselves by wearing the thread of the twice-born, and by refusing to be slaves; in fact, society shall be all "mouth" and mixed castes.[1] The courts of justice shall be disused; the great works of peace shall no longer be undertaken; wars shall last six weeks, and their causes shall be clean forgotten; the useful arts and great sciences shall die starved; there shall be no Gems of Science; there shall be a hospital for destitute kings, those, at least, who do not lose their heads, and no Vikrama——

A severe shaking stayed for a moment the Vampire's tongue.

---

1 The Brahman, or priest, is supposed to proceed from the mouth of Brahma, the creating person of the Triad ; the Khshatriyas (soldiers) from his arms ; the Vaishyas (enterers into business) from his thighs ; and the Shudras, "who take refuge in the Brahmans," from his feet. Only high caste men should assume the thread at the age of puberty.

He presently resumed.   Briefly, building tanks;
feeding Brahmans ; lying when one ought to lie; suicide ;
the burning of widows, and the burying of live children,
shall become utterly unfashionable.

The consequence of this singular degeneracy, O
mighty Vikram, will be that strangers shall dwell beneath
the roof tree in Bharat Khanda (India), and impure barbarians shall call the land their own.   They come from a
wonderful country, and I am most surprised that they
bear it.   The sky which ought to be gold and blue is
there grey, a kind of dark white ; the sun looks deadly
pale, and the moon as if he were dead.[1]   The sea, when
not dirty green, glistens with yellowish foam, and as you
approach the shore, tall ghastly cliffs, like the skeletons of
giants, stand up to receive or ready to repel.   During the
greater part of the sun's Dakhshanayan (southern declina-
tion) the country is covered with a sort of cold white stuff
which dazzles the eyes ; and at such times the air is obscured with what appears to be a shower of white feathers
or flocks of cotton.   At other seasons there is a pale glare
produced by the mist clouds which spread themselves
over the lower firmament.   Even the faces of the people
are white; the men are white when not painted blue; the
women are whiter, and the children are whitest : these
indeed often have white hair.

"Truly," exclaimed Dharma Dhwaj, "says the proverb, 'Whoso seeth the world telleth many a lie.'"

At present (resumed the Vampire, not heeding the
interruption), they run about naked in the woods, being
merely Hindu outcastes.   Presently they will change—
the wonderful white Pariahs !   They will eat all food
indifferently, domestic fowls, onions, hogs fed in the street,
donkeys, horses, hares, and (most horrible !) the flesh of
the sacred cow.   They will imbibe what resembles meat

---

1 Soma, the moon, I have said, is masculine in India.

of colocynth, mixed with water, producing a curious frothy liquid, and a fiery stuff which burns the mouth, for their milk will be mostly chalk and pulp of brains; they will ignore the sweet juices of fruits and sugar-cane, and as for the pure element they will drink it, but only as medicine, They will shave their beards instead of their heads, and stand upright when they should sit down, and squat upon a wooden frame instead of a carpet, and appear in red and black like the children of Yama.[1] They will never offer sacrifices to the manes of ancestors, leaving them after their death to fry in the hottest of places. Yet will they perpetually quarrel and fight about their faith ; for their tempers are fierce, and they would burst if they could not harm one another. Even now the children, who amuse themselves with making puddings on the shore, that is to say, heaping up the sand, always end their little games with "punching," which means shutting the hand and striking one another's heads, and it is soon found that the children are the fathers of the men.

These wonderful white outcastes will often be ruled by female chiefs, and it is likely that the habit of prostrating themselves before a woman who has not the power of cutting off a single head, may account for their unusual degeneracy and uncleanness. They will consider no occupation so noble as running after a jackal; they will dance for themselves, holding on to strange women, and they will take a pride in playing upon instruments, like young music girls.

The women, of course, relying upon the aid of the female chieftains, will soon emancipate themselves from the rules of modesty. They will eat with their husbands and with other men, and yawn and sit carelessly before them showing the backs of their heads. They will impudently quote the words, "By confinement at home, even under affectionate and observant guardians,

---

1 Pluto.

women are not secure, but those are really safe who are
guarded by their own inclinations " ; as the poet sang—

Woman obeys one only word, her heart.

They will not allow their husbands to have more than one
wife, and even the single wife will not be his slave when
he needs her services, busying herself in the collection of
wealth, in ceremonial purification, and feminine duty ; in
the preparation of daily food and in the superintendence
of household utensils.   What said Rama of Sita his wife ?
" If I chanced to be angry, she bore my impatience like
the patient earth without a murmur; in the hour of necessity she cherished me as a mother does her child ; in the
moments of repose she was a lover to me; in times of
gladness she was to me as a friend."   And it is said, "a
religious wife assists her husband in his worship with a
spirit as devout as his own.   She gives her whole mind to
make him happy ; she is as faithful to him as a shadow to
the body, and she esteems him, whether poor or rich,
good or bad, handsome or deformed.   In his absence or
his sickness she renounces every gratification ; at his
death she dies with him, and he enjoys heaven as the
fruit of her virtuous deeds.   Whereas if she be guilty of
many wicked actions and he should die first, he must
suffer much for the demerits of his wife."

But these women will talk aloud, and scold as the
braying ass, and make the house a scene of variance, like
the snake with the ichneumon, the owl with the crow, for
they have no fear of losing their noses or parting with
their ears.   They will (O my mother !) converse with
strange men and take their hands ; they will receive
presents from them, and, worst of all, they will show their
white faces openly without the least sense of shame ; they
will ride publicly in chariots and mount horses, whose
points they pride themselves upon knowing, and eat
and drink in crowded places—their husbands looking on
the while, and perhaps even leading them through the

streets. And she will be deemed the pinnacle of the pagoda of perfection, that most excels in wit and shamelessness, and who can turn to water the livers of most men. They will dance and sing instead of minding their children, and when these grow up they will send them out of the house to shift for themselves, and care little if they never see them again.[1] But the greatest sin of all will be this : when widowed they will ever be on the look-out for a second husband, and instances will be known of women fearlessly marrying three, four, and five times.[2] You would think that all this licence satisfies them. But no ! The more they have the more their weak minds covet. The men have admitted them to an equality, they will aim at an absolute superiority, and claim respect and homage ; they will eternally raise tempests about their rights, and if anyone should venture to chastise them as they deserve, they would call him a coward and run off to the judge.

The men will, I say, be as wonderful about their women as about all other matters. The sage of Bharat Khanda guards the frail sex strictly, knowing its frailty, and avoids teaching it to read and write, which it will assuredly use for a bad purpose. For women are ever subject to the god[3] with the sugar-cane bow and string of bees, and arrows tipped with heating blossoms, and to him they will ever surrender man, dhan, tan—mind, wealth, and body. When, by exceeding cunning, all human precautions have been made vain, the wise man bows to Fate, and he forgets, or he tries to forget, the past. Whereas this race of white Pariahs will purposely

---

1 Nothing astonishes Hindus so much as the apparent want of affection between the European parent and child.

2 A third marriage is held improper and baneful to a Hindu woman. Hence, before the nuptials they betroth the man to a tree, upon which the evil expends itself, and the tree dies.

3 Kama.

lead their women into every kind of temptation, and, when an accident occurs, they will rage at and accuse them, killing ten thousand with a word, and cause an uproar, and talk scandal and be scandalized, and go before the magistrate, and make all the evil as public as possible. One would think they had in every way done their duty to their women !

And when all this change shall have come over them, they will feel restless and take flight, and fall like locusts upon the Aryavartta (land of India). Starving in their own country, they will find enough to eat here, and to carry away also. They will be mischievous as the saw with which ornament-makers trim their shells, and cut ascending as well as descending. To cultivate their friendship will be like making a gap in the water, and their partisans will ever fare worse than their foes. They will be selfish as crows, which, though they eat every kind of flesh, will not permit other birds to devour that of the crow.

In the beginning they will hire a shop near the mouth of mother Ganges, and they will sell lead and bullion, fine and coarse woollen cloths, and all the materials for intoxication. Then they will begin to send for soldiers beyond the sea, and to enlist warriors in Zambudwipa (India). They will from shopkeepers become soldiers : they will beat and be beaten ; they will win and lose ; but the power of their star and the enchantments of their Queen Kompani, a daina or witch who can draw the blood out of a man and slay him with a look, will turn everything to their good. Presently the noise of their armies shall be as the roaring of the sea ; the dazzling of their arms shall blind the eyes like lightning ; their battle-fields shall be as the dissolution of the world ; and the slaughter-ground shall resemble a garden of plantain trees after a storm. At length they shall spread like the march of a host of ants over the land. They will

15—2

swear, " Dehar Ganga[1]!" and they hate nothing so much as being compelled to destroy an army, to take and loot a city, or to add a rich slip of territory to their rule. And yet they will go on killing and capturing and adding region to region, till the Abode of Snow (Himalaya) confines them to the north, the Sindhu-naddi (Indus) to the west, and elsewhere the sea. Even in this, too, they will demean themselves as lords and masters, scarcely allowing poor Samudradevta[2] to rule his own waves.

Raja Vikram was in a silent mood, otherwise he would not have allowed such ill-omened discourse to pass uninterrupted. Then the Baital, who in vain had often paused to give the royal carrier a chance of asking him a curious question, continued his recital in a dissonant and dissatisfied tone of voice.

By my feet and your head,[3] O warrior king ! it will fare badly in those days for the Rajas of Hindustan, when the red-coated men of Shaka[4] shall come amongst them. Listen to my words.

In the Vindhya Mountain there will be a city named Dharmapur, whose king will be called Mahabul. He will be a mighty warrior, well-skilled in the dhanur-veda (art of war),[5] and will always lead his own armies to the field. He will duly regard all the omens, such as a storm at the beginning of the march, an earthquake, the implements of war dropping from the hands of the soldiery, screaming vultures passing over or walking near the army, the clouds and the sun's rays waxing red, thunder in a clear sky, the

---

1 An oath, meaning, "From such a falsehood preserve me, Ganges!"

2 The Indian Neptune.

3 A highly insulting form of adjuration.

4 The British Islands—according to Wilford.

5 Literally the science (veda) of the bow (dhanush). This weapon, as everything amongst the Hindus, had a divine origin; it was of three kinds—the common bow, the pellet or stone bow, and the crossbow or catapult.

moon appearing small as a star, the dropping of blood from the clouds, the falling of lightning bolts, darkness filling the four quarters of the heavens, a corpse or a pan of water being carried to the right of the army, the sight of a female beggar with dishevelled hair, dressed in red, and preceding the vanguard, the starting of the flesh over the left ribs of the commander-in-chief, and the weeping or turning back of the horses when urged forward.

He will encourage his men to single combats, and will carefully train them to gymnastics. Many of the wrestlers and boxers will be so strong that they will often beat all the extremities of the antagonist into his body, or break his back, or rend him into two pieces. He will promise heaven to those who shall die in the front of battle, and he will have them taught certain dreadful expressions of abuse to be interchanged with the enemy when commencing the contest. Honours will be conferred on those who never turn their backs in an engagement, who manifest a contempt of death, who despise fatigue, as well as the most formidable enemies, who shall be found invincible in every combat, and who display a courage which increases before danger, like the glory of the sun advancing to his meridian splendour.

But King Mahabul will be attacked by the white Pariahs, who, as usual, will employ against him gold, fire, and steel. With gold they will win over his best men, and persuade them openly to desert when the army is drawn out for battle. They will use the terrible " fire weapon,[1]" large and small tubes, which discharge flame and smoke, and bullets as big as those hurled by the bow of Bharata.[2] And instead of using swords and shields, they will fix daggers to the end of their tubes, and thrust with them like lances.

---

1 It is a disputed point whether the ancient Hindus did or did not know the use of gunpowder.

2 It is said to have discharged balls, each 6,400 pounds in weight.

Mahabul, distinguished by valour and military skill, will march out of his city to meet the white foe. In front will be the ensigns, bells, cows'-tails, and flags, the latter painted with the bird Garura,[1] the bull of Shiva, the Bauhinia tree, the monkey-god Hanuman, the lion and the tiger, the fish, an alms-dish, and seven palm-trees. Then will come the footmen armed with fire-tubes, swords and shields, spears and daggers, clubs, and bludgeons. They will be followed by fighting men on horses and oxen, on camels and elephants. The musicians, the water-carriers, and lastly the stores on carriages, will bring up the rear.

The white outcastes will come forward in a long thin red thread, and vomiting fire like the Jwalamukhi.[2] King Mahabul will receive them with his troops formed in a circle; another division will be in the shape of a half-moon; a third like a cloud, whilst others shall represent a lion, a tiger, a carriage, a lily, a giant, and a bull. But as the elephants will all turn round when they feel the fire, and trample upon their own men, and as the cavalry defiling in front of the host will openly gallop away; Mahabul, being thus without resource, will enter his palanquin, and accompanied by his queen and their only daughter, will escape at night-time into the forest.

The unfortunate three will be deserted by their small party, and live for a time on jungle food, fruits and roots; they will even be compelled to eat game. After some days they will come in sight of a village, which Mahabul will enter to obtain victuals. There the wild Bhils, famous for long years, will come up, and surrounding the party, will bid the Raja throw down his arms. Thereupon Mahabul, skilful in aiming, twanging and wielding

---

1 A kind of Mercury, a god with the head and wings of a bird, who is the Vahan or vehicle of the second person of the Triad, Vishnu.

2 The celebrated burning springs of Baku, near the Caspian, are so called. There are many other " fire mouths."

the bow on all sides, so as to keep off the bolts of the enemy, will discharge his bolts so rapidly, that one will drive forward another, and none of the barbarians will be able to approach.   But he will have failed to bring his quiver containing an inexhaustible store of arms, some of which, pointed with diamonds, shall have the faculty of returning again to their case after they have done their duty. The conflict will continue three hours, and many of the Bhils will be slain: at length a shaft will cleave the king's skull, he will fall dead, and one of the wild men will come up and cut off his head.

When the queen and the princess shall have seen that Mahabul fell dead, they will return to the forest weeping and beating their bosoms.   They will thus escape the Bhils, and after journeying on for four miles, at length they will sit down wearied, and revolve many thoughts in their minds.

They are very lovely (continued the Vampire), as I see them with the eye of clear-seeing.   What beautiful hair ! it hangs down like the tail of the cow of Tartary, or like the thatch of a house ; it is shining as oil, dark as the clouds, black as blackness itself.   What charming faces ! likest to water-lilies, with eyes as the stones in unripe mangos, noses resembling the beaks of parrots, teeth like pearls set in corals, ears like those of the red-throated vulture, and mouths like the water of life. What excellent forms ! breasts like boxes containing essences, the unopened fruit of plantains or a couple of crabs ; loins the width of a span, like the middle of the viol ; legs like the trunk of an elephant, and feet like the yellow lotus.

And a fearful place is that jungle, a dense dark mass of thorny shrubs, and ropy creepers, and tall canes, and tangled brake, and gigantic gnarled trees, which groan wildly in the night wind's embrace.   But a wilder horror urges the unhappy women on ; they fear the polluting touch of the Bhils; once more they rise and plunge deeper into its gloomy depths.

The day dawns. The white Pariahs have done their usual work. They have cut off the hands of some, the feet and heads of others, whilst many they have crushed into shapeless masses, or scattered in pieces upon the ground. The field is strewed with corpses, the river runs red, so that the dogs and jackals swim in blood; the birds of prey sitting on the branches, drink man's life from the stream, and enjoy the sickening smell of burnt flesh.

Such will be the scenes acted in the fair land of Bharat.

Perchance two white outcastes, father and son, who with a party of men are scouring the forest and slaying everything, fall upon the path which the women have taken shortly before. Their attention is attracted by footprints leading towards a place full of tigers, leopards, bears, wolves, and wild dogs. And they are utterly confounded when, after inspection, they discover the sex of the wanderers.

"How is it," shall say the father, "that the footprints of mortals are seen in this part of the forest?"

The son shall reply, "Sir, these are the marks of women's feet: a man's foot would not be so small."

"It is passing strange," shall rejoin the elder white Pariah, "but thou speakest truth. Certainly such a soft and delicate foot cannot belong to anyone but a woman."

"They have only just left the track," shall continue the son, "and look! this is the step of a married woman. See how she treads on the inside of her sole, because of the bending of her ankles." And the younger white outcaste shall point to the queen's footprints.

"Come, let us search the forest for them," shall cry the father, "what an opportunity of finding wives fortune has thrown in our hands. But no! thou art in error," he shall continue, after examining the track pointed out by his son, "in supposing this to be the sign of a matron. Look at the other, it is much longer; the toes have scarcely touched the ground, whereas the marks of the heels are deep. Of a truth *this* must be the married woman." And the elder white outcaste shall point to the footprints of the princess.

" Then," shall reply the son, who admires the shorter foot, " let us first seek them, and when we find them, give to me her who has the short feet, and take the other to wife thyself."

Having made this agreement they shall proceed on their way, and presently they shall find the women lying on the earth, half dead with fatigue and fear. Their legs and feet are scratched and torn by brambles, their ornaments have fallen off, and their garments are in strips. The two white outcastes find little difficulty, the first surprise over, in persuading the unhappy women to follow them home, and with great delight, conformably to their arrangement, each takes up his prize on his horse and rides back to the tents. The son takes the queen, and the father the princess.

In due time two marriages come to pass; the father, according to agreement, espouses the long foot, and the son takes to wife the short foot. And after the usual interval, the elder white outcaste, who had married the daughter, rejoices at the birth of a boy, and the younger white outcaste, who had married the mother, is gladdened by the sight of a girl.

Now then, by my feet and your head, O warrior king Vikram, answer me one question. What relationship will there be between the children of the two white Pariahs ?

Vikram's brow waxed black as a charcoal-burner's, when he again heard the most irreverent oath ever proposed to mortal king. The question presently attracted his attention, and he turned over the Baital's words in his head, confusing the ties of filiality, brotherhood, and relationship, and connection in general.

" Hem ! " said the warrior king, at last perplexed, and remembering, in his perplexity, that he had better hold his tongue—" ahem ! "

" I think your majesty spoke ? " asked the Vampire, in an inquisitive and insinuating tone of voice.

" Hem ! " ejaculated the monarch.

The Baital held his peace for a few minutes, coughing once or twice impatiently. He suspected that the extraordinary nature of this last tale, combined with the use of the future tense, had given rise to a taciturnity so unexpected in the warrior king. He therefore asked if Vikram the Brave would not like to hear another little anecdote.

"This time the king did not even say "hem!" Having walked at an unusually rapid pace, he distinguished at a distance the fire kindled by the devotee, and he hurried towards it with an effort which left him no breath wherewith to speak, even had he been so inclined.

"Since your majesty is so completely dumbfoundered by it, perhaps this acute young prince may be able to answer my question?" insinuated the Baital, after a few minutes of anxious suspense.

But Dharma Dhwaj answered not a syllable.

CONCLUSION.

At Raja Vikram's silence the Baital was greatly surprised, and he praised the royal courage and resolution to the skies. Still he did not give up the contest at once.

"Allow me, great king," pursued the Demon, in a dry tone of voice, "to wish you joy. After so many failures you have at length succeeded in repressing your loquacity. I will not stop to enquire whether it was humility and self-restraint which prevented your answering my last question, or whether it was mere ignorance and inability. Of course I suspect the latter, but to say the truth your condescension in at last taking a Vampire's advice, flatters me so much, that I will not look too narrowly into cause or motive."

Raja Vikram winced, but maintained a stubborn silence, squeezing his lips lest they should open involuntarily.

"Now, however, your majesty has mortified, we will suppose, a somewhat exacting vanity, I also will in my turn forego the pleasure which I had anticipated in seeing you a corpse and in entering your royal body for a short time, just to know how queer it must feel to be a king. And what is more, I will now perform my original promise, and you shall derive from me a benefit which none but myself can bestow. First, however, allow me to ask you, will you let me have a little more air?"

Dharma Dhwaj pulled his father's sleeve, but this

time Raja Vikram required no reminder : wild horses or
the executioner's saw, beginning at the shoulder, would
not have drawn a word from him. Observing his
obstinate silence, the Baital, with an ominous smile, continued :

"Now give ear, O warrior king, to what I am about
to tell thee, and bear in mind the giant's saying, 'A man
is justified in killing one who has a design to kill him.'
The young merchant Mal Deo, who placed such magnificent presents at your royal feet, and Shanta-Shil the
devotee saint, who works his spells, incantations, and
magical rites in a cemetery on the banks of the Godaveri
river, are, as thou knowest, one person—the terrible Jogi,
whose wrath your father aroused in his folly, and whose
revenge your blood alone can satisfy. With regard to
myself, the oilman's son, the same Jogi, fearing lest I
might interfere with his projects of universal dominion,
slew me by the power of his penance, and has kept me
suspended, a trap for you, head downwards from the
siras-tree.

"That Jogi it was, you now know, who sent you to
fetch me back to him on your back. And when you cast
me at his feet he will return thanks to you and praise
your valour, perseverance and resolution to the skies. I
warn you to beware. He will lead you to the shrine of
Durga, and when he has finished his adoration he will say
to you, 'O great king, salute my deity with the eight-
limbed reverence.'"

Here the Vampire whispered for a time and in a low
tone, lest some listening goblin might carry his words if
spoken out loud to the ears of the devotee Shanta-Shil.

At the end of the monologue a rustling sound was
heard. It proceeded from the Baital, who was disengag-
ing himself from the dead body in the bundle, and the
burden became sensibly lighter upon the monarch's back.

The departing Baital, however, did not forget to bid

farewell to the warrior king and to his son. He compli-
mented the former for the last time, in his own way, upon
the royal humility and the prodigious self-mortification
which he had displayed—qualities, he remarked, which
never failed to ensure the proprietor's success in all the
worlds.

There he found the Jogi.

Raja Vikram stepped out joyfully, and soon reached
the burning ground. There he found the Jogi, dressed in
his usual habit, a deerskin thrown over his back, and
twisted reeds instead of a garment hanging round his
loins. The hair had fallen from his limbs and his skin
was bleached ghastly white by exposure to the elements.
A fire seemed to proceed from his mouth, and the matted

locks dropping from his head to the ground were changed by the rays of the sun to the colour of gold or saffron. He had the beard of a goat and the ornaments of a king ; his shoulders were high and his arms long, reaching to his knees : his nails grew to such a length as to curl round the ends of his fingers, and his feet resembled those of a tiger. He was drumming upon a skull, and incessantly exclaiming, " Ho, Kali ! ho, Durga ! ho, Devi ! "

As before, strange beings were holding their carnival in the Jogi's presence. Monstrous Asuras, giant goblins, stood grimly gazing upon the scene with fixed eyes and motionless features. Rakshasas and messengers of Yama, fierce and hideous, assumed at pleasure the shapes of foul and ferocious beasts. Nagas and Bhutas, partly human and partly bestial, disported themselves in throngs about the upper air, and were dimly seen in the faint light of the dawn. Mighty Daityas, Bramha-daityas, and Pretas, the size of a man's thumb, or dried up like leaves, and Pisachas of terrible power guarded the place. There were enormous goats, vivified by the spirits of those who had slain Brahmans ; things with the bodies of men and the faces of horses, camels and monkeys ; hideous worms containing the souls of those priests who had drunk spirituous liquors ; men with one leg and one ear, and mischievous blood-sucking demons, who in life had stolen church property. There were vultures, wretches that had violated the beds of their spiritual fathers, restless ghosts that had loved low-caste women, shades for whom funeral rites had not been performed, and who could not cross the dread Vaitarani stream,[1] and vital souls fresh from the horrors of Tamisra, or utter darkness, and the Usipatra Vana, or the sword-leaved forest. Pale spirits, Alayas, Gumas, Baitals, and Yakshas,[2] beings of a base

---

1 The Hindu Styx.

2 From Yaksha, to eat ; as Rakshasas are from Raksha, to preserve.—See Hardy's *Manual of Buddhism*, p. 57.

and vulgar order, glided over the ground, amongst corpses and skeletons animated by female fiends, Dakinis, Yoginis, Hakinis, and Shankinis, which were dancing in frightful revelry. The air was filled with supernatural sights and sounds, cries of owls and jackals, cats and crows, dogs, asses, and vultures, high above which rose the clashing of the bones with which the Jogi sat drumming upon the skull before him, and tending a huge cauldron of oil whose smoke was of blue fire. But as he raised his long lank arm, silver-white with ashes, the demons fled, and a momentary silence succeeded to their uproar. The tigers ceased to roar and the elephants to scream; the bears raised their snouts from their foul banquets, and the wolves dropped from their jaws the remnants of human flesh. And when they disappeared, the hooting of the owl, and ghastly "ha! ha!" of the curlew, and the howling of the jackal died away in the far distance, leaving a silence still more oppressive.

As Raja Vikram entered the burning-ground, the hollow sound of solitude alone met his ear. Sadly wailed the wet autumnal blast. The tall gaunt trees groaned aloud, and bowed and trembled like slaves bending before their masters. Huge purple clouds and patches and lines of glaring white mist coursed furiously across the black expanse of firmament, discharging threads and chains and lozenges and balls of white and blue, purple and pink lightning, followed by the deafening crash and roll of thunder, the dreadful roaring of the mighty wind, and the torrents of plashing rain. At times was heard in the distance the dull gurgling of the swollen river, interrupted by explosions, as slips of earth-bank fell headlong into the stream. But once more the Jogi raised his arm and all was still: nature lay breathless, as if awaiting the effect of his tremendous spells.

The warrior king drew near the terrible man, unstrung his bundle from his back, untwisted the portion which he held, threw open the cloth, and exposed to Shanta-Shil's glittering eyes the corpse, which had now recovered its proper form—that of a young child. Seeing it, the devotee was highly pleased, and thanked Vikram the Brave, extolling his courage and daring above any monarch that had yet lived. After which he repeated certain charms facing towards the south, awakened the dead body, and placed it in a sitting position. He then in its presence sacrificed to his goddess, the White One,[1] all that he had ready by his side—betel leaf and flowers, sandal wood and unbroken rice, fruits, perfumes, and the flesh of man untouched by steel. Lastly, he half filled his skull with burning embers, blew upon them till they shot forth tongues of crimson light, serving as a lamp, and motioning the Raja and his son to follow him, led the way to a little fane of the Destroying Deity erected in a dark clump of wood, outside and close to the burning-ground.

They passed through the quadrangular outer court of the temple whose piazza was hung with deep shade.[2] In silence they circumambulated the small central shrine, and whenever Shanta-Shil directed, Raja Vikram entered the Sabha, or vestibule, and struck three times upon the gong, which gave forth a loud and warning sound.

They then passed over the threshold, and looked into the gloomy inner depths. There stood Smashana-Kali,[3]

---

1 Shiva is always painted white, no one knows why. His wife Gauri has also a European complexion. Hence it is generally said that the sect popularly called "Thugs," who were worshippers of these murderous gods, spared Englishmen, the latter being supposed to have some *rapport* with their deities.

2 The Hindu shrine is mostly a small building, with two inner compartments, the vestibule and the Garbagriha, or adytum, in which stands the image.

3 Meaning Kali of the cemetery (Smashana); another form of Durga.

the goddess, in her most horrid form. She was a naked and very black woman, with half-severed head, partly cut and partly painted, resting on her shoulder; and her tongue lolled out from her wide yawning mouth[1]; her eyes were red like those of a drunkard; and her eyebrows were of the same colour : her thick coarse hair hung like a mantle to her heels. She was robed in an elephant's hide, dried and withered, confined at the waist with a belt composed of the hands of the giants whom she had slain in war : two dead bodies formed her earrings, and her necklace was of bleached skulls. Her four arms supported a scimitar, a noose, a trident, and a ponderous mace. She stood with one leg on the breast of her husband, Shiva, and she rested the other on his thigh. Before the idol lay the utensils of worship, namely, dishes for the offerings, lamps, jugs, incense, copper cups, conches and gongs ; and all of them smelt of blood.

As Raja Vikram and his son stood gazing upon the hideous spectacle, the devotee stooped down to place his skull-lamp upon the ground, and drew from out his ochre-coloured cloth a sharp sword which he hid behind his back.

" Prosperity to thine and thy son's for ever and ever, O mighty Vikram !" exclaimed Shanta-Shil, after he had muttered a prayer before the image. " Verily thou hast right royally redeemed thy pledge, and by the virtue of thy presence all my wishes shall presently be accomplished. Behold ! the Sun is about to drive his car over the eastern hills, and our task now ends. Do thou reverence before this my deity, worshipping the earth

---

[1] Not being able to find victims, this pleasant deity, to satisfy her thirst for the curious juice, cut her own throat that the blood might spout up into her mouth. She once found herself dancing on her husband, and was so shocked that in surprise she put out her tongue to a great length, and remained motionless. She is often represented in this form.

through thy nose, and so prostrating thyself that thy eight limbs may touch the ground.[1] Thus shall thy glory and splendour be great; the Eight Powers[2] and the Nine Treasures shall be thine, and prosperity shall ever remain under thy roof-tree."

Raja Vikram, hearing these words, recalled suddenly to mind all that the Vampire had whispered to him. He brought his joined hands open up to his forehead, caused his two thumbs to touch his brow several times, and replied with the greatest humility,

"O pious person! I am a king ignorant of the way to do such obeisance. Thou art a spiritual preceptor: be pleased to teach me and I will do even as thou desirest."

Then the Jogi, being a cunning man, fell into his own net. As he bent him down to salute the goddess, Vikram, drawing his sword, struck him upon the neck so violent a blow, that his head rolled from his body upon the ground. At the same moment Dharma Dhwaj, seizing his father's arm, pulled him out of the way in time to escape being crushed by the image, which fell with the sound of thunder upon the floor of the temple.

A small thin voice in the upper air was heard to cry, "A man is justified in killing one who has the desire to kill him." Then glad shouts of triumph and victory were heard in all directions. They proceeded from the celestial choristers, the heavenly dancers, the mistresses of the gods, and the nymphs of Indra's Paradise, who left their beds of gold and precious stones, their seats glorious as the meridian sun, their canals of crystal water, their perfumed groves, and their gardens where the wind ever

---

1 This ashtanga, the most ceremonious of the five forms of Hindu salutation, consists of prostrating and of making the eight parts of the body—namely, the temples, nose and chin, knees and hands—touch the ground.

2 "Sidhis," the personified Powers of Nature. At least, so we explain them; but people do not worship abstract powers.

blows in softest breezes, to applaud the valour and good
fortune of the warrior king.

At last the brilliant god, Indra himself, with the
thousand eyes, rising from the shade of the Parigat tree,
the fragrance of whose flowers fills the heavens, appeared
in his car drawn by yellow steeds and cleaving the thick
vapours which surround the earth—whilst his attendants
sounded the heavenly drums and rained a shower of

As he bent him down to salute the goddess.

blossoms and perfumes—bade the Vikramajit the Brave
ask a boon.

The Raja joined his hands and respectfully replied,
"O mighty ruler of the lower firmament, let this my
history become famous throughout the world!"

"It is well," rejoined the god. "As long as the sun
and moon endure, and the sky looks down upon the
ground, so long shall this thy adventure be remembered
over all the earth. Meanwhile rule thou mankind."

Thus saying, Indra retired to the delicious Amrawati.[1] Vikram took up the corpses and threw them into the cauldron which Shanta-Shil had been tending. At once two heroes started into life, and Vikram said to them, " When I call you, come ! "

With these mysterious words the king, followed by his son, returned to the palace unmolested. As the Vampire had predicted, everything was prosperous to him, and he presently obtained the remarkable titles, Sakaro, or foe of the Sakas, and Sakadhipati-Vikramaditya.

And when, after a long and happy life spent in bringing the world under the shadow of one umbrella, and in ruling it free from care, the warrior king Vikram entered the gloomy realms of Yama, from whom for mortals there is no escape, he left behind him a name that endured amongst men like the odour of the flower whose memory remains long after its form has mingled with the dust.[2]

---

1 The residence of Indra, king of heaven, built by Wishwa-Karma, the architect of the gods.

2 In other words, to the present day, whenever a Hindu novelist, romancer, or tale writer seeks a peg upon which to suspend the texture of his story, he invariably pitches upon the glorious, pious, and immortal memory of that Eastern King Arthur, Vikramaditya, shortly called Vikram.

Opinions of the Press.

" It will be impossible in a paragraph or two to give any adequate idea of the mass of information and entertainment it contains."— *Saturday Review.*

" Every episode is so vividly described that the reader is compelled to follow the story with increasing interest, and cannot fail to obtain, almost unconsciously, a vast amount of valuable information."—*Dundee Advertiser.*

" Burton never wrote anything more captivating. Those who excite and incite like him, and make a ceiling and stone walls a prison while you read, are rare, just as rare as he was himself."— *Sketch.*

" This is one of those books which, when once read, are never forgotten, and are always re-read with pleasure."—*St. James's Budget.*

" Even Burton never wrote anything better than his ' Pilgrimage to Mecca.' After years one's appetite returns to it, and on a second reading one is more than ever struck by the amount of marvel and of peril which he takes for granted, and mentions as mere circumstance. It is a great book of travels."—*Bookman.*

" The narrative is one of absorbing interest....Those who know the book of old will welcome the present handsome edition, and those who do not know it may be congratulated on the pleasure in store for them."—*Glasgow Herald.*

II.—A Mission to Gelele, King of Dahome."
Memorial Edition. Complete in 2 vols. Price Twelve Shillings, *net.*

Opinions of the Press.

" Of all Burton's books this account of his hazardous mission to Dahomey is one of the least known; it brings out, in a very marked manner, the writer's unfailing tact and resource in dealing with savage peoples."—*Daily Graphic.*

" Carefully edited and excellently got up."—*Glasgow Herald.*

" The style is more colloquial than that of the ' Pilgrimage to Mecca,' but it is none the less readable and attractive. The effect produced by the book is that of a clever man talking over his adventures after dinner, or in a club smoking-room."—*Manchester Guardian.*

" An uncompromising account of a race which has, perhaps, been sentimentalised over more than any other.—*Star.*

BOOKS OF RELATED INTEREST

How Ganesh Got His Elephant Head
by Harish Johari and Vatsala Sperling

The Magical Adventures of Krishna
How a Mischief Maker Saved the World
by Vatsala Sperling

Walking the World in Wonder
A Children's Herbal
by Ellen Evert Hopman

The Ancient Celtic Festivals
and How We Celebrate Them Today
by Clare Walker Leslie and Frank E. Gerace

Tai Chi for Kids
Move with the Animals
by Stuart Alve Olson

The Journey of Tunuri and the Blue Deer
A Huichol Indian Story
by James Endredy

The Monkeys and the Mango Tree
Teaching Stories of the Saints and Sadhus of India
by Harish Johari

Like a Fish in Water
Yoga for Children
by Isabelle Koch

Inner Traditions • Bear & Company
P.O. Box 388
Rochester, VT 05767
1-800-246-8648
www.InnerTraditions.com

Or contact your local bookseller